Better Homes and Gardens®

CHRISTMAS COOKING
FROM THE HEART™

Simple Celebrations

Meredith® Consumer Marketing
Des Moines, Iowa

Our seal assures you that every recipe in *Christmas Cooking from the Heart*™ has been tested in the Better Homes and Gardens® Test Kitchen. This means that each recipe is practical and reliable, and meets our high standards of taste appeal. We guarantee your satisfaction with this book for as long as you own it.

All of us at Meredith® Consumer Marketing are dedicated to providing you with information and ideas to enhance your home. We welcome your comments and suggestions. Write to us at: Meredith Consumer Marketing, 1716 Locust St., Des Moines, IA 50309-3023. *Christmas Cooking from the Heart* is available by mail. To order editions from past years, call 800/627-5490.

Cover Photography:
Front cover: Dutch Mocha Chocolate Cake (80), Sweet Cherry Truffles (117), Painted Cookies (106), Star Mint Meringues (111), Coconut Macaroons (107), Linzer Pinwheels (107), French Filled Macaroons (108), Double-Chocolate Peppermint Biscotti (110), Red Velvet Shortbread Cookies (102), Chocolate-Cherry-Walnut-Thumbprints (98)

Better Homes and Gardens®

CHRISTMAS COOKING
FROM THE HEART™

MEREDITH CORPORATION CONSUMER MARKETING
Senior Vice President, Consumer Marketing: David Ball
Consumer Product Marketing Director: Steve Swanson
Consumer Product Marketing Manager: Wendy Merical
Senior Production Manager: George Susral

WATERBURY PUBLICATIONS, INC.
Editorial Director: Lisa Kingsley
Creative Director: Ken Carlson
Associate Editor: Tricia Bergman
Associate Design Director: Doug Samuelson, Bruce Yang
Graphic Designer: Mindy Samuelson
Contributing Copy Editor: Peg Smith
Contributing Proofreaders: Gretchen Kauffman, Terri Fredrickson
Contributing Indexer: Elizabeth T. Parson

BETTER HOMES AND GARDENS® MAGAZINE
Editor in Chief: Gayle Goodson Butler
Art Director: Michael D. Belknap
Deputy Editor, Food and Entertaining: Nancy Wall Hopkins
Senior Food Editor: Richard Swearinger
Associate Food Editor: Erin Simpson
Editorial Assistant: Renee Irey

MEREDITH PUBLISHING GROUP
President: Tom Hardy
Vice President, Manufacturing: Bruce Heston

MEREDITH CORPORATION
President and Chief Executive Officer: Stephen M. Lacy

In Memoriam: E.T. Meredith III (1933–2003)

table of
contents

Cinnamon Twists, page 71

simple celebrations

Wherever—and whenever—family and friends gather to celebrate, there is an abundance of wonderful food. The holidays, of course, have their own familiar dishes and flavors that make the season so special. *Christmas Cooking from the Heart* features traditional foods—some straightforward, some with a twist—perfect for celebrating occasions from Thanksgiving through New Year's. Each year, the culinary experts in the *Better Homes and Gardens®* Test Kitchen come up with fresh new ways for you to enjoy your favorite holiday recipes for appetizers, entrées, desserts, and edible gifts. Use this volume of *Christmas Cooking from the Heart* to create a memorable holiday season. Follow helpful tips to plan, prepare, and organize the busiest days of the year, simply but special. Taking time to shop and cook in advance so you can enjoy the celebration with family and friends is the greatest gift you can give yourself—and those you love. Happy holidays!

Chicken-and-Raisin-Stuffed Mushrooms, page 39

Cranberry-Pistachio Toffee, page 121

Holiday Orange-Eggnog Punch, page 134

Herb-Crusted Pork Tenderloin
with Red Currant Sauce, page 10

holiday feast

Of all the meals you look forward to throughout the year, this one is the pinnacle of celebratory dining—the holiday feast. Whether you host an intimate gathering for family and friends or a big hungry crowd, these recipes are perfect. Choose a main course—smoked beef rib roast, savory lamb roast, or maple-glazed turkey—then fill in with fresh salads and indulgent sides.

Roast Pork with Cherry Glaze, page 11

Pepper and Garlic-Studded Smoked Beef Rib Roast

Peppercorn blend usually consists of dried black, green, white, and pink peppercorns, which are not actually true peppercorns but rather the dried berries of a type of rose plant.

PREP **30 minutes** SOAK **1 hour** GRILL **2 hours**
STAND **15 minutes** MAKES **14 servings**

2   cups hickory or mesquite wood chips
1   6- to 6½-pound beef rib roast
5   cloves garlic, quartered lengthwise
1   tablespoon olive oil
3   tablespoons peppercorn melange, cracked
1   tablespoon kosher salt or coarse sea salt

1. Soak wood chips in enough water to cover for at least 1 hour before using.
2. Trim fat from meat. With a small sharp knife, make 20 small holes, about 1 inch deep, evenly spaced in the roast. Insert a piece of garlic in each hole. Brush roast with olive oil. Rub peppercorn melange and salt over the roast. Pat gently to hold in place. Insert a meat thermometer into center of meat without touching bone.

3. For a charcoal grill, arrange medium coals around a drip pan. Test for medium-low heat above pan. Sprinkle wood chips over coals. Place roast, bone side down, on grill rack over drip pan. Cover; grill until meat thermometer registers desired doneness. Allow 2 to 2¾ hours for medium-rare (135°F) or 2½ to 3¼ hours for medium doneness (150°F). (For a gas grill, preheat grill. Reduce heat to medium-low. Adjust for indirect cooking. Add wood chips according to manufacturer's directions. Grill as above, except place meat on a rack in a roasting pan.)
4. Remove meat from grill. Cover with foil and let stand for 15 minutes before slicing. (Meat temperature will rise 10°F during standing.)
PER SERVING *281 cal., 16 g total fat (6 g sat. fat), 92 mg chol., 221 mg sodium, 1 g carbo., 0 g fiber, 31 g pro.*

Roasted Lamb with Olive Tapenade

Tie the leg of lamb before roasting to hold its shape and carve it neatly for serving. Use 100%-cotton kitchen string and tie it in 1- or 2-inch increments the length of the roast.

PREP **30 minutes** ROAST **1 hour 30 minutes**
STAND **15 minutes** OVEN **325°F** MAKES **8 servings**

1   cup pitted kalamata olives
1   tablespoon snipped fresh parsley
1   tablespoon olive oil
1   teaspoon finely shredded lemon peel
2   teaspoons lemon juice
1   teaspoon snipped fresh rosemary
1   teaspoon snipped fresh thyme
¼   teaspoon black pepper
2   cloves garlic, minced
1   3½- to 4-pound boneless leg of lamb, rolled and tied
⅓   cup dry red wine
1   teaspoon kosher salt
1   teaspoon black pepper

1. For olive tapenade, in a food processor combine olives, parsley, oil, lemon peel, lemon juice, rosemary, thyme, the ¼ teaspoon pepper, and garlic. Cover and process until finely chopped, stopping to scrape down processor sides as necessary. Set aside.
2. Preheat oven to 325°F. Untie and unroll roast. Trim fat. If necessary, place meat, boned side up, between 2 pieces of plastic wrap and pound meat with a meat mallet to an even thickness. Spread olive mixture over cut surface of meat. Roll up; tie securely with 100%-cotton kitchen string.
3. Place roast, seam side down, on a rack in a shallow roasting pan. In a small bowl combine red wine, kosher salt, and the 1 teaspoon pepper. Roast for 1½ to 2 hours or until an instant-read thermometer inserted into the center of the roast registers 135°F for medium-rare doneness; baste with red wine mixture several times

Pepper-and-Garlic-Studded Smoked Beef Rib Roast

until the last 10 minutes of roasting. Discard any remaining red wine mixture.

4. Remove roast from oven. Cover with foil and let stand for 15 minutes before slicing. (Meat temperature after standing should be 145°F.) Remove strings and slice meat.

PER SERVING *313 cal., 14 g total fat (4 g sat. fat), 124 mg chol., 549 mg sodium, 2 g carbo., 1 g fiber, 41 g pro.*

Cranberry and Citrus-Glazed Pork Roast

The citrus- and sage-infused cranberry sauce serves as glaze while roasting and sauce for serving the pork.

PREP **15 minutes** ROAST **1 hour 15 minutes**
STAND **15 minutes** OVEN **325°F**
MAKES **10 to 12 servings**

¼   teaspoon salt
¼   teaspoon black pepper
¼   teaspoon ground sage
1   2½- to 3-pound boneless pork top loin roast
      (single loin)
1   16-ounce can whole or jellied cranberry sauce
½   teaspoon finely shredded orange peel
⅓   cup orange juice
¼   teaspoon ground sage

1. Preheat oven to 325°F. For rub, in a small bowl combine the salt, pepper, and ¼ teaspoon sage. Sprinkle rub evenly all over pork roast; rub in mixture with your fingers. Place meat on a rack in a shallow roasting pan. Insert an oven-going meat thermometer into center of roast. Roast, uncovered, for 45 minutes.

2. Meanwhile, for sauce, in a medium saucepan combine cranberry sauce, orange peel, orange juice, and ¼ teaspoon sage. Bring to boiling; reduce heat. Simmer, uncovered, about 10 minutes or until mixture has thickened slightly.

3. Spoon about ¼ cup of the sauce over pork. Roast meat, uncovered, for 30 to 45 minutes more or until meat thermometer registers 150°F. Remove from oven. Cover meat loosely with foil; let stand for 15 minutes before slicing. (Meat temperature after standing should be 160°F.) Serve remaining sauce with meat.

PER SERVING *285 cal., 12 g total fat (4 g sat. fat), 66 mg chol., 120 mg sodium, 19 g carbo., 1 g fiber, 23 g pro.*

Herb-Crusted Pork Tenderloin with Red Currant Sauce

1. Preheat oven to 425°F. Trim any fat from meat. Brush meat evenly with Dijon mustard. Sprinkle meat with salt and pepper. In a shallow dish combine rosemary, thyme, and sage. Roll meat in the mixed herbs, pressing herbs on all sides of meat.

2. In a very large nonstick skillet brown tenderloin in hot oil over medium-high heat, turning to brown all sides. Transfer tenderloin to a rack in a shallow roasting pan. Roast for 25 minutes or until an instant-read thermometer inserted in pork registers 155°F and juices run clear. Remove from oven; cover with foil and let stand 15 minutes (meat temperature will rise to 160°F).

3. For currant sauce, in a small saucepan combine jelly, vinegar, and butter. Heat and stir until jelly is melted. Remove from heat. Stir in horseradish, lemon peel, and juice.

4. To serve, line a serving platter with watercress. Slice pork and arrange on the watercress; spoon some of the currant sauce over pork. Serve remaining sauce on the side.

PER SERVING *256 cal., 9 g total fat (3 g sat. fat), 73 mg chol., 294 mg sodium, 20 g carbo., 1 g fiber, 23 g pro.*

Pork Roast with Cherry Glaze

Aromatic cardamom is a member of the ginger family.

PREP **45 minutes** ROAST **2 hours 30 minutes**
STAND **15 minutes** OVEN **350°/400°F**
MAKES **8 servings**

2   tablespoons coriander seeds
1   4½- to 5-pound boneless pork shoulder roast
3   to 4 cups freshly pressed apple juice or good-quality apple cider
2   sticks cinnamon
6   green cardamom pods
1   red onion, cut into wedges
1   yellow onion, cut into wedges
2   cups dried tart red cherries or dried cranberries
¼   cup loosely packed fresh thyme leaves
½   cup fresh parsley, chopped

1. Preheat oven to 350°F. In a skillet toast coriander seeds over medium-high heat about 1½ minutes or until fragrant, shaking pan often. Transfer to a dish to cool. Grind seeds in a coffee or spice grinder until they resemble coarse meal.

2. Rub pork with *salt*, freshly ground *black pepper*, and ground coriander seeds. Place on rack in a large roasting pan. Add 3 cups of the apple juice, the cinnamon, and cardamom to pan. Roast 1½ hours or until the pork reaches an internal temperature of 140°F. Remove from oven. Transfer pork to a large platter; cover to keep warm. Pour pan juices through a mesh strainer into large liquid measuring cup. Return

Herb-Crusted Pork Tenderloin with Red Currant Sauce

Like arugula, watercress has a delightfully peppery bite. Use the greens interchangeably in this recipe.

PREP **30 minutes** ROAST **25 minutes**
STAND **15 minutes** OVEN **425°F** MAKES **4 servings**

1   1- to 1¼-pound pork tenderloin
2   to 3 teaspoons Dijon mustard
    Salt and freshly ground black pepper
1   tablespoon snipped fresh rosemary
2   teaspoons snipped fresh thyme
2   teaspoons snipped fresh sage
1   tablespoon olive oil
⅓   cup red currant jelly
1   tablespoon white wine vinegar
2   teaspoons butter, softened
1   teaspoon prepared horseradish
¼   teaspoon finely shredded lemon peel
½   teaspoon lemon juice
3   cups watercress, tough stems removed

pork to pan along with onions. Increase oven to 400°F.

3. Meanwhile, for Cherry Glaze, skim fat from strained pan juices (if necessary, add additional apple juice to equal 2½ cups). Transfer to large saucepan. Add dried cherries. Place over medium-high heat. Simmer 10 to 15 minutes or until cherries rehydrate and liquid is consistency of syrup.

4. Brush pork with ¼ cup of the Cherry Glaze. Return to oven. Roast 1 hour or until pork reaches internal temperature of 165°F and onions begin to brown (cover loosely with foil if pork browns too quickly). Remove from oven; cover with foil. Let stand 15 minutes.

5. To serve, place pork on a warm platter. Arrange roasted onions around pork. Stir half of the fresh thyme and parsley into the Cherry Glaze. Carefully spoon some of the glaze over pork. Sprinkle remaining herbs. Serve with Cherry Glaze.

PER SERVING *559 cal., 17 g total fat (6 g sat. fat,), 146 mg chol., 265 mg sodium, 42 g carbo., 5 g fiber, 51 g pro.*

Pork Roast with Cherry Glaze

Maple-Glazed Roast Turkey

Maple-Glazed Roast Turkey

Allow 3 to 4 days for the turkey to thaw in the refrigerator. If it's still a bit icy when you take it out to roast, place the turkey in its original wrapping in the sink and cover it with cold water. Change the water every 30 minutes until completely thawed.

PREP **30 minutes** ROAST **3 hours** STAND **15 minutes** OVEN **325°F** MAKES **18 servings**

1	12- to 14-pound whole turkey (thawed if frozen)
¼	cup olive oil
2	tablespoons finely snipped fresh parsley
1	tablespoon finely snipped fresh sage leaves
1	tablespoon snipped fresh thyme
3	large cloves garlic, minced
¼	teaspoon freshly ground black pepper
1	medium apple, quartered and seeded
1	lemon, quartered and seeded
¼	cup pure maple syrup or honey
2	tablespoons butter
1	recipe Apple Cider Sauce

1. Preheat oven to 325°F. Remove neck and giblets from the turkey. Rinse turkey body cavity; pat dry with paper towels.

2. In a small bowl combine the olive oil, parsley, sage, thyme, garlic, 1 teaspoon kosher *salt* or ½ teaspoon *salt,* and black pepper. Rub some of the olive oil and herb blend into the body cavity of the turkey. Loosen skin from breast and rub some of the remaining mixture on meat under breast skin. Rub any remaining herb mixture on skin. Place the apple and lemon into the body cavity of the turkey.

3. Skewer turkey neck skin to back. Tie legs to tail with 100%-cotton kitchen string or tuck the ends of the drumsticks under the band of skin across the tail. Twist the wing tips under the back.

4. Place the turkey, breast side up, on a rack in a shallow roasting pan. Insert a meat thermometer into the center of 1 of the inside thigh muscles, thermometer not touching bone. Cover turkey loosely with foil, leaving some space between the bird and foil. Loosely press foil over legs and neck. Roast for 2 hours.

5. For glaze, in a small saucepan heat and stir maple syrup and butter until butter is melted.

6. Remove turkey from oven. Cut the string between the drumsticks so the thighs will cook evenly. Remove the foil to let the bird brown. Brush about one-third of the glaze over turkey. Return turkey to oven and roast for 60 to 90 minutes more or until meat thermometer registers 180°F and juices run clear after piercing the thickest part of the inner thigh, brushing twice more with remaining glaze.

7. Remove turkey from oven and cover loosely with foil. Let stand for 15 minutes before carving. Carve turkey in thin slices and serve with Apple Cider Sauce.

Apple Cider Sauce In a medium saucepan combine one 14-ounce can chicken broth, 1 cup apple cider, 1 cup chopped onion, ⅓ cup maple syrup, 2 tablespoons cider vinegar, and 2 bay leaves. Bring to boiling; reduce heat. Simmer, covered, for 15 minutes or until onion is very soft. Remove the bay leaves; discard. In a large saucepan melt 3 tablespoons butter over medium heat. Stir in 3 tablespoons all-purpose flour and ¼ teaspoon ground white pepper. Carefully add hot cider mixture all at once. Cook and stir over medium heat until thickened and bubbly. Add 1 teaspoon snipped fresh sage. Cook and stir 1 minute more. Makes 3½ cups.

PER SERVING *393 cal., 15 g total fat (5 g sat. fat), 191 mg chol., 320 mg sodium, 9 g carbo., 1 g fiber, 51 g pro.*

No-Drippings Gravy

The name of this recipe says it all. When your roasted bird doesn't yield much drippings or when you bring home a rotisserie chicken and would like gravy to go with it, this recipe comes to the rescue.

START TO FINISH 15 minutes   MAKES 3 cups

⅓   cup butter
⅓   cup all-purpose flour
3   cups chicken broth
¼   teaspoon black pepper
     Coarse kosher salt or table salt
     Fresh parsley (optional)

1. In a medium saucepan melt butter over medium heat. Stir in flour until smooth. Add chicken broth and pepper. Cook and stir until thickened and bubbly. Cook and stir for 1 minute more. Season to taste with salt. If desired, garnish with parsley.
PER ¼ CUP *62 cal., 5 g total fat (3 g sat. fat), 14 mg chol., 317 mg sodium, 3 g carbo., 0 g fiber, 1 g pro.*

Brandy-Cream Gravy

Do little to the holiday bird before roasting if you plan to make this elegant gravy with drippings. Just a drizzle over the carved meat adds richness and terrific flavor.

PREP 15 minutes   BAKE 1 hour   COOK 1 hour
OVEN 325°F   MAKES 2½ cups

1   large head garlic
1   teaspoon olive oil
1   turkey gizzard
1   turkey neck, halved
2   cups water
     Pan drippings from roasted turkey or chicken
¼   cup all-purpose flour
2   tablespoons brandy
⅓   cup whipping cream
1   teaspoon lemon juice
½   teaspoon snipped fresh thyme
     Salt
     Black pepper

1. Preheat oven to 325°F. Peel away the dry outer layers of skin from the garlic head, leaving inner skin and cloves intact. Cut off the pointed top portion (about ¼ inch), leaving the bulb intact but exposing individual cloves. Place the garlic head, cut side up, in a custard cup. Drizzle with olive oil. Cover with foil and bake about 1 hour or until the cloves feel soft when pressed. Set aside garlic head just until cool enough to handle. Squeeze out the garlic paste from individual cloves. Set aside.

2. For giblet broth, rinse gizzard and neck. In a medium saucepan combine the water, gizzard, and neck. Bring to boiling; reduce heat. Cover and simmer about 1 hour or until tender. Discard neck and gizzard. Line a colander or sieve with two layers of 100%-cotton cheesecloth. Set colander or sieve in a heatproof bowl; carefully pour boiled mixture into lined colander or sieve.

3. Pour drippings from turkey or chicken into a fat separator or into a large glass measuring cup. If using a fat separator, pour off fat into a glass measuring cup. (If using a large measuring cup, use a spoon to skim and reserve fat from drippings.) Pour ¼ cup of the fat into a medium saucepan; discard remaining fat.

4. Add enough of the giblet broth to the drippings to equal 1⅔ cups. Stir flour into fat in saucepan. Carefully stir brandy into mixture before pan is over heat. Add drippings mixture and whipping cream all at once to flour mixture in saucepan. Cook and stir mixture over medium heat until thickened and bubbly. Cook and stir for 1 minute more. Stir in the roasted garlic paste, lemon juice, and thyme. Season to taste with salt and pepper. Heat through. Serve gravy in a gravy boat or bowl.
PER ¼ CUP *135 cal., 10 g total fat (4 g sat. fat,), 48 mg chol., 45 mg sodium, 4 g carbo., 0 g fiber, 6 g pro.*

Brandy-Cream Gravy

Fresh Cranberry Compote

Serve this sweet-tart compote solo or with a tiny scoop of vanilla ice cream and a simple butter cookie or shortbread.

PREP 15 minutes STAND 6 hours MAKES 6 cups

2   12-ounce packages fresh cranberries
2   oranges, seeded and coarsely chopped
1   cup Granny Smith apple, peeled, cored, and coarsely chopped (1 large)
¾   cups Grand Marnier or orange juice
1   cup sugar
2   whole cinnamon sticks
½   teaspoon fresh shaved nutmeg

1. Place cranberries, oranges, and apple in a food processor (in batches if needed). Pulse 8 to 10 times or until mixture is coarsely chopped. Transfer cranberry mixture to a large bowl; add Grand Marnier, sugar, cinnamon, and nutmeg. Mix well; cover with plastic and let stand at room temperature for at least 6 hours or overnight (refrigerate if using orange juice option).
2. Taste cranberry mixture and adjust sweetness with additional sugar as desired. Cover and refrigerate up to 2 weeks. Remove cinnamon sticks before serving.
PER ¼ CUP *76 cal., 0 g total fat, 0 mg chol., 1 mg sodium, 17 g carbo., 2 g fiber, 0 g pro.*

Crimson Cranberry Chutney

Serve this gorgeous jewel-tone chutney with roast pork or poultry.

PREP 10 minutes COOK 12 minutes COOL 30 minutes
CHILL up to 3 days STAND 30 minutes MAKES 3½ cups

1¼   cups granulated sugar
½   cup orange juice
1   12-ounce package cranberries (3 cups)
1   cup peeled, cored, and chopped apples
1   cup golden raisins
¼   cup packed brown sugar
2   teaspoons minced fresh ginger

1. In a 3-quart saucepan combine granulated sugar and orange juice. Cook and stir over medium-high heat until sugar is dissolved. Bring to boiling without stirring.
2. Stir in cranberries, apples, raisins, brown sugar, and fresh ginger. Return to boiling. Reduce heat to medium and simmer, uncovered, for 5 minutes or until berries have popped and mixture starts to thicken, stirring occasionally. Remove from heat; cool about 30 minutes. Cover and refrigerate for up to 3 days.
3. Let chutney stand at room temperature for 30 minutes before serving.
PER 2 TABLESPOONS *68 cal., 0 g total fat, 0 mg chol., 2 mg sodium, 18 g carbo., 1 g fiber, 0 g pro.*

Bordelaise Sauce

This French sauce of beef broth, wine, shallot, and parsley is customarily served with broiled or roasted meats.

START TO FINISH 40 minutes MAKES 1 cup

1¼   cups reduced-sodium beef broth
¾   cup dry red wine
2   tablespoons finely chopped shallot or onion
3   tablespoons butter or margarine, softened
1   tablespoon all-purpose flour
¼   teaspoon salt
1   tablespoon snipped fresh parsley (optional)

1. In a medium saucepan stir together broth, wine, and shallot. Bring just to boiling; reduce heat. Simmer, uncovered, skimming the surface often with a spoon, for 25 to 30 minutes or until reduced to 1 cup.
2. With a fork, in a small bowl stir together butter and flour. Whisk butter mixture into wine mixture, 1 teaspoon at a time, whisking constantly (mixture will thicken). Cook and stir for 1 minute more. Stir in salt and, if desired, parsley. Serve with beef or lamb.
PER 2 TABLESPOONS *64 cal., 4 g total fat (3 g sat. fat), 11 mg chol., 173 mg sodium, 2 g carbo., 0 g fiber, 1 g pro.*

Corn, Sage, and Toasted Corn Bread Pudding

Toasting the corn bread before making the stuffing does two good things: It gives the corn bread a nice toasty flavor and creates a crust that holds the shape of the cubes when combined with wet ingredients.

PREP 30 minutes BAKE 1 hour 5 minutes
COOK 15 minutes STAND 10 minutes OVEN 350°F
MAKES 12 servings

8   cups cubed corn bread*
2   tablespoons butter
4   cups sliced mushrooms (cremini, stemmed shiitake, oyster, or button)
1   medium onion, chopped
2   cloves garlic, minced
2   cups fresh corn kernels (4 ears) or frozen corn, thawed
3   tablespoons snipped fresh sage or 1 tablespoon dried leaf sage, crushed
5   eggs
2¾   cups milk
½   teaspoon salt
¼   teaspoon black pepper

1. Preheat oven to 350°F. Spread cubed bread in a 15×10×1-inch baking pan. Bake, uncovered, for 15 minutes or until lightly toasted, stirring once. Cool slightly.

2. Meanwhile, in an extra-large skillet cook and stir mushrooms, onion, and garlic in melted butter until tender. Add corn and sage; cook 2 minutes more. Remove from heat. Gently stir in toasted bread cubes. Transfer to a greased 3-quart rectangular or oval baking dish.

3. In a medium bowl combine eggs, milk, salt, and pepper. Pour over bread mixture. Bake, covered, for 30 minutes. Uncover and bake 20 to 30 minutes more or until pudding is browned and puffed and center is set. Cool 10 minutes before serving.

*Prepare two 8-ounce packages of corn muffin mix. Pour into two greased 8×8×2-inch baking pans. Bake in a 400°F oven for 20 minutes. Cool in pan on wire rack. Let stand overnight before cubing.

PER SERVING *299 cal., 13 g total fat (2 g sat. fat), 125 mg chol., 492 mg sodium, 39 g carbo., 1 g fiber, 0 g pro.*

Corned Beef, Onion, and Marbled Rye variation
Substitute 8 cups marbled rye bread for the corn bread. Use half a 16-ounce package small frozen whole onions or 1 large onion, chopped, in place of the mushrooms and chopped onion; use 2 medium pears, peeled and chopped, in place of the corn; use 1 teaspoon caraway seeds in place of the sage; and stir in 1 cup chopped cooked corned beef.

Wild Mushroom Bread Pudding

Served with a crisp green salad, this mushroom-and-cheese side dish makes a delicious meatless main dish as well.

PREP **30 minutes** BAKE **35 minutes** CHILL **2 hours**
OVEN **325°F** MAKES **8 servings**

3	cups sliced assorted fresh wild mushrooms (such as cremini, portobello, chanterelle, and/or stemmed shiitake or oyster) (8 ounces)
2	medium shallots, sliced (¼ cup)
3	cloves garlic, minced
2	tablespoons olive oil
¼	cup dry sherry or dry white wine
8	ounces rosemary or onion focaccia, cut into 1-inch pieces (about 6 cups)
4	eggs, lightly beaten
2	cups half-and-half or light cream
1	cup shredded Gruyère cheese (4 ounces)
1	tablespoon snipped fresh thyme
1	tablespoon snipped fresh rosemary
½	teaspoon salt
½	teaspoon coarsely ground black pepper

1. Grease eight 10-ounce individual casseroles; set aside. In a large skillet cook mushrooms, shallots, and garlic in hot oil over medium heat about 5 minutes or until tender. Carefully add sherry. Simmer, uncovered, until liquid is nearly evaporated. Transfer mixture to a large bowl. Stir in focaccia pieces.

Wild Mushroom Bread Pudding

2. In a medium bowl combine eggs, half-and-half, cheese, thyme, rosemary, salt, and pepper. Pour egg mixture over focaccia mixture, pressing with a wooden spoon to moisten all of the bread.

3. Divide pudding mixture among the prepared casseroles. Cover and chill for 2 to 24 hours.

4. Preheat oven to 325°F. Bake, uncovered, for 35 to 40 minutes or until a knife inserted near the centers comes out clean.

PER SERVING *289 cal., 18 g total fat (8 g sat. fat) 146 mg chol., 366 mg sodium, 18 g carbo., 1 g fiber, 13 g pro.*

Sage, Sweet Pepper, and Couscous Dressing

½ teaspoon freshly ground black pepper
¼ teaspoon salt
Fresh sage leaves (optional)

1. In a large saucepan heat 1 tablespoon olive oil over medium heat. Add Israeli couscous; cook about 5 minutes or until golden, stirring occasionally. Add vegetable broth. Bring to boiling; reduce heat. Simmer, covered, for 8 to 10 minutes or until couscous is tender and most of the liquid is absorbed. Remove from heat; set aside.
2. Meanwhile, in a large skillet cook sweet peppers, celery, and finely chopped onions (if using) in 2 tablespoons hot olive oil over medium heat for 5 to 6 minutes or until vegetables are tender, stirring occasionally. Stir in green onions (if using), snipped or dried sage, orange peel, poultry seasoning, black pepper, and salt; cook and stir for 1 minute more.
3. Add vegetable mixture to Israeli couscous; toss lightly to combine. Transfer to a serving bowl. If desired, garnish with sage leaves. Serve immediately.
PER SERVING *193 cal., 6 g total fat (1 g sat. fat), 0 mg chol., 382 mg sodium, 32 g carbo., 3 g fiber, 5 g pro.*

Barley-Wild Rice Pilaf with Pistachios

Wild rice isn't really rice at all but rather the seed of an aquatic grass that grows in shallow rivers and streams. Rinse both the barley and wild rice to remove any dirt or grit that may linger after processing.

PREP 20 minutes COOK 5 to 6 hours (low) or 2½ to 3 hours (high) STAND 10 minutes MAKES 12 servings

¾ cup regular barley (not quick-cooking)
¾ cup wild rice
2 14.5-ounce cans diced tomatoes with basil, garlic, and oregano
1 cup finely chopped celery (2 stalks)
½ cup finely chopped onion (1 medium)
4 cloves garlic, minced
1 teaspoon chopped fresh rosemary
½ teaspoon cracked black pepper
¼ teaspoon salt
2 14.5-ounce cans chicken broth
¼ cup coarsely chopped pistachios

1. Rinse and drain barley and wild rice. In a 3½- or 4-quart slow cooker combine barley, wild rice, undrained tomatoes, celery, onion, garlic, rosemary, pepper, and salt. Pour broth over all in cooker.
2. Cover and cook on low-heat setting for 5 to 6 hours or on high-heat setting for 2½ to 3 hours. If possible, remove ceramic liner from cooker or turn off cooker. Let stand, covered, for 10 minutes before serving. Top with pistachios.
PER SERVING *128 cal., 2 g total fat (0 g sat. fat), 1 mg chol., 675 mg sodium, 24 g carbo., 3 g fiber, 5 g pro.*

Sage, Sweet Pepper, and Couscous Dressing

Israeli couscous, also called pearl couscous, is a large-grain round pasta that originates in the Middle East. Cooked, it has a wonderfully chewy texture. Toasting it in hot oil in the pan before adding the cooking liquid gives it a nutty taste.

START TO FINISH 30 minutes MAKES 8 servings

1 tablespoon olive oil
1½ cups Israeli couscous
2½ cups vegetable broth
2 cups coarsely chopped red, orange, and/or yellow sweet peppers (2 large)
1½ cups coarsely chopped celery (3 stalks)
1 cup thinly sliced green onions (8) or finely chopped onions (2 medium)
2 tablespoons olive oil, butter, or margarine
3 tablespoons snipped fresh sage or 1 tablespoon dried sage, crushed
1 teaspoon finely shredded orange peel
½ teaspoon poultry seasoning

Walnut-Lemon Rice Pilaf

This supersimple pilaf starts with two pouches of cooked brown rice, so it can be ready in a flash.

START TO FINISH **20 minutes** MAKES **8 servings**

1 cup coarsely chopped walnuts
2 small yellow sweet peppers, cut into bite-size strips
1 small red onion, cut into slivers
4 cloves garlic, minced
4 teaspoons olive oil
2 8.8-ounce pouches cooked brown rice
½ cup coarsely chopped fresh parsley
1 teaspoon finely shredded lemon peel
¼ cup lemon juice

1. In a large dry skillet heat walnuts over medium heat for 3 to 5 minutes or until lightly toasted, stirring frequently. Remove from skillet; set aside. In the same skillet cook sweet peppers, onion, and garlic in hot oil over medium heat for 5 minutes or just until tender, stirring occasionally.
2. Add rice to skillet. Cook and stir to heat through. Stir in nuts, parsley, lemon peel, lemon juice, and ¼ teaspoon *salt.*

PER SERVING *238 cal., 14 g total fat (1 g sat. fat), 0 mg chol., 152 mg sodium, 26 g carbo., 2 g fiber, 5 g pro.*

Walnut-Lemon Rice Pilaf

Pomegranate Rice

Some supermarkets sell pomegranate seeds in the refrigerator section of the produce department. They're more expensive than buying whole fruit, but buying the fruit already seeded makes cooking with them decidedly tidier.

PREP **20 minutes** COOK **14 minutes** STAND **10 minutes**
MAKES **6 to 8 servings**

1   shallot, chopped
1   tablespoon canola oil
1   cup jasmine or long grain white rice
2   teaspoons grated fresh ginger
⅛   teaspoon ground cinnamon
1   14.5-ounce can reduced-sodium chicken broth
¼   cup water
½   cup roasted salted pistachio nuts
1   cup pomegranate seeds*
     Lemon peel strips

1. In a large saucepan cook chopped shallot in hot oil over medium heat for 3 to 5 minutes or just until tender, stirring occasionally. Add rice, ginger, and cinnamon. Cook and stir for 5 minutes or until rice begins to brown.
2. Carefully add broth and water to rice. Bring to boiling; reduce heat. Simmer, covered, for 14 minutes. Remove from heat; let stand, covered, for 10 minutes or until the liquid is absorbed.

3. Stir in nuts and pomegranate seeds. Sprinkle with lemon peel.
*To remove seeds from pomegranates, score an X in the top of each pomegranate. Break each apart into quarters. Working in a bowl of cool water, immerse each quarter and loosen the seeds from the white membrane with your fingers. Discard peel and membrane. Drain the seeds. You can freeze pomegranate seeds in sealed freezer containers for up to 1 year.
PER SERVING *235 cal., 8 g total fat (1 g sat. fat), 0 mg chol., 203 mg sodium, 38 g carbo., 3 g fiber, 5 g pro.*

Risotto-Style Orzo with Butternut Squash and Pancetta

Pancetta is a cured, unsmoked Italian bacon flavored with salt and spices and formed into a roll. It's usually sold in very thin round slices. If you can't find it, substitute American-style bacon.

START TO FINISH **50 minutes** MAKES **12 servings**

8   ounces pancetta, cut into ¼-inch pieces
3   tablespoons butter
3   tablespoons olive oil
1½   cups chopped onions
3   large cloves garlic, minced
4   pounds butternut squash, peeled, seeded, and cut into ½-inch pieces
2   14-ounce cans reduced-sodium chicken broth
1   cup dry white wine
4   cups water
2   cups dried orzo pasta (rosamarina)
1   cup grated Parmesan cheese (4 ounces)
2   tablespoons snipped fresh sage
       Salt
       Freshly ground black pepper

1. In a Dutch oven cook pancetta over medium heat until crisp and brown. Using a slotted spoon, remove pancetta and drain on paper towels. Drain fat from pan.
2. Add butter and oil to Dutch oven. Increase heat to medium-high; add onions and garlic. Cook for 6 to 7 minutes or until onions are tender, stirring frequently. Stir in squash.
3. Add 1 cup of the broth and the wine. Bring to boiling; reduce heat. Simmer, uncovered, about 12 minutes or until squash is nearly tender and liquid is absorbed.
4. Meanwhile, in a large saucepan combine the remaining broth and the water. Bring to boiling; stir in orzo. Cook according to package directions; drain. Add cooked pancetta, cooked orzo, Parmesan cheese, and sage to squash mixture; stir gently to combine. Season to taste with salt and pepper. Transfer mixture to a serving bowl.
PER SERVING *356 cal., 16 g total fat (6 g sat. fat), 29 mg chol., 728 mg sodium, 40 g carbo., 4 g fiber, 12 g pro.*

Pomegranate Rice

Thyme Potatoes au Gratin

Thyme Potatoes au Gratin

This decadent gratin is made with a generous amount of whipping cream, butter, red potatoes, and Parmesan cheese. It's fabulous with roast beef.

PREP 40 minutes BAKE 1 hour 35 minutes
STAND 10 minutes OVEN 350°F MAKES 8 servings

3   cups whipping cream
1   large clove garlic, minced
2   tablespoons butter, softened
4   pounds red potatoes, peeled and thinly sliced
4   ounces Parmesan cheese, grated
1   teaspoon salt
2   tablespoons snipped fresh thyme
¼   teaspoon freshly grated nutmeg
¼   teaspoon freshly ground pepper
    Shaved Parmesan, snipped fresh parsley, dried tomato slices (optional)

1. Preheat oven to 350°F. In a medium saucepan combine cream and garlic; bring to simmering over medium heat. Simmer, uncovered, 5 minutes; do not boil. Remove from heat.

2. Generously butter a 3- or 3½-quart baking dish. Layer one-third of the potato slices. In a small bowl combine grated cheese, salt, thyme, nutmeg, and pepper. Sprinkle one-third of the cheese mixture; pour one-third of the hot cream. Repeat layers twice. Cover with foil.

3. Bake 1¼ to 1½ hours, until potatoes are almost tender and liquid is mostly absorbed. Uncover; bake 20 to 30 minutes more, until liquid is absorbed and potatoes are browned and moist. If dish is broiler-safe, broil 3 to 4 inches from heat for 2 to 3 minutes, until top is crisp and brown. Let stand for 10 minutes. If desired, top with shaved Parmesan, snipped fresh parsley, and/or dried tomato slices.

To Make Ahead Prepare through Step 2. Cover and chill up to 2 days before baking. Remove from refrigerator and let stand 20 minutes at room temperature. Heat oven to 350°F. Continue as directed. (Some darkening on the edges of the potatoes may have occurred during refrigeration. This is to be expected because as raw potatoes are exposed to air; it is not harmful and does not impact the taste of the potatoes.)

PER SERVING *382 cal., 27 g total fat (17 g sat. fat), 96 mg chol., 384 mg sodium, 29 g carbo., 2 g fiber, 8 g pro.*

Creamed Corn Casserole

2. In a large saucepan cook sweet peppers and onion in hot butter until tender. Stir in corn and black pepper. In a medium bowl whisk together soup, cream cheese spread, and milk. Stir soup mixture into corn mixture. Transfer to the prepared casserole.

3. Bake, covered, for 50 to 55 minutes or until corn mixture is heated through, stirring once.

PER ½ CUP *169 cal., 9 g total fat (4 g sat. fat), 26 mg chol., 270 mg sodium, 21 g carbo., 3 g fiber, 5 g pro.*

Cheddar Mashed Potatoes

These twice-cooked creamy, cheesy mashed potatoes are finished in a slow cooker, so you can turn attention to other tasks as they cook.

PREP **40 minutes** COOK **3 to 4 hours** (low)
MAKES **8 servings**

3 pounds russet potatoes, peeled and cut into 2-inch chunks
2 teaspoons coarse salt
6 ounces cream cheese, cut up
½ cup unsalted butter, cut up
½ teaspoons freshly ground black pepper
   Nonstick cooking spray
1 cup shredded sharp cheddar cheese (4 ounces)

1. In a 4-quart Dutch oven cook potatoes and 1 teaspoon of the salt, covered, in enough boiling water to cover for 15 minutes or until tender; drain. Mash with a potato masher or beat with an electric mixer on low. Stir in cream cheese, butter, the remaining 1 teaspoon salt, and black pepper.

2. Lightly coat the inside of a 3½- or 4-quart slow cooker with cooking spray. Spoon potato mixture into prepared slow cooker. Cover and cook on low-heat setting for 3 to 4 hours, stirring in cheddar cheese the last 30 minutes of cooking.

Easy Add-Ins Just before serving, stir in chopped green onions, chives, or parsley.

PER SERVING *332 cal., 24 g total fat (15 g sat. fat), 69 mg chol., 522 mg sodium, 23 g carbo., 2 g fiber, 8 g pro.*

Herbed Root Vegetable Cobbler

This savory cobbler features potatoes, rutabagas, carrots, and onions—seasoned and bubbling under a crown of Herbed Parmesan Dumplings.

PREP **45 minutes** BAKE **1 hour 12 minutes**
STAND **20 minutes** OVEN **400°F** MAKES **12 servings**

1 pound Yukon gold potatoes, cut into 1-inch pieces
1 pound rutabagas, peeled and cut into 1-inch pieces
4 medium carrots, cut into 1-inch pieces
2 medium parsnips, peeled and cut into 1-inch pieces
1 small red onion, cut into thin wedges
2 cloves garlic, minced

Creamed Corn Casserole

To make this side dish in a slow cooker, prepare the recipe as directed, except do not thaw the corn and omit the butter. In a 3½- or 4-quart slow cooker combine frozen corn, sweet pepper, onion, and black pepper. Whisk together the soup, cheese spread, and milk. Pour over the corn mixture in cooker. Cover and cook on low-heat setting for 8 to 10 hours or on high-heat setting for 4 to 5 hours. Stir before serving.

PREP **15 minutes** BAKE **50 minutes** OVEN **375°F**
MAKES **12 servings**

   Nonstick cooking spray
2 16-ounce packages frozen whole kernel corn
2 cups chopped red and/or green sweet peppers
1 cup chopped onion (1 large)
1 tablespoon butter or margarine
¼ teaspoon black pepper
1 10.75-ounce can condensed cream of celery soup
1 8-ounce tub cream cheese spread with chives and onion or cream cheese spread with garden vegetables
¼ cup milk

1. Preheat oven to 375°F. Lightly coat a 2-quart baking dish with cooking spray; set aside. Place corn in a colander. Run under cool water to thaw; drain. Set aside.

1   cup chicken broth
1½   teaspoons dried fines herbes, herbes de Provence, or Italian seasoning, crushed
½   teaspoon salt
¼   teaspoon black pepper
1   4- to 5.2-ounce container semisoft cheese with garlic and herbs
1   recipe Herbed Parmesan Dumplings

1. Preheat oven to 400°F. In an ungreased 3-quart baking dish combine potatoes, rutabagas, carrots, parsnips, onion, and garlic.

2. In a small bowl combine broth, fines herbes, salt, and pepper. Pour over vegetables, stirring to coat. Bake, covered, for 1 hour or until vegetables are nearly tender. Carefully uncover vegetables; stir in semisoft cheese.

3. Drop Herbed Parmesan Dumplings into 12 mounds on top of hot vegetables. Bake, uncovered, for 12 to 15 minutes more or until a toothpick inserted in centers of dumplings comes out clean. Let stand for 20 minutes before serving.

Herbed Parmesan Dumplings In a medium bowl stir together 1½ cups all-purpose flour; 2 teaspoons baking powder; 1½ teaspoons dried fines herbes, herbes de Provence, or Italian seasoning, crushed; and ½ teaspoon salt. Using a pastry blender, cut in 6 tablespoons butter until mixture resembles coarse crumbs. Stir in ¼ cup finely shredded Parmesan cheese. In a small bowl combine 2 lightly beaten eggs and ⅓ cup milk. Add all at once to flour mixture, stirring just until moistened.

PER SERVING *235 cal., 11 g total fat (6 g sat. fat), 61 mg chol., 424 mg sodium, 29 g carbo., 4 g fiber, 6 g pro.*

Herbed Root Vegetable Cobbler

Butternut-Hazelnut Gratin

Butternut-Hazelnut Gratin

To make soft bread crumbs, tear one or two slices of white, French, or whole wheat bread into 1-inch pieces then place them a food processor. Pulse until crumbly. One slice of bread yields about ½ cup of bread crumbs.

PREP **30 minutes** BAKE **1 hour** STAND **10 minutes** OVEN **350°F** MAKES **8 servings**

2   tablespoons butter
2   tablespoons pure maple syrup
2   medium onions, cut into thin wedges
1   tablespoon snipped fresh sage
3   cloves garlic, minced
¼   teaspoon salt
1   2- to 2½-pound butternut squash
½   teaspoon salt
¼   teaspoon black pepper
1   cup crumbled goat cheese (chèvre) (4 ounces)
1   cup coarse soft bread crumbs
⅓   cup hazelnuts (filberts), toasted and chopped (see note, page 87)
1   tablespoon butter, melted

1. Preheat oven to 350°F. Lightly grease a 2-quart baking dish; set aside. In a large skillet heat the 2 tablespoons butter and maple syrup over medium-low heat. Add onions; cook about 15 minutes or until very tender and golden, stirring occasionally. Stir in sage, garlic, and the ¼ teaspoon salt.
2. Meanwhile, halve squash lengthwise; seed and peel squash. Cut crosswise into ¼-inch slices. Sprinkle with the ½ teaspoon salt and the pepper.
3. Arrange squash in the prepared baking dish. Top with onion mixture and cheese. Bake, covered, for 50 to 55 minutes or until squash is nearly tender.
4. In a small bowl combine bread crumbs and hazelnuts; stir in melted butter. Sprinkle on squash mixture. Bake, uncovered, for 10 to 15 minutes more or until squash is tender and crumbs are lightly browned. Let stand for 10 minutes before serving.
PER SERVING *221 cal., 13 g total fat (7 g sat. fat), 26 mg chol., 342 mg sodium, 22 g carbo., 3 g fiber, 7 g pro.*

Warm Fingerling Potato Salad

This warm vinaigrette-dressed salad cooks conveniently in the microwave.

PREP **15 minutes** COOK **7 minutes** MAKES **4 servings**

1   pound fingerling or new potatoes, halved
1   cup fresh green beans, trimmed and cut into 2-inch pieces
¼   teaspoon salt
3   tablespoons olive oil
1   shallot, chopped
2   tablespoons white or red wine vinegar
2   tablespoons snipped fresh parsley

2 teaspoons Dijon mustard
1 teaspoon snipped fresh rosemary or ¼ teaspoon
   dried rosemary, crushed
⅛ teaspoon salt
⅛ teaspoon black pepper
¼ cup pitted niçoise olives, halved

1. Place potatoes in a 1½-quart microwave-safe
casserole dish. Top with green beans. Sprinkle with the
¼ teaspoon salt. Cover and microwave on high for 7 to
9 minutes or until potatoes are tender, stirring once.
Drain potato mixture.
2. For vinaigrette, in a large screw-top jar combine the
oil, shallot, vinegar, parsley, mustard, rosemary, the
⅛ teaspoon salt, and pepper. Cover and shake well.
3. In a bowl combine potato mixture, vinaigrette, and
olives; toss gently to coat. Transfer salad to a serving
bowl. Serve immediately or chill completely and
serve cold.
PER SERVING *202 cal., 12 g total fat (1 g sat. fat), 0 mg
chol., 333 mg sodium, 21 g carbo., 4 g fiber, 4 g pro.*

Sweet Potatoes with Pecans and Blue Cheese

While they're still warm from the oven, wedges
of sweet potatoes and onion are drizzled with a
homemade vinaigrette and sprinkled with candied
pecans and blue cheese.

PREP 30 minutes COOK 2 minutes ROAST 37 minutes
OVEN 375°F MAKES 6 servings

2 large sweet potatoes, peeled and cut lengthwise
   into thin wedges (1½ pounds)
1 small sweet onion, cut into 1-inch pieces (⅓ cup)
4 tablespoons olive oil
½ teaspoon salt
¼ teaspoon black pepper
1 tablespoon butter
⅓ cup pecan pieces
1 tablespoon packed light brown sugar
4 teaspoons cider vinegar
1½ teaspoons honey
1 clove garlic, minced (½ teaspoon)
2 tablespoons crumbled blue cheese or finely
   shredded white cheddar cheese

1. Preheat oven to 375°F. In a 15×10×1-inch baking pan
combine sweet potatoes and onion pieces. Drizzle with
2 tablespoons of the olive oil; sprinkle the salt and
pepper. Toss gently to combine. Spread potato mixture
in a single layer. Bake for 30 to 35 minutes or until
vegetables are tender, stirring once.
2. Meanwhile, in a small skillet melt butter over medium
heat. Stir in pecan pieces, brown sugar, and ¼ teaspoon
salt. Cook and stir for 2 to 3 minutes or until pecans are
coated in the brown sugar mixture. Remove from heat;
spread on foil and cool completely.

Sweet Potatoes with
Pecans and Blue Cheese

3. For dressing, in a small bowl whisk together the
vinegar, honey, garlic, ¼ teaspoon *salt,* and ¼ teaspoon
pepper. Slowly whisk in remaining 2 tablespoons olive
oil until combined. Whisk in 1 tablespoon of the
blue cheese.
4. To serve, transfer potatoes and onions to a serving
plate. Drizzle with dressing. Sprinkle with pecans and
remaining blue cheese.
PER SERVING *241 cal., 16 g total fat (3 g sat. fat), 7 mg
chol., 487 mg sodium, 23 g carbo., 3 g fiber, 3 g pro.*

Brussels Sprouts with Frizzled Prosciutto

If you like, substitute 4 slices of chopped bacon for the prosciutto and olive oil. Cook the bacon in the skillet, leaving just enough—about 1 tablespoon—of the drippings in the pan to cook the shallots and Brussels sprouts.

PREP 30 minutes COOK 20 minutes
MAKES 12 servings

2½	pounds Brussels sprouts
1	tablespoon olive oil
4	ounces thinly sliced prosciutto
3	tablespoons butter
½	cup thinly sliced shallots or chopped onion
½	teaspoon salt
¼	teaspoon freshly ground black pepper
1	tablespoon red wine vinegar

1. Trim stems and remove any wilted outer leaves from Brussels sprouts; wash. Cut any large sprouts in half lengthwise.
2. In a large Dutch oven bring a large amount of salted water to boiling. Carefully add Brussels sprouts and cook for 6 to 8 minutes just until tender (centers should be slightly firm). Drain and spread in a shallow baking pan.
3. When ready to serve, heat oil in a large skillet over medium-high heat. Add prosciutto to skillet, half at a time, and cook until crisp; remove from skillet. Reduce heat to medium. Add butter and shallots to skillet. Cook and stir about 2 minutes or until shallots begin to soften.
4. Add Brussels sprouts, salt, and pepper to skillet. Cook and stir Brussels sprouts about 6 minutes (8 minutes if chilled) or until heated through. Add vinegar and stir to coat. Transfer Brussels spouts to a serving bowl. Top with prosciutto and serve.

PER SERVING *92 cal., 5 g total fat (2 g sat. fat), 15 mg chol., 391 mg sodium, 8 g carbo., 3 g fiber, 5 g pro.*

Brussels Sprouts with Frizzled Prosciutto

Creamy Spinach

Flavor the sauce for this creamy spinach dish with a teaspoon or two of coarse-grained Dijon mustard, if you like, added along with the whipping cream. Cooked crumbled bacon makes a nice garnish.

START TO FINISH **20 minutes** MAKES **4 servings**

4   6-ounce packages prewashed fresh baby spinach; two 9-ounce packages fresh spinach (large stems removed); or two 10-ounce packages frozen chopped spinach, thawed
½   cup chopped onion (1 medium)
2   to 3 cloves garlic, minced
2   tablespoons butter
1   cup whipping cream
½   teaspoon black pepper
¼   teaspoon salt
¼   teaspoon ground nutmeg

1. In a large saucepan cook fresh spinach (if using) in rapidly boiling salted water for 1 minute. Drain well, squeezing out excess liquid. Pat dry with paper towels. Snip spinach with kitchen shears to coarsely chop; set aside. (If using frozen spinach, drain well, squeezing out excess liquid.)
2. In a large skillet cook onion and garlic in hot butter about 5 minutes or until onion is tender. Stir in whipping cream, pepper, salt, and nutmeg. Bring mixture to boiling; cook, uncovered, for 3 to 5 minutes or until cream begins to thicken. Add spinach. Simmer, uncovered, until desired consistency, stirring occasionally. Serve immediately.
PER SERVING *312 cal., 29 g total fat (18 g sat. fat), 97 mg chol., 345 mg sodium, 11 g carbo., 4 g fiber, 7 g pro.*

Double-Gingered Orange Carrots

Here's a neat trick: Use a very sharp vegetable peeler to thinly shave the ginger.

PREP **10 minutes** COOK **20 minutes**
MAKES **8 servings**

3   pounds baby carrots with tops trimmed or 2 pounds small to medium carrots
4   teaspoons olive oil
½   cup orange juice
2   1-inch pieces fresh ginger, peeled and shaved or cut into very thin slices
¼   teaspoon salt
¼   cup chopped, toasted hazelnuts (see note, page 87)
2   tablespoons chopped crystallized ginger

1. Halve baby carrots lengthwise. Quarter small carrots lengthwise; cut crosswise into 3-inch pieces.
2. In a nonstick skillet cook carrots in hot olive oil over medium heat for 10 minutes, stirring once. Add orange juice, fresh ginger, and salt; toss to coat. Cook, covered,

Double-Gingered Orange Carrots

for 6 to 8 minutes or until carrots are tender. Uncover; cook for 2 minutes more or until liquid is reduced by half.
3. To serve, sprinkle with nuts and crystallized ginger.
PER SERVING *109 cal., 5 g total fat (1 g sat. fat), 0 mg chol., 224 mg sodium, 16 g carbo., 4 g fiber, 2 g pro.*

Green Beans with Sage and
Shiitake Mushrooms

Green Beans with Sage and Shiitake Mushrooms

Always discard the stems of shiitake mushrooms—they're very woody and inedible.

PREP **15 minutes** COOK **14 minutes**
MAKES **8 to 10 servings**

2   pounds green beans, trimmed
2   tablespoons olive oil
2   tablespoons butter
3   to 4 cloves garlic, thinly sliced
12   ounces shiitake mushrooms, stemmed and halved
3   tablespoons chopped fresh sage
      Coarse sea salt or kosher salt and freshly ground black pepper

1. Bring a large saucepan of salted water to boiling. Add the green beans. Return to boiling; reduce heat. Cook, covered, for 3 to 4 minutes just until tender. Drain green beans in a colander. Run cold water over the beans until chilled to stop the cooking and keep the beans bright green. Set aside. (Or cover and chill beans up to 24 hours.)
2. In a very large skillet heat the olive oil and butter over medium heat. Add the garlic and cook, stirring often, until it is just golden. Add the mushrooms and continue to cook for 6 to 8 minutes until mushrooms are soft and cooked through, stirring often. Add the reserved beans. Toss and heat through, 5 to 8 minutes. Add sage, salt, and pepper to taste.
PER SERVING *112 cal., 6 g total fat (2 g sat. fat), 8 mg chol., 150 mg sodium, 14 g carbo., 4 g fiber, 3 g pro.*

Garlic and Parsleyed Green Beans

Before adding the chilled green beans to the skillet, pat them dry with clean paper towels. Getting water in hot oil or butter causes spattering, which can burn.

PREP **25 minutes** COOK **10 minutes**
MAKES **6 to 8 servings**

1½   pounds green beans, washed and both ends trimmed
3   tablespoons unsalted butter
2   teaspoons fresh garlic, finely chopped with a good pinch of salt
2   tablespoons snipped fresh parsley
      Salt and freshly ground black pepper to taste

1. Fill a large saucepan with water and bring to boiling. Add 1 tablespoon *salt* and the beans. Cook, uncovered, for 5 to 8 minutes or just until beans are tender yet vibrant green. Drain the beans and immediately submerge them in a bowl of lightly salted ice water; drain well.
2. In a large skillet heat butter over medium-high heat until melted and foaming. Add the beans; cook and stir until heated through. Add the garlic and parsley.

Maple-Glazed Baked Apples

Season to taste with salt and pepper. Cook and stir for 1 minute.
PER SERVING *90 cal., 6 g total fat (4 g sat. fat), 15 mg chol., 80 mg sodium, 9 g carbo., 4 g fiber, 2 g pro.*

Maple-Glazed Baked Apples

Serve these old-fashioned baked apples drizzled with whipping cream or topped with a scoop of vanilla bean ice cream.

PREP **20 minutes** BAKE **40 minutes** OVEN **350°F**
MAKES **6 servings**

6   small apples (such as Jonathan, Jonagold, or Winesap)
½   cup apple juice or apple cider
2   tablespoons maple syrup
1   tablespoon butter
6   3-inch cinnamon sticks

1. Preheat oven to 350°F. Using a melon baller, core apples, leaving the bottoms intact. Using a small sharp knife, cut off a strip of peel around the top of each apple. Place apples in a 2-quart casserole or baking dish.
2. In a small saucepan combine apple juice, maple syrup, and butter. Bring to boiling. Pour hot juice mixture over apples. Insert a cinnamon stick into the center of each apple.
3. Bake for 40 to 45 minutes or until apples are tender, brushing tops of apples occasionally with juice mixture in casserole.
PER SERVING *69 cal., 2 g total fat (1 g sat. fat), 5 mg chol., 25 mg sodium, 14 g carbo., 2 g fiber, 0 g pro.*

Good Greens Winter Soup

Kale is one of the most nutritious greens on the planet. It's loaded with vitamins A and C, folic acid, calcium, and iron. Eat this good-for-you soup to counter all of the cookies you've been eating.

START TO FINISH **35 minutes** MAKES **8 servings**

2   leeks, trimmed, halved, and sliced, or 1 medium onion, chopped
2   stalks celery, chopped
2   cloves garlic, minced
1   tablespoon olive oil
3   14.5-ounce cans reduced-sodium chicken broth
1   14.5-ounce can diced tomatoes with basil, garlic, and oregano, undrained
4   cups coarsely shredded kale
2   medium zucchini, halved lengthwise and sliced crosswise
¼   teaspoon salt
¼   teaspoon black pepper
1   5-ounce package baby spinach
½   cup chopped fresh parsley or fresh basil (optional)
2   tablespoons red wine vinegar
    Finely grated Parmesan cheese (optional)

1. In a 5- to 6-quart Dutch oven cook leeks, celery, and garlic in hot oil over medium heat for 10 minutes or until tender and just starting to brown.
2. Stir in broth, tomatoes, kale, zucchini, salt, and pepper. Bring to boiling; reduce heat. Cover and simmer for 5 minutes or just until vegetables are tender, stirring once. Stir in spinach, parsley, and vinegar just before serving. If desired, serve with Parmesan cheese.

PER CUP *90 cal., 2 g total fat (0 g sat. fat), 0 mg chol., 737 mg sodium, 14 g carbo., 2 g fiber, 5 g pro.*

Good Greens Winter Soup

Smoked Sausage-Lentil Soup

This hearty and humble legume-based soup is a nice main dish for a casual gathering. Keep a pot simmering on the stove for guests to serve themselves. Serve it with a crisp green salad and warm rolls or crusty bread.

PREP 25 minutes COOK 25 minutes
MAKES 10 servings

2   small fennel bulbs
8   cloves garlic, minced
2   tablespoons olive oil
¾   cup onion, chopped (1 large)
2   cups carrots, chopped (4 medium)
12   cups water
2½   cups brown lentils, rinsed and drained
2   teaspoons salt
½   teaspoon black pepper
12   ounces cooked smoked sausage, cut into ½-inch-thick pieces
⅓   cup red wine vinegar

1. Cut off fennel stalks. If desired, reserve some of the fennel leaves as a garnish; discard fennel stalks. Remove any wilted outer layers and chop enough of the fennel bulbs to measure 2 cups.
2. In a 4- to 6-quart Dutch oven cook and stir garlic in hot oil over medium heat for 1 minute. Add onion; cook until golden brown, stirring occasionally. Add the 2 cups fennel and the carrots; cook until tender, stirring occasionally. Add the water, lentils, salt, and pepper. Bring to boiling; reduce heat. Simmer, uncovered, for 25 to 30 minutes or until lentils are tender.
3. Meanwhile, in a large skillet cook sausage until browned. Using a slotted spoon, transfer sausage to lentil mixture. Stir in vinegar. If desired, garnish with the reserved fennel leaves.
PER SERVING *347 cal., 14 g total fat (4 g sat. fat), 23 mg chol., 1,314 mg sodium, 34 g carbo., 20 g fiber, 22 g pro.*

Christmas Potato Soup

An immersion blender is a handy tool for blending soup without having to transfer hot soup between a Dutch oven and food processor or blender.

PREP 25 minutes ROAST 25 minutes COOK 20 minutes
OVEN 425°F MAKES 8 servings

15   cloves garlic, peeled
½   teaspoon olive oil
6   slices bacon
4   medium leeks, sliced
2   14.5-ounce cans reduced-sodium chicken broth
1½   cups water
2   pounds round red potatoes, peeled and chopped
½   teaspoon salt
¼   teaspoon black pepper

Smoked Sausage-Lentil Soup

       Water (optional)
½   cup sour cream (optional)
       Snipped chives (optional)

1. Preheat oven to 425°F. Place garlic cloves in a custard cup; drizzle with olive oil. Cover with foil. Roast in oven 25 to 35 minutes or until cloves feel soft when pressed; set aside.
2. Meanwhile, in a Dutch oven cook bacon over medium heat until crisp; drain on paper towels. Crumble bacon; set aside.
3. Cook leeks in the bacon drippings for 5 minutes or until softened but not browned. Add broth, water, potatoes, salt, and pepper. Bring to boiling, reduce heat. Simmer, uncovered, 10 to 12 minutes. Stir in garlic.
4. Use an immersion blender to process the soup until smooth. (Or pour half the soup mixture into a food processor or blender. Cover and process or blend until smooth. Repeat with remaining soup. Return soup to Dutch oven.)
5. Add bacon to soup and heat through. If desired, thin with water to desired consistency. Ladle into bowls; if desired, top with sour cream and sprinkle with chives.
PER CUP *224 cal., 13 g total fat (4 g sat. fat), 19 mg chol., 627 mg sodium, 20 g carbo., 2 g fiber, 7 g pro.*

Beet Salad with Goat Cheese and Walnuts

Beet Salad with Goat Cheese and Walnuts

For an especially festive touch, make this salad with Chioggia beets (also called candy cane beets for their red and white stripes).

START TO FINISH **15 minutes** MAKES **16 servings**

16 cups mixed baby salad greens
1   cup bottled balsamic vinaigrette salad dressing
4   8¼-ounce cans tiny whole beets or 8 small cooked beets, chilled
¼   cup snipped fresh basil or fresh parsley
½   teaspoon black pepper
½   cup coarsely chopped walnuts, toasted (see note, page 119)
4   ounces semisoft goat cheese (chèvre), crumbled

1. Place greens in a large salad bowl. Drizzle some of the dressing over greens, gently tossing to mix. Set aside.
2. Drain and cut up beets. In a medium bowl combine beets, basil, and pepper. Drizzle with some of the salad dressing; toss to coat.
3. To serve, divide salad greens among salad plates. Spoon beet mixture onto center of the salad greens. Sprinkle salads with walnuts and goat cheese.
PER SERVING *147 cal., 10 g total fat (3 g sat. fat), 7 mg chol., 571 mg sodium, 11 g carbo., 3 g fiber, 6 g pro.*

Waldorf Wilted Salad

Bok choy stems add subtle flavor and an unconventional texture to this traditional apple and walnut salad.

START TO FINISH **25 minutes** MAKES **6 servings**

10 cups mesclun mix or field greens
3 cups ½-inch pieces bok choy stems
½ cup walnuts, toasted and coarsely chopped (see note, page 119)
⅓ cup olive oil
⅓ cup rice vinegar
2 tablespoons chopped shallot
1 tablespoon Dijon mustard
1 teaspoon sugar
⅛ teaspoon salt
⅛ teaspoon freshly ground pepper
3 Granny Smith apples, cored, cut into wedges
3 hard-cooked eggs, cut into wedges

1. In a large bowl toss greens, bok choy, and nuts. Set aside.
2. For dressing, in a small saucepan combine oil, vinegar, shallot, mustard, sugar, salt, and pepper. Bring to boiling; remove from heat. Carefully pour warm dressing over salad; toss lightly. Cover bowl with a large dinner plate for 1 to 2 minutes or just until greens begin to wilt. Remove plate. Add apples and eggs; toss lightly. Serve immediately.

PER SERVING *276 cal., 21 g total fat (3 g sat. fat), 106 mg chol., 174 mg sodium, 17 g carbo., 4 g fiber, 7 g pro.*

Mesclun Salad with Roasted Pears

This salad is a delicious combination of contrasting tastes and textures. Sweet fruit balances the tang of blue cheese; tender roasted pears and strawberries complement the crisp greens and toasted pecans.

PREP **20 minutes** ROAST **20 minutes** OVEN **425°F**
MAKES **12 servings**

2 pounds Bosc pears, peeled, cored, and sliced ¼ inch thick (6 medium)
1 tablespoon olive oil
½ teaspoon salt
¼ teaspoon freshly ground black pepper
¼ cup olive oil
2 tablespoons sherry vinegar or balsamic vinegar
2 teaspoons finely chopped shallot
1 teaspoon honey
2 5-ounce bags mesclun or spring salad mix (12 cups)
2 cups sliced fresh strawberries
3 ounces blue cheese, crumbled
¾ cup pecan halves, toasted (see note, page 119) (optional)

1. Preheat oven to 425°F. Line a 15×10×1-inch baking pan with foil. Place pear slices in prepared pan. Drizzle with 1 tablespoon oil. Sprinkle with ¼ teaspoon of the salt and ⅛ teaspoon of the pepper; toss to coat. Arrange slices in a single layer. Roast pear slices, uncovered, for 20 to 25 minutes or until golden and edges are crisp and brown, gently turning and rearranging once. Watch closely the last few minutes of roasting to prevent from burning. Cool pears in pan on a wire rack.
2. For dressing, in a screw-top jar combine ¼ cup olive oil, vinegar, shallots, honey, the remaining ¼ teaspoon salt, and the remaining ⅛ teaspoon pepper. Cover and shake well.
3. On individual salad plates arrange greens, pear slices, strawberries, blue cheese, and, if desired, pecans. Drizzle with dressing.

PER SERVING *129 cal., 8 g total fat (2 g sat. fat), 5 mg chol., 198 mg sodium, 13 g carbo., 2 g fiber, 2 g pro.*

Mesclun Salad with Roasted Pears

Apple Fennel Salad

Apple Fennel Salad

To remove the edible pomegranate seeds (also called arils), cut off the crown of the fruit, then lightly score the rind five or six times from top to bottom. Submerge the cut fruit in a bowl of cold water to soak for 5 minutes, then hold the fruit under water to prevent the juice from spattering and staining; break apart the sections. The seeds will sink to the bottom of the bowl. Remove and discard the rind and membrane. Drain and pat the seeds dry.

START TO FINISH **40 minutes**
MAKES **8 to 10 servings**

1   pomegranate
3   lemons
5   cups tart, crisp green and/or red apples, such as Granny Smith (4 medium)
2   cups fennel bulbs, trimmed, fronds reserved (2 medium)
6   tablespoons canola oil
2   tablespoons mayonnaise
3   to 4 tablespoons snipped fresh parsley
    Coarse salt and freshly ground black pepper

1. Remove seeds from pomegranate; set aside. Squeeze the juice from 1 of the lemons into a large salad bowl. Halve and core the apples, leaving skin intact. Thinly slice the apples and toss with the lemon juice in the bowl; set aside.
2. Halve the fennel bulbs. Core and thinly slice each bulb. Add the fennel to the apples. Toss to combine; set aside. Coarsely chop some of the reserved fennel fronds (about ¼ cup); set aside.
3. Finely shred the yellow portion of peel from the 2 remaining lemons into a small bowl. Juice the lemons and add juice to peel. Whisk the oil into the juice and the peel. Whisk in the mayonnaise. Season with salt and pepper.
4. To serve, drain apples and fennel; return to bowl. Add pomegranate seeds, reserved fennel fronds, and parsley. Pour dressing over salad and toss to coat.
To Make-Ahead Prepare as above, except do not add the pomegranate seeds; cover and chill up to 24 hours. Sprinkle with the seeds just before serving.
PER SERVING *182 cal., 13 g total fat (1 g sat. fat), 1 mg chol., 174 mg sodium, 19 g carbo., 5 g fiber, 2 g pro.*

Pink Grapefruit Stacked Salad

Pink Grapefruit Stacked Salad

Winter is peak season for citrus because it is especially juicy and sweet this time of year. This gorgeous salad alternates slices of pink and white grapefruit on a bed of spinach topped with pomegranate seeds.

START TO FINISH **30 minutes** MAKES **8 servings**

3	medium pink grapefruit
3	medium white grapefruit
½	cup apricot nectar
2	tablespoons hazelnut oil or walnut oil
1	tablespoon snipped fresh mint or ½ teaspoon dried mint, crushed
⅛	teaspoon salt
⅛	teaspoon cracked black pepper
4	cups fresh baby spinach leaves or shredded fresh spinach leaves
½	cup chopped walnuts, toasted (see note, page 119)
¼	cup pomegranate seeds (optional)*

1. Peel the grapefruit, removing all of the white pith. Cut flesh from each grapefruit to form square pieces (reserve grapefruit trimmings for another use). Slice each square crosswise into 4 slices. Set slices aside.

2. For dressing, in a small bowl whisk together apricot nectar, oil, mint, salt, and pepper.

3. To serve, line individual salad plates with spinach. For each serving, stack 3 slices of the grapefruit, alternating colors, on the spinach leaves. Drizzle with dressing. Sprinkle with walnuts and, if desired, pomegranate seeds.

*****Note** If pomegranate seeds aren't available, substitute snipped dried cranberries or dried tart cherries.

PER SERVING *147 cal., 9 g total fat (1 g sat. fat), 0 mg chol., 56 mg sodium, 18 g carbo., 4 g fiber, 3 g pro.*

savory
bites.
and sips

Bite-size nibbles and noshes make for especially social eating. Because they're portable and usually can be held with fingers, guests can mix and mingle while enjoying stuffed mushrooms, savory little meatballs, appetizer tarts, and creamy dips and spreads. Make one or two recipes as a prelude to dinner—or set out an appetizer buffet as dinner.

Goat Cheese-Olive Tart, page 41

Italian Mini Meatballs

1. Preheat oven to 350°F. For meatballs, in a large bowl combine egg, bread crumbs, dry salad dressing mix, crushed red pepper, and garlic. Add ground beef, Italian sausage, pineapple, green chile peppers, and mozzarella cheese; mix well. Shape into 48 meatballs.

2. In a 15×10×1-inch baking pan arrange meatballs in a single layer. Bake, uncovered, for 20 minutes. Drain well. Transfer meatballs to a 3½- or 4-quart slow cooker.

3. For sauce, in a medium bowl combine bottled salad dressing, pineapple preserves, and chili sauce. Pour over meatballs in cooker. Cover and cook on low-heat setting for 3 to 4 hours or on high-heat setting for 1½ to 2 hours.

4. Stir gently before serving. Serve meatballs with wooden toothpicks.

Note To make uniform shape meatballs, pat the meat mixture into an 8×6-inch rectangle on a piece of waxed paper. Cut the meat into 1-inch cubes, then use your hands to roll each cube in a ball.

PER APPETIZER *62 cal., 4 g total fat (1 g sat. fat), 14 mg chol., 165 mg sodium, 4 g carbo., 0 g fiber, 3 g pro.*

Cranberry-Sauced Sausages

To make these cocktail sausages in a slow cooker, combine cranberry sauce, ketchup, lemon juice, dry mustard, and allspice in a 1½- or 2-quart slow cooker. Stir in the sausage links. Cover and cook on low-heat setting for 4 hours or on high-heat setting for 2 hours.

PREP **10 minutes** COOK **10 minutes**
MAKES **16 servings**

1	16-ounce can jellied cranberry sauce
⅔	cup ketchup
2	tablespoons lemon juice
1	teaspoon dry mustard
¼	teaspoon ground allspice
1	16-ounce package small cooked smoked sausage links

1. In a large saucepan combine cranberry sauce, ketchup, lemon juice, dry mustard, and allspice. Stir in sausage links. Cook over medium-high heat until heated through, stirring occasionally.

2. Serve immediately or keep warm, covered, in a 1½- or 2-quart slow cooker on warm setting or low-heat setting up to 2 hours.

PER SERVING *134 cal., 7 g total fat (3 g sat. fat), 20 mg chol., 393 mg sodium, 13 g carbo., 1 g fiber, 4 g pro.*

Italian Mini Meatballs

Meatballs are always a hit at holiday parties. Crushed pineapple and fruit preserves add a touch of sweetness to these saucy little bites.

PREP **30 minutes** BAKE **20 minutes**
COOK **3 to 4 hours (low) or 1½ to 2 hours (high)**
OVEN **350°F** MAKES **48 appetizers**

1	lightly beaten egg
⅓	cup fine dry bread crumbs
1	0.7-ounce envelope Italian dry salad dressing mix
½	teaspoon crushed red pepper
2	cloves garlic, minced
1	pound lean ground beef
8	ounces bulk Italian sausage
¼	cup canned crushed pineapple, well drained
¼	cup canned diced green chile peppers, well drained
¼	cup shredded mozzarella cheese (1 ounce)
½	cup bottled Italian salad dressing
½	cup pineapple or plum preserves
½	cup bottled chili sauce

Sesame Beef Kabobs

Sweet peppers and fresh pea pods give these Asian-flavor beef kabobs fresh crunch.

PREP **30 minutes** MARINATE **4 hours**
GRILL **14 minutes** MAKES **30 servings**

12　ounces boneless beef top sirloin steak, cut
　　1 inch thick
2　tablespoons soy sauce
2　tablespoons toasted sesame oil
2　tablespoons sliced green onion (1)
1½　teaspoons sugar
1½　teaspoons dry sherry (optional)
2　cloves garlic, minced
½　teaspoon sesame seeds
½　teaspoon crushed red pepper
2　small red and/or orange sweet peppers, quartered
　　and seeded
¾　cup fresh pea pods, trimmed and halved
　　crosswise diagonally
　　Sesame seeds
4　limes, cut into wedges

1. Trim fat from meat. Place meat in a resealable plastic bag set in a shallow dish.
2. For marinade, in a small bowl combine soy sauce, sesame oil, green onion, sugar, sherry, (if using), garlic, ½ teaspoon sesame seeds, and crushed red pepper. Pour marinade over meat. Seal bag; turn to coat meat. Marinate in the refrigerator for 4 to 24 hours, turning bag occasionally. Drain meat, discarding marinade.
3. For a charcoal grill, grill meat on the rack of an uncovered grill directly over medium coals for 14 to 18 minutes for medium-rare (145°F) or 18 to 22 minutes for medium (160°F), turning once halfway through grilling. While the meat is grilling, add sweet pepper quarters to grill. Grill for 4 to 5 minutes or until lightly charred, turning once halfway through grilling. (For a gas grill, preheat grill. Reduce heat to medium. Place meat, then sweet pepper quarters, on grill rack over heat. Cover and grill as above.) Cut meat and sweet pepper quarters into 1-inch pieces.
4. Meanwhile, in a small saucepan cook pea pods in a small amount of boiling water for 2 to 4 minutes or until crisp-tender; drain.
5. To serve, thread meat pieces, sweet pepper pieces, and pea pods onto wooden skewers. Sprinkle with additional sesame seeds and serve with lime wedges.
PER APPETIZER *38 cal., 2 g total fat (1 g sat. fat), 5 mg chol., 74 mg sodium, 2 g carbo., 0 g fiber, 3 g pro.*

Sesame Beef Kabobs

Shrimp-and-Bacon-Stuffed Baby Potatoes

1. Preheat oven to 425°F. Cut potatoes in half lengthwise. Using small melon baller or very small spoon, scoop out potato flesh, leaving ¼ inch shells. Cut a thin slice from the bottom of each potato half so it stands upright. Place potatoes, cut sides up, in a 15×10×1-inch baking pan.
2. In a small bowl combine mustard, oil, and 1 teaspoon seafood seasoning. Brush insides of potato shells with mustard mixture. Bake about 30 minutes or until potatoes are tender.
3. Meanwhile, for filling, in a small bowl combine shrimp, cream cheese, Gouda cheese, bacon, and 1 teaspoon seafood seasoning. Spoon filling into potato shells, mounding slightly.
4. Bake for 12 to 15 minutes more or until filling is heated through and cheese is melted. Serve warm or at room temperature. If desired, garnish with chives.
*Note If seasoning is coarse, crush before using.
PER APPETIZER *63 cal., 4 g total fat (2 g sat. fat), 24 mg chol., 168 mg sodium, 3 g carbo., 0 g fiber, 4 g pro.*

Teriyaki Chicken Rumaki

The original version of this mock Polynesian appetizer popular in the 1950s called for chicken livers. Although this version uses chicken breast, you could substitute fresh sea scallops or shrimp for the chicken breast.

PREP **25 minutes** SOAK **30 minutes**
BAKE **24 minutes** OVEN **375°F** MAKES **24 servings**

12 slices bacon, halved crosswise
1 pound skinless, boneless chicken breast halves, cut into 24 (1½-inch) pieces
6 green onions, trimmed and each cut into 4 pieces
1 cup thin red sweet pepper strips (1 medium)
⅓ cup teriyaki glaze

1. Soak 4- to 6-inch wooden skewers in water for at least 30 minutes. Drain before using.
2. Preheat oven to 375°F. Wrap bacon around chicken pieces. Thread each skewer with a bacon-wrapped chicken piece, a green onion piece, and a sweet pepper strip. Place in a 15×10×1-inch baking pan.
3. Bake for 8 minutes. Brush with teriyaki glaze. Bake about 16 minutes more or until bacon is cooked through.
PER SERVING *114 cal., 9 g total fat (3 g sat. fat), 24 mg chol., 325 mg sodium, 1 g carbo., 0 g fiber, 7 g pro.*

Shrimp-and-Bacon-Stuffed Baby Potatoes

If bacon makes everything better, how about tender and tiny new potatoes baked with bacon, shrimp, and cheese filling? Absolutely irresistible.

PREP **35 minutes** BAKE **42 minutes**
OVEN **425°F** MAKES **28 appetizers**

14 tiny new potatoes (about 1¼ pounds)
2 tablespoons Dijon mustard
1 tablespoon olive oil
1 teaspoon seafood seasoning*
1 7- to 8-ounce package frozen peeled cooked shrimp, thawed, drained, and chopped
½ of an 8-ounce package cream cheese, softened
1 cup shredded Gouda cheese (4 ounces)
5 slices bacon, crisp-cooked, drained, and crumbled
1 teaspoon seafood seasoning*
¼ cup snipped fresh chives (optional)

Chicken and Raisin-Stuffed Mushrooms

Stuffed mushrooms are classic party fare. These sweet and savory bites offer a tantalizing departure from the standard cream-cheese-filled version.

PREP 30 minutes BAKE 13 minutes
OVEN 425°F MAKES 15 mushrooms

15 large fresh mushrooms (2½ to 3 inches in diameter)
3 tablespoons butter
¼ cup thinly sliced green onions (2)
1 clove garlic, minced
¾ cup finely chopped cooked chicken or turkey (about 4 ounces)
2 tablespoons fine dry bread crumbs
2 tablespoons grated Parmesan cheese
2 tablespoons finely chopped smoke-flavor almonds
2 tablespoons chopped golden raisins
1 tablespoon snipped fresh parsley
    Olive oil

1. Preheat oven to 425°F. Remove and discard stems from mushrooms. Set mushroom caps aside.
2. For filling, in a small saucepan melt butter over medium heat. Add green onions and garlic; cook and stir about 2 minutes or until tender. Remove from heat. Stir in chicken, bread crumbs, cheese, almonds, raisins, and parsley. Set filling aside.
3. Place mushrooms, stemmed sides down, in a 15×10×1-inch baking pan. Bake for 5 minutes. Turn mushrooms stem sides up. Brush mushrooms with oil. Divide filling among mushrooms. Bake for 8 to 10 minutes more or until heated through.
PER MUSHROOM *60 cal., 4 g total fat (2 g sat. fat), 13 mg chol., 65 mg sodium, 3 g carbo., 0 g fiber, 3 g pro.*

Chicken-and-Raisin-Stuffed Mushrooms

Bacon-Pecan Tassies

1. Preheat oven to 325°F. For pastry, in a medium bowl combine ½ cup butter and cream cheese. Beat with an electric mixer on medium until smooth. Stir in flour. Divide dough in 24 pieces; shape in balls. Press balls onto the bottoms and up the sides of 24 ungreased 1¾-inch muffin cups. Set aside.
2. For filling, in a medium bowl beat egg, brown sugar, and 1 tablespoon melted butter until combined. Stir in pecans and bacon. Spoon 1 heaping teaspoon of the filling into each pastry-lined muffin cup.
3. Bake for 25 to 30 minutes or until pastry is golden brown and filling is puffed. Cool slightly in pan. Carefully transfer tassies to a wire rack; cool. If desired, sprinkle with chives.
PER TASSIE *118 cal., 8 g total fat (4 g sat. fat), 25 mg chol., 62 mg sodium, 11 g carbo., 0 g fiber, 2 g pro.*

Avocado Pesto-Stuffed Tomatoes

These savory little stuffed tomatoes are elegant. Serve them in place of veggies and dip.

PREP **40 minutes** STAND **30 minutes**
MAKES **30 stuffed tomatoes**

30 cherry tomatoes (about 1¼ pints)
½ medium avocado, seeded, peeled, and cut up
2 ounces cream cheese, softened
2 tablespoons homemade or purchased basil pesto
1 teaspoon lemon juice
    Snipped fresh basil (optional)

1. Line a large baking sheet with paper towels; set aside. Cut a thin slice from the bottom of each tomato so it stands upright. Cut a thin slice from the top of each tomato. Carefully hollow out the cherry tomatoes with a small measuring spoon or melon baller. Invert tomatoes on baking sheet. Let stand for 30 minutes.
2. In a food processor combine avocado, cream cheese, pesto, and lemon juice. Cover and process until mixture is smooth. Spoon into a pastry bag fitted with a large plain round or open star tip.
3. Place tomatoes, open sides up, on a serving platter. Pipe avocado mixture into the tomato shells. Serve immediately or loosely cover and chill up to 4 hours. Sprinkle with basil before serving.
PER STUFFED TOMATO *18 cal., 1 g total fat (1 g sat. fat), 2 mg chol., 16 mg sodium, 1 g carbo., 0 g fiber, 0 g pro.*

Bacon-Pecan Tassies

What happens when a little bacon and cream cheese is added to a classic cookie? It becomes an irresistible appetizer to nibble with a glass of wine.

PREP **30 minutes** BAKE **25 minutes**
OVEN **325°F** MAKES **24 tassies**

½ cup butter, softened
1 3-ounce package cream cheese, softened
1 cup all-purpose flour
1 egg
¾ cup packed brown sugar
1 tablespoon butter, melted
½ cup coarsely chopped pecans
2 slices bacon, crisp-cooked, drained, and crumbled
    Snipped fresh chives (optional)

Goat Cheese-Olive Tart

A warm wedge of this rustic French-style tart is delicious with a glass of chilled white wine.

PREP **25 minutes** BAKE **30 minutes**
OVEN **375°F** MAKES **6 to 8 servings**

½ of a 15-ounce package (1 crust) rolled refrigerated unbaked piecrust
1   cup finely chopped leek (white part only)
½ cup finely chopped fennel
1   tablespoon olive oil
¾ cup crumbled aged goat cheese (chèvre) or shredded Parmesan cheese (3 ounces)
¾ cup coarsely chopped Gaeta, kalamata, or other Italian olives
1   tablespoon snipped fresh thyme

1. Allow piecrust to stand according to package directions. Preheat oven to 375°F. Line a large baking sheet with parchment paper. Place piecrust on the prepared baking sheet; roll into an 11-inch circle. Set aside.
2. For filling, in a medium skillet cook leek and fennel in hot oil over medium heat for 5 to 6 minutes or until tender, stirring occasionally. Remove from heat. Stir in cheese, olives, and thyme. Cool slightly.
3. Spread filling in center of pastry, within 1½ inches of pastry edges. Fold pastry edges over filling.
4. Bake for 30 to 35 minutes or until pastry is golden brown. Cut into wedges and serve warm.
PER SERVING *272 cal., 18 g total fat (7 g sat. fat), 18 mg chol., 347 mg sodium, 21 g carbo., 1 g fiber, 5 g pro.*

Bacon-Filled Medjool Dates

If there is a perfect flavor combination, it is these sweet-salty-savory stuffed dates. Who can stop at just one?

PREP **25 minutes** BAKE **12 minutes**
OVEN **375°F** MAKES **24 filled dates**

6   slices bacon
½ cup whole almonds or pecan halves, toasted and chopped
½ cup finely shredded Manchego or Parmesan cheese (2 ounces)
24 unpitted whole Medjool dates (about 1 pound)
3   tablespoons honey
1   teaspoon snipped fresh thyme

1. Preheat oven to 375°F. In a large skillet cook bacon over medium heat until crisp. Remove bacon and drain on paper towels. Crumble bacon. In a small bowl combine bacon, almonds, and cheese.
2. Cut a slit along 1 side of each date; spread open and remove pit. Spoon about 1 tablespoon of the bacon mixture into each date; press date to shape around filling (filling will be exposed). Arrange dates, filling sides up, on an ungreased baking sheet.
3. Bake for 12 to 15 minutes or until heated through and cheese is lightly browned. Cool slightly.
4. Before serving, drizzle warm dates with honey and sprinkle with thyme.
PER DATE *112 cal., 3 g total fat (1 g sat. fat), 4 mg chol., 79 mg sodium, 21 g carbo., 2 g fiber, 2 g pro.*

Bacon-Filled Medjool Dates

Blue Cheese-Apricot Bites

2. Meanwhile, in a small bowl combine Gorgonzola cheese and cream cheese. Beat with an electric mixer on medium until smooth.

3. Spoon about ¾ teaspoon of the cheese mixture on top of each dried apricot. Sprinkle with nuts. If desired, garnish with additional fresh rosemary.

PER SERVING *33 cal., 2 g total fat (1 g sat. fat), 5 mg chol., 24 mg sodium, 3 g carbo., 0 g fiber, 1 g pro.*

Ricotta, Gorgonzola, and Honey Spread

Although any honey will do for drizzling over this spread, a specialty honey made from avocado blossoms, buckwheat, orange blossoms, or sage will impart it with the distinct flavor of the source of the honey.

PREP **25 minutes** CHILL **1 hour** MAKES **36 servings**

- 1 15-ounce carton whole milk ricotta cheese
- 6 ounces Gorgonzola cheese, crumbled
- ½ teaspoon snipped fresh thyme or ¼ teaspoon dried thyme, crushed
- ¼ teaspoon snipped fresh rosemary or ⅛ teaspoon dried rosemary, crushed
- 1 tablespoon honey
- 36 toasted baguette slices
  Sliced apples, fresh thyme, and/or toasted walnuts (see note, page 119)
  Honey

1. In a large mixing bowl beat ricotta with an electric mixer on medium for 2 minutes. Stir in Gorgonzola, ½ teaspoon fresh thyme, and ¼ teaspoon fresh rosemary until combined. Fold in 1 tablespoon honey just until combined. Spoon spread into a serving bowl. Cover and chill 1 to 24 hours.

2. To serve, spread on baguette slices and top with apple slices, thyme, and/or walnuts. Drizzle with honey.

PER 1 TABLESPOON *91 cal., 3 g total fat (2 g sat. fat), 10 mg chol., 182 mg sodium, 12 g carb., 1 g fiber, 4 g pro.*

Italian Grinder Dip

Garlic toasts are topped with a savory combination of ground beef, sausage, and well-seasoned tomato sauce—and taste like the classic sandwiches you can get at your favorite Italian restaurant.

PREP **25 minutes** COOK **4 to 5 hours (low) or 2 to 2½ hours (high)** MAKES **22 servings**

- 1 pound ground beef
- 1 pound bulk Italian sausage
- 1 cup chopped onion (1 large)
- 3 cloves garlic, minced
- ¾ cup chopped green sweet pepper (1 medium)
- 1 4-ounce can (drained weight) sliced mushrooms, drained

Blue Cheese-Apricot Bites

Topped with crunchy candied walnuts, these fruit and cheese bites offer the sweetness of apricots complemented by tangy blue cheese.

START TO FINISH **25 minutes** MAKES **16 servings**

- 2 teaspoons butter
- 2 tablespoons finely chopped walnuts
- 2 teaspoons sugar
- ½ teaspoon snipped fresh rosemary or ¼ teaspoon dried rosemary, finely crushed
- ¼ cup crumbled Gorgonzola, Roquefort, or other blue cheese (1 ounce)
- 1 ounce cream cheese
- 16 dried apricots
  Snipped fresh rosemary (optional)

1. In a small skillet melt butter over medium heat. Add walnuts and sugar; cook and stir for 2 to 3 minutes or until walnuts are lightly toasted. Stir in ½ teaspoon fresh or ¼ teaspoon dried rosemary; cook and stir for 30 seconds more. Transfer nuts to a foil-lined baking sheet; cool.

1 teaspoon fennel seeds, crushed
1 teaspoon dried oregano, crushed
1 teaspoon dried basil, crushed
½ teaspoon crushed red pepper
1 14- or 15-ounce can pizza sauce
  Sliced garlic bread and/or ciabatta bread, toasted
  Shredded mozzarella cheese

1. In a skillet cook ground beef, sausage, onion, and garlic over medium-high heat until meat is brown. Drain off fat.
2. In a 3½- or 4-quart slow cooker combine meat mixture, sweet pepper, mushrooms, fennel seeds, oregano, basil, and crushed red pepper. Stir in pizza sauce.
3. Cover and cook on low-heat setting for 4 to 5 hours or on high-heat setting for 2 to 2½ hours. Serve on toasted bread and sprinkle with cheese.
PER 3 TABLESPOONS *148 cal., 12 g total fat (4 g sat. fat), 32 mg chol., 217 mg sodium, 3 g carbo., 1 g fiber, 7 g pro.*

Beet Hummus

Cooked beets give this garlicky bean dip a gorgeous red hue and earthy flavor.

START TO FINISH **20 minutes** MAKES **16 servings**

1 15-ounce can cannellini beans (white kidney beans), rinsed and drained
1 8-ounce package refrigerated cooked whole baby beets or one 15-ounce can small whole beets, drained
¼ cup tahini (sesame seed paste)
2 tablespoons lemon juice
1 tablespoon prepared horseradish
2 cloves garlic, minced
½ teaspoon salt
¼ cup olive oil
  Chopped hard-cooked egg
  Snipped fresh parsley
  Cucumber slices, jicama slices, and/or celery sticks

1. In a blender or food processor combine beans, beets, tahini, lemon juice, horseradish, garlic, and salt. Cover and blend or process until nearly smooth. With the motor running, add oil in a thin, steady stream through the opening in the lid.
2. Transfer hummus to a serving bowl. If desired, cover and chill up to 24 hours. Garnish with hard-cooked egg and parsley. Serve with cucumber, jicama, and/or celery.
PER 2 TABLESPOONS *79 cal., 6 g total fat (1 g sat. fat), 13 mg chol., 126 mg sodium, 6 g carbo., 2 g fiber, 3 g pro.*

Beet Hummus

Club Sandwich Dip

Cooked bacon is handy to have in your refrigerator, and cooking it yourself saves money over buying it precooked. Cook a package of bacon to the desired crispness, then drain and cool on paper towels. Lightly wrap in clean paper towels or waxed paper, then store in the refrigerator in a tightly sealed plastic bag. When you need bacon, heat it in the microwave on a paper towel-lined plate for 30 seconds. It will be crisp and taste just cooked.

PREP 20 minutes COOK 1 to 2 hours (high)
MAKES 20 servings

1   pound smoked turkey, chopped
8   ounces cooked ham, chopped
8   ounces process Swiss or American cheese, torn
1   8-ounce package cream cheese, cut up
1   cup light mayonnaise
2   teaspoons Dijon mustard
6   slices bacon, crisp-cooked, drained, and crumbled
½   cup cherry or grape tomatoes, coarsely chopped
    Whole wheat toast points and/or assorted cut-up vegetables

1. In a 3- or 3½-quart slow cooker combine turkey, ham, process cheese, cream cheese, mayonnaise, and mustard.
2. Cover and cook on high-heat setting for 1 to 2 hours or until cheeses are melted, stirring after 1 hour.
3. Serve immediately or keep warm, covered, on warm setting or low-heat setting up to 2 hours, stirring occasionally. Before serving, stir in half the bacon. Top with the remaining bacon and tomatoes. Serve with toast points and/or assorted cut-up vegetables.
PER ¼ CUP *177 cal., 13 g total fat (6 g sat. fat), 46 mg chol., 578 mg sodium, 3 g carbo., 0 g fiber, 11 g pro.*

Ricotta Dip for Fruit

Serve this sweet dip alongside a savory spread or dip to cover all the flavor bases. Kids love it!

PREP 15 minutes CHILL 4 hours
MAKES 12 servings

½   cup low-fat ricotta cheese*
4   ounces cream cheese, softened
3   tablespoons orange juice
2   tablespoons powdered sugar
1   6-ounce container vanilla low-fat yogurt
6   cups cubed cantaloupe, cubed honeydew melon, pineapple chunks, and/or strawberries

Club Sandwich Dip

Ricotta Dip for Fruit

1. For dip, in a blender or food processor combine ricotta cheese, cream cheese, orange juice, and powdered sugar. Cover and blend or process until smooth. In a medium bowl stir together cheese mixture and yogurt. Cover and chill dip 4 hours.
2. Serve with assorted fresh fruit.
*Note For a richer, creamier dip, substitute whole milk ricotta cheese for low-fat ricotta cheese.
PER 2 TABLESPOONS *94 cal., 4 g total fat (3 g sat. fat), 14 mg chol., 72 mg sodium, 12 g carbo., 1 g fiber, 3 g pro.*

Crunchy Cracker Snack Mix

Munching on something salty and crunchy while sipping a glass of wine is welcome at casual gatherings. This supersimple mix takes only minutes to make and can be stored at room temperature up to 1 week.

PREP **10 minutes** BAKE **25 minutes**
OVEN **300°F** MAKES **52 servings**

5   cups wheat stick crackers
4   cups bite-size cheese crackers
3   cups pretzel twists
2   cups mixed nuts
½   cup butter, melted
1   0.6- to 0.7-ounce envelope cheese-garlic or Italian dry salad dressing mix

1. Preheat oven to 300°F. In a large roasting pan combine wheat crackers and cheese crackers. Bake about 5 minutes or until warm. Gently stir in pretzels and mixed nuts.

Crunchy Cracker Snack Mix

2. Pour melted butter over mixture. Sprinkle with salad dressing mix; toss gently to coat. Bake for 20 minutes more, stirring once.
3. Spread mixture onto a large sheet of foil to cool. Store in an airtight container at room temperature up to 1 week.
PER ¼ CUP *80 cal., 6 g total fat (2 g sat. fat), 165 mg chol., 165 mg sodium, 5 g carbo., 1 g fiber, 2 g pro.*

White Chocolate Snack Mix

Coffeehouse Mocha Punch

White Chocolate Snack Mix

This sweet snack mix is perfect to bag and wrap with a pretty ribbon to give as a gift to coworkers, teachers, and coaches.

START TO FINISH **45 minutes** MAKES **56 servings**

2   cups bite-size wheat or rice square cereal, bite-size shredded wheat biscuits, or bite-size shredded wheat biscuits with raisin filling
2   cups broken graham crackers, graham crackers with cinnamon-sugar topping, or chocolate-covered graham crackers
2   cups pretzel sticks
2   cups broken rice cakes
1   cup tiny marshmallows
1   cup raisins or mixed dried fruit bits
1   cup whole or slivered almonds or cashews
1   pound white baking chocolate, chopped
⅓   cup whipping cream
1   tablespoon light-color corn syrup
½   teaspoon almond extract

1. Line an extra-large baking sheet with waxed paper or parchment paper; set aside. In an extra-large bowl gently combine cereal, graham crackers, pretzels, rice cakes, marshmallows, raisins, and nuts.
2. In a medium saucepan combine white chocolate, whipping cream, and corn syrup. Cook and stir over low heat until nearly melted; remove from heat and stir gently until smooth. Stir in almond extract.
3. Pour warm chocolate mixture over cereal mixture; toss gently to coat. Immediately spread mixture on the prepared baking sheet. Cool until chocolate is set (up to 12 hours). Break into pieces.
PER ¼ CUP *105 cal., 5 g total fat (2 g sat. fat), 4 mg chol., 75 mg sodium, 14 g carbo., 1 g fiber, 2 g pro.*

Coffeehouse Mocha Punch

For a nonalcoholic version of this fun dessert punch, substitute an additional ½ cup of strong brewed coffee, chilled, for the liqueur.

START TO FINISH **20 minutes** MAKES **6 servings**

2   cups chocolate-flavor milk
1   cup strong brewed coffee, chilled
½   cup coffee liqueur
1   pint coffee-flavor ice cream or chocolate ice cream, softened (2 cups)
1   pint vanilla ice cream, softened (2 cups)
     Whipped cream (optional)
     Ground cinnamon (optional)

1. In a large punch bowl stir together chocolate milk, coffee, and liqueur. Add small scoops of the ice creams. Using a wire whisk, lightly beat mixture until smooth.
2. If desired, top servings with whipped cream and sprinkle with cinnamon.
PER 9 OUNCE *325 cal., 12 g total fat (8 g sat. fat), 44 mg chol., 123 mg sodium, 39 g carbo., 1 g fiber, 6 g pro.*

Mulled Cranberry Punch

Keep this warming, spiced punch in the slow cooker on low for 2 hours to stay at just the right temperature for the duration of the party.

PREP **15 minutes** COOK **4 to 6 hours (low) or 2 to 2½ hours (high)** MAKES **12 servings**

1   orange
8   inches stick cinnamon, broken
8   whole cloves
4   whole allspice
1   32-ounce bottle cranberry juice
1   11.5-ounce can frozen white grape-raspberry juice concentrate
4   cups water

1. Use a vegetable peeler to remove several 2- to 3-inch-long sections of orange peel from the orange, avoiding the white pith. Juice the orange; set aside
2. For a spice bag, cut a 6-inch square from a double thickness of 100%-cotton cheesecloth. Place orange peel, cinnamon, cloves, and allspice in the center of the square. Bring the corners together and tie closed with 100%-cotton kitchen string.
3. In a 3½- to 4-quart slow cooker combine cranberry juice, juice concentrate, the water, orange juice, and spice bag.
4. Cover and cook on low-heat setting for 4 to 6 hours or on high-heat setting for 2 to 2½ hours. Remove and discard spice bag. Serve immediately or keep warm on low-heat setting up to 2 hours.
PER 6 OUNCES *114 cal., 0 g total fat, 0 mg chol., 7 mg sodium, 29 g carbo., 1 g fiber, 0 g pro.*

Mulled Cranberry Punch

bountiful breakfast

The holidays are a delicious reason to forgo the typical bran cereal and wheat toast or yogurt and fruit breakfast for a bit more indulgence. Arouse sleepyheads from beds with homemade cream cheese and apple Danish, hearty egg casserole, savory or sweet pancakes, or a basketful of warm and buttery bacon-and-cheese biscuits.

Eggs Benedict Strata, page 50

49

Egg 'n' Bacon Breakfast Casserole

2. Meanwhile, grease a 2-quart baking dish; set aside. Spread 1 side of bread slices with butter. Cut bread into 1-inch cubes. Place half the bread cubes in the prepared baking dish. Sprinkle with half the bacon. Top with the remaining bread cubes and remaining bacon; sprinkle with cheese and green onions.

3. In a bowl whisk together eggs, whipping cream, dry mustard, salt, and pepper. Gradually pour egg mixture over layers in dish. Cover with plastic wrap and chill at least 2 hours.

4. Preheat oven to 325°F. Bake egg casserole, uncovered, for 50 to 55 minutes or until a knife inserted near center comes out clean. Let stand 10 minutes before serving.

PER SERVING *763 cal., 55 g total fat (29 g sat. fat) , 356 mg chol., 1,312 mg sodium, 29 g carbo., 2 g fiber, 25 g pro.*

Eggs Benedict Strata

This is a simple way to serve Eggs Benedict for a crowd. The sauce is mock hollandaise, made with sour cream, Dijon mustard, and milk. Effortless and delicious!

PREP **30 minutes** STAND **8 hours + 10 minutes** CHILL **2 hours** BAKE **55 minutes** OVEN **325°F** MAKES **6 servings**

8   slices whole wheat or whole grain white bread
6   cups baby spinach leaves or torn fresh kale
2   teaspoons canola oil
4   ounces Canadian-style bacon (about 7 slices), torn into bite-size pieces
4   eggs, beaten
2   egg whites, beaten
¼   cup light sour cream
2   tablespoons all-purpose flour
1   teaspoon finely shredded lemon peel
1   teaspoon dry mustard
¼   teaspoon black pepper
1⅔   cups fat-free milk
⅓   cup light sour cream
2   teaspoons Dijon mustard
1   to 2 tablespoons fat-free milk
    Fresh thyme sprigs (optional)

1. Place bread slices in a single layer on a wire rack; cover loosely with a clean kitchen or paper towel and let stand 8 to 12 hours or until dry. (Or place in a 15×10×1-inch baking pan; bake in 300°F oven for 10 to 15 minutes or until dry, turning once.) Tear slices in large pieces.

2. In a very large nonstick skillet cook spinach in hot oil over medium heat for 1 to 2 minutes or just until spinach is wilted, turning frequently with tongs. (If using kale, cook for 6 to 8 minutes or just until tender.) Coarsely chop spinach or kale.

Egg 'n' Bacon Breakfast Casserole

Green onions flavor this rich and hearty breakfast dish. Serve with fresh fruit and coffee or tea.

PREP **25 minutes** CHILL **2 hours** BAKE **50 minutes** STAND **10 minutes** OVEN **325°F** MAKES **6 servings**

1   pound bacon, coarsely chopped, or bulk pork sausage
6   1-inch slices French bread
2   tablespoons butter, softened
1   cup shredded Colby-Jack or American cheese (4 ounces)
½   cup chopped green onions (4)
6   eggs, lightly beaten
1½   cups whipping cream, half-and-half, light cream, or whole milk
¾   to 1 teaspoon dry mustard
½   teaspoon salt
¼   teaspoon black pepper

1. In a large skillet cook bacon over medium heat until crisp. Drain bacon on paper towels; discard drippings. (If using sausage, cook over medium-high heat until brown. Drain off fat.)

3. In a lightly greased 2-quart rectangular baking dish arrange half the bread pieces. Top with the spinach and Canadian-style bacon. Top with remaining bread pieces.

4. In a medium bowl whisk together the eggs, egg whites, ¼ cup sour cream, flour, lemon peel, dry mustard, and pepper. Stir in 1⅔ cups milk until well combined. Evenly pour over the layers in dish. Cover and chill for 2 to 24 hours.

5. Preheat oven to 325°F. Bake strata, uncovered, for 55 to 60 minutes or until a knife inserted near center comes out clean. Let stand for 10 minutes before serving.

6. Meanwhile, in a small bowl stir together ⅓ cup sour cream, mustard, and milk to make drizzling consistency. Drizzle sauce over strata to serve. Garnish with fresh thyme.

PER SERVING 241 cal., 9 g total fat (3 g sat. fat), 158 mg chol., 521 mg sodium, 23 g carbo., 3 g fiber, 17 g pro.

Tomato, Spinach, and Feta Strata

With whole grain bread, lots of fresh vegetables, and just a little bit of low-fat feta for flavor, this strata is a healthful choice for a holiday brunch.

PREP **30 minutes** CHILL **4 hours**
BAKE **1 hour 10 minutes** STAND **10 minutes**
OVEN **325°F** MAKES **6 servings**

    Nonstick cooking spray
4   cups cubed whole grain bread
1   pound fresh asparagus, trimmed and cut into
    1-inch pieces
1   cup chopped onion
2   cups fresh baby spinach
6   eggs
1   cup fat-free milk
⅛   teaspoon sea salt or kosher salt
⅛   teaspoon freshly ground black pepper
2   plum tomatoes, thinly sliced
½   cup reduced-fat feta cheese
¼   cup snipped fresh basil

1. Coat a 2-quart rectangular baking dish with cooking spray. Arrange half the bread cubes in the prepared baking dish.

2. In a covered medium saucepan cook asparagus and onion in a small amount of boiling water for 2 to 3 minutes or just until tender; stir in spinach. Immediately drain well. Spoon half the asparagus mixture on bread in baking dish. Top with the remaining bread cubes and remaining asparagus mixture. Set aside.

3. In a large bowl whisk together eggs, milk, salt, and pepper. Evenly pour over mixture in baking dish. With the back of a large spoon, lightly press down layers.

Arrange tomato slices on top. Top with feta cheese and basil. Cover with foil; refrigerate for 4 to 24 hours.

4. Preheat oven to 325°F. Bake, covered, for 30 minutes. Uncover; bake about 40 minutes more or until center registers 180°F when tested with an instant-read thermometer (there will be some liquid in center that will be absorbed during standing). Let stand on a wire rack for 10 minutes before serving.

PER SERVING 247 cal., 9 g total fat (3 g sat. fat), 216 mg chol., 419 mg sodium, 27 g carbo., 7 g fiber, 18 g pro.

Tomato, Spinach, and Feta Strata

Pork and Apple Casserole

The inspiration for this sweet and savory breakfast casserole came from scrapple—the Pennsylvania Dutch specialty made with pork scraps, cornmeal, and seasonings.

PREP **25 minutes** BAKE **30 minutes** OVEN **400°F**
MAKES **6 servings**

1   pound bulk pork sausage
1⅓ cups chopped apples (2 medium)
1⅓ cups packaged corn bread stuffing mix
1   tablespoon dried minced onion
2   eggs, lightly beaten
1¼ cups apple juice or apple cider
½   cup shredded cheddar cheese (2 ounces)

1. Preheat oven to 400°F. Grease a 2-quart square baking dish; set aside. In a large skillet cook sausage over medium heat until brown. Drain off fat. Stir in apples, stuffing mix, and dried onion. In a small bowl combine eggs and apple juice. Add to sausage mixture; toss gently to combine. Transfer sausage mixture to the prepared baking dish.
2. Bake, covered, for 20 minutes. Stir casserole and sprinkle with cheese. Bake, uncovered, about 10 minutes more or until heated through.
PER SERVING *429 cal., 29 g total fat (11 g sat. fat), 138 mg chol., 776 mg sodium, 24 g carbo., 2 g fiber, 17 g pro.*

Mushroom-Olive Frittata

Cremini mushrooms are immature portobello mushrooms. White button mushrooms are good substitutes when portobellos are not available.

PREP **30 minutes** BROIL **2 minutes**
STAND **5 minutes** MAKES **4 servings**

1   tablespoon olive oil
1   cup sliced fresh cremini mushrooms
2   cups coarsely shredded fresh Swiss chard or
     spinach
1   large shallot, thinly sliced
4   eggs*
2   egg whites*
2   teaspoons snipped fresh rosemary or ½ teaspoon
     dried rosemary, crushed
¼   teaspoon ground black pepper
⅛   teaspoon salt
¼   cup thinly sliced, pitted kalamata olives
⅓   cup shredded Parmesan cheese

1. Preheat broiler. In a medium broilerproof nonstick skillet cook mushrooms in hot oil over medium heat for 3 minutes, stirring occasionally. Add Swiss chard and shallot. Cook about 5 minutes or until mushrooms and chard are tender, stirring occasionally.
2. Meanwhile, in a medium bowl whisk together eggs, egg whites, rosemary, pepper, and salt. Pour egg mixture over vegetables in skillet. Cook over medium heat. As mixture sets, run a spatula around edge of skillet, lifting egg mixture so the uncooked portion flows beneath. Continue cooking and lifting until egg mixture is almost set and surface is just slightly moist.
3. Sprinkle with olives; top with cheese. Broil about 4 inches from the heat about 2 minutes or until top is lightly browned and center is set. Let stand for 5 minutes before serving.
***Note** If desired, substitute 1¼ cups refrigerated or frozen egg product, thawed, for the 4 eggs and 2 egg whites.
PER SERVING *165 cal., 11 g total fat (3 g sat. fat), 216 mg chol., 416 mg sodium, 4 g carbo., 1 g fiber, 12 g pro.*

Pork and Apple Casserole

Mushroom-Olive Frittata

Smoked Salmon Platter with Dilled Crème Fraîche

This colorful, fresh platter is delicious for brunch or a light lunch. Serve it with champagne or sparkling dry cider.

START TO FINISH **25 minutes** MAKES **12 servings**

1   7- to 8-ounce container crème fraîche or sour cream
2   teaspoons snipped fresh dill
1   24-ounce piece hot-smoked salmon
2   hard-cooked eggs, chopped
½   cup finely chopped red onion (1 medium)
½   cup radishes, cut into thin bite-size strips
⅓   cup drained capers
    Fresh dill sprigs
    Lemon wedges
    Crostini and/or assorted crackers

1. For crème fraîche sauce, in a small bowl combine crème fraîche and snipped dill. Set aside.
2. Place salmon on a serving platter. Arrange mounds of hard-cooked eggs, red onion, radishes, and capers around salmon. Garnish with dill sprigs and lemon wedges. Serve with crème fraîche sauce and crostini and/or assorted crackers.
PER SERVING *210 cal., 9 g total fat (4 g sat. fat,), 63 mg chol., 754 mg sodium, 16 g carbo., 1 g fiber, 15 g pro.*

Kale-Goat Cheese Frittata

This elegant frittata made with vitamin-packed kale is also a lovely light supper served with a green salad and crusty bread.

START TO FINISH **25 minutes** MAKES **6 servings**

2   cups coarsely torn fresh kale
1   medium onion, halved and thinly sliced
2   teaspoons olive oil
6   eggs
4   egg whites
¼   teaspoon salt
⅛   teaspoon black pepper
¼   cup drained oil-packed dried tomatoes, sliced
1   ounce goat cheese, crumbled

1. Preheat broiler. In 10-inch ovenproof nonstick skillet cook and stir kale and onion in hot oil over medium heat for 10 minutes until onion is tender.
2. Meanwhile, in medium bowl whisk together eggs, egg whites, salt, and pepper. Pour over kale mixture in skillet. Cook over medium-low heat. As egg mixture sets, run a spatula around the edge of the skillet, lifting egg mixture so the uncooked portion flows beneath. Continue cooking and lifting until egg mixture is almost set but still glossy and moist.
3. Sprinkle egg mixture with dried tomatoes and goat cheese. Broil 4 to 5 inches from heat for 1 to 2 minutes or until eggs are set. Cut into wedges to serve.
PER SERVING *145 cal., 9 g total fat (3 g sat. fat), 216 mg chol., 242 mg sodium, 6 g carbo., 1 g fiber, 11 g pro.*

Easy Chocolate-Almond Croissants

These simply impressive croissants are fun to make for a holiday bake sale.

PREP **25 minutes** BAKE **15 minutes**
OVEN **350°F** MAKES **8 croissants**

½ of an 8-ounce can almond paste, cut in small pieces
¼ cup whipping cream, divided
4 ounces special dark baking chocolate, chopped
1 8-ounce package refrigerated crescent rolls (8)
1 egg, lightly beaten
1 tablespoon water
¼ cup sliced almonds
1 tablespoon powdered sugar

Easy Chocolate-Almond Croissants

1. Preheat oven to 350°F. Lightly grease a baking sheet; set aside. For filling, in a medium mixing bowl combine almond paste and 1 tablespoon of the cream. Beat with an electric mixer on medium until nearly smooth. Add the remaining cream, 1 tablespoon at a time, beating until nearly smooth. Stir in chocolate.
2. Unroll dough and separate at perforations into 8 triangles. Spoon filling onto wide ends of dough triangles; spread slightly. Starting at the wide end of each triangle, roll up dough around filling toward the point. Place, point sides down, on the prepared baking sheet; curve the ends.
3. In a small bowl combine egg and the water. Brush dough lightly with egg mixture; sprinkle with almonds.
4. Bake for 15 to 17 minutes or until golden brown. Transfer to a wire rack; cool slightly. Sprinkle lightly with powdered sugar. Serve warm.
PER CROISSANT *296 cal., 19 g total fat (6 g sat. fat), 37 mg chol., 261 mg sodium, 28 g carbo., 2 g fiber, 6 g pro.*

Apple-Cheese Danish

Good choices for cooking apples include Granny Smith, Jonathan, Golden Delicious, McIntosh, and Newtown Pippin.

PREP **45 minutes** BAKE **47 minutes**
COOL **45 minutes** OVEN **375°F** MAKES **12 servings**

1 17.3-ounce package (2 sheets) frozen puff pastry sheets, thawed
2½ pounds cooking apples, peeled, cored, and thinly sliced (about 7 cups)
2 tablespoons butter
1 cup granulated sugar
2 tablespoons all-purpose flour
1 teaspoon ground cinnamon
⅛ teaspoon ground nutmeg
1 8-ounce package cream cheese, softened
1 egg
1 teaspoon vanilla
Milk
2 tablespoons coarse sugar

1. Preheat oven to 375°F. Lightly grease a 15×10×1-inch baking pan; set aside. On a lightly floured surface unfold 1 pastry sheet and roll into a 15×10-inch rectangle. Transfer to the prepared baking pan, pressing dough to edges of pan. Bake about 12 minutes or until golden brown (pastry will puff and shrink from sides of pan). Cool on a wire rack.
2. Meanwhile, in an extra-large skillet cook apples in hot butter over medium heat about 8 minutes or just until crisp-tender, stirring occasionally. In a small bowl combine ½ cup of the granulated sugar, the flour, ½ teaspoon of the cinnamon, and the nutmeg. Sprinkle over apples. Cook and stir over medium-low heat for 2 minutes more; set aside.

3. In a medium mixing bowl combine cream cheese and the remaining ½ cup granulated sugar. Beat with an electric mixer on medium until smooth. Beat in egg and vanilla just until combined. Carefully spread cream cheese mixture on baked pastry to within 1 inch of the edges. Spoon apple mixture on cream cheese mixture.

4. On a lightly floured surface unfold the remaining pastry sheet and roll into a 13×9-inch rectangle (rolled pastry is large enough to completely cover apple mixture). Place on apple mixture. Lightly press edges of top pastry to edges of bottom pastry. Lightly brush pastry with milk. Using a sharp knife, cut a few slits in pastry to allow steam to escape. In a small bowl combine coarse sugar and the remaining ½ teaspoon cinnamon; sprinkle over pastry.

5. Bake for 35 to 40 minutes or until pastry is slightly puffed and golden brown. Cool on wire rack about 45 minutes. Serve slightly warm. Store any leftovers in the refrigerator.

PER SERVING *438 cal., 25 g total fat (4 g sat. fat), 44 mg chol., 184 mg sodium, 51 g carbo., 5 g pro.*

Gingerbread with Lemon-Butter Sauce

Glazed with lemon sauce and garnished with candied lemon, homey gingerbread is transformed into an elegant dessert.

PREP **20 minutes** BAKE **35 minutes**
OVEN **350°F** MAKES **9 servings**

1½ cups all-purpose flour
¼ cup packed dark brown sugar
¾ teaspoon ground cinnamon
¾ teaspoon ground ginger
½ teaspoon baking powder
½ teaspoon baking soda
⅛ teaspoon ground allspice
½ cup shortening
½ cup molasses
½ cup water
1 egg
¼ cup finely snipped crystallized ginger
1 recipe Lemon-Butter Sauce
1 recipe Candied Lemon Slices (optional)

1. Preheat oven to 350°F. Grease and lightly flour a 2-quart square baking dish; set aside.

2. In a large mixing bowl stir together flour, brown sugar, cinnamon, ground ginger, baking powder, baking soda, and allspice. Add shortening, molasses, the water, and egg. Beat with an electric mixer on low to medium until combined. Beat on high for 2 minutes. Stir in crystallized ginger. Pour batter into the prepared baking dish, spreading evenly.

3. Bake for 35 to 40 minutes or until a toothpick inserted near center comes out clean.

Gingerbread with Lemon-Butter Sauce

4. Serve warm with Lemon-Butter Sauce. If desired, garnish with Candied Lemon Slices.

Lemon-Butter Sauce In a saucepan combine ¼ cup granulated sugar and 1 tablespoon cornstarch. Stir in ¾ cup half-and-half and 2 tablespoons butter. Cook and stir over medium heat until mixture is bubbly. Reduce heat; cook and stir for 1 minute more. Remove from heat. Stir in ¼ teaspoon finely shredded lemon peel, 3 tablespoons lemon juice, and 2 tablespoons finely snipped crystallized ginger. Serve warm.

PER SERVING *345 cal., 17 g total fat (6 g sat. fat), 38 mg chol., 96 mg sodium, 46 g carbo., 4 g pro.*

Candied Lemon Slices Cut 2 small lemons into thin slices; discard seeds. In a large skillet bring 1 cup light-color corn syrup to boiling over medium heat. Stir in lemon slices. Return to boiling; reduce heat. Simmer, uncovered, until lemons are tender, turning occasionally; cool.

Bacon-Cheddar Cornmeal Biscuits

Bacon-Cheddar Cornmeal Biscuits

Rouse sleepyheads from their slumber with a whiff of these bacon and cheese biscuits baking in the oven. It will be a good morning indeed.

PREP 20 minutes BAKE 10 minutes
OVEN 425°F MAKES 16 biscuits

1¾ cups all-purpose flour
½ cup cornmeal
1 tablespoon baking powder
¼ cup butter
¾ cup shredded cheddar cheese (3 ounces)
4 slices bacon, crisp-cooked and crumbled
⅔ cup milk
1 egg, lightly beaten
2 tablespoons snipped fresh chives

1. Preheat oven to 350°F. In a large bowl combine flour, cornmeal, and baking powder. Using a pastry blender, cut butter into flour mixture until butter is the size of small peas. Add cheese, bacon, milk, egg, and chives; stir until moistened.

2. Turn out dough onto floured surface. Knead lightly 4 to 6 strokes or just until dough holds together. Pat or roll dough to an 8-inch square that is ½ inch thick. Using a sharp knife, cut sixteen 2-inch squares. Transfer to a lightly greased baking sheet; brush with additional milk.
3. Bake for 10 to 12 minutes or until golden brown. Remove; cool on a wire rack.
PER BISCUIT *133 cal., 6 g total fat (3 g sat.), 29 mg chol., 177 mg sodium, 15 g carbo., 1 g fiber, 5 g pro.*

Baked Stuffed French Toast

This cream cheese and dried fruit-filled French toast is similar to strata. Assemble and chill it overnight to bake and serve warm in the morning.

PREP 25 minutes CHILL 2 hours BAKE 30 minutes
OVEN 375°F MAKES 4 servings

8 ¾-inch slices French bread
1 recipe Cream Cheese Filling
4 eggs, lightly beaten
1 cup milk
1 cup orange juice

1. Place half the bread slices in a 3-quart baking dish. Spread with Cream Cheese Filling. Top with the remaining bread slices.

2. In a bowl combine eggs, milk, and orange juice. Pour egg mixture evenly over bread stacks, covering all the tops. Cover and chill for 2 to 24 hours.

3. Preheat oven to 375°F. Line a 15×10×1-inch baking pan with parchment paper or nonstick foil. Arrange bread stacks in the prepared baking pan. Bake, uncovered, for 30 to 35 minutes or until golden, turning once.

Cream Cheese Filling In a medium bowl combine one 8-ounce package cream cheese, ½ cup snipped dried apricots or golden raisins, and 1 teaspoon ground cinnamon.

PER SERVING *550 cal., 27 g total fat (14 g sat. fat), 279 mg chol., 695 mg sodium, 59 g carbo., 3 g fiber, 20 g pro.*

Pumpkin Pancakes

The warm caramel topping for these spiced pumpkin flapjacks gets flavor and crunch from toasted coconut and pecans.

PREP 15 minutes BAKE 2 minutes per batch
MAKES about 16 pancakes

2   cups all-purpose flour
3   tablespoons packed brown sugar
1   tablespoon baking powder
½   teaspoon salt
½   teaspoon pumpkin pie spice or ground cinnamon (optional)
1¾   cups milk
3   eggs, lightly beaten
¾   cup canned pumpkin
¼   cup vegetable oil
1   recipe Caramel-Coconut Topping (optional)

1. In a large bowl combine flour, brown sugar, baking powder, salt, and pumpkin pie spice (if desired). In a medium bowl combine milk, eggs, pumpkin, and oil. Add egg mixture all at once to flour mixture. Stir just until moistened (batter should be slightly lumpy).

2. Heat a lightly greased griddle or large heavy skillet over medium heat. For each pancake, pour ¼ cup batter onto griddle. Cook for 1 to 2 minutes on each side or until golden, turning to second sides when tops are bubbly and edges are slightly dry. Serve warm. If desired, serve with Caramel-Coconut Topping.

PER PANCAKE *128 cal., 5 g total fat (1 g sat. fat), 42 mg chol., 167 mg sodium, 17 g carbo., 1 g fiber, 4 g pro.*

Caramel-Coconut Topping In a small saucepan combine 1⅓ cups caramel ice cream topping, 1 cup toasted shredded coconut, and ½ cup toasted chopped pecans (see note, page 119). Heat over low heat until warm.

PER 2½ TABLESPOONS *55 cal., 2 g total fat (1 g sat. fat), 0 mg chol., 48 g sodium, 10 g carbo., 1 g fiber, 0 g pro.*

Parmesan-Cornmeal Pancakes

Break out of the pancake routine with these savory griddle cakes. Serve them with crisp bacon and wedges of ripe melon for a hearty breakfast.

PREP 15 minutes BAKE 2 to 4 minutes per batch MAKES about 16 pancakes

1   cup all-purpose flour
¾   cup yellow cornmeal
⅓   cup grated Parmesan cheese
1   tablespoon sugar (optional)
1   teaspoon salt
1¾   cups buttermilk
2   eggs, lightly beaten
2   tablespoons cooking oil
⅓   cup finely chopped green onions (optional)

1. In a bowl combine flour and other dry ingredients. In a second bowl combine remaining ingredients. Stir buttermilk mixture into flour mixture until slightly lumpy.

2. Heat a lightly greased griddle or heavy skillet over medium heat. For each pancake, pour ¼ cup batter onto griddle. Cook until golden; turn when tops are bubbly and edges are slightly dry (1 to 2 minutes per side). If desired, top pancakes with finely chopped green onions.

PER PANCAKE *92 cal., 3 g total fat (1 g sat. fat), 29 mg chol., 216 mg sodium, 12 g carbo., 1 g fiber, 4 g pro.*

Parmesan-Cornmeal Pancakes and Pumpkin Pancakes

Multigrain Waffles and Fruit

Marmalade adds a bittersweetness to the warm berry sauce for the waffles. Substitute another jam or preserves, such as raspberry, strawberry, or apricot.

PREP 25 minutes BAKE per waffle baker directions MAKES 12 servings

1	cup all-purpose flour
1	cup whole wheat flour
½	cup oat flour
1	tablespoon baking powder
1	tablespoon packed brown sugar
½	teaspoon baking soda
¼	teaspoon salt
1¾	cups milk
2	eggs, lightly beaten
½	cup canola oil
1	tablespoon finely shredded orange peel
½	cup orange marmalade
3	cups fresh berries (such as blueberries, sliced strawberries, and/or raspberries)

Multi-Grain Waffles and Fruit

1. In a large bowl stir together all-purpose flour, whole wheat flour, oat flour, baking powder, brown sugar, baking soda, and salt. Make a well in center of flour mixture; set aside.

2. In a medium bowl combine milk, eggs, oil, and orange peel. Add egg mixture all at once to flour mixture. Stir just until moistened (batter should be slightly lumpy).

3. Lightly grease and preheat a Belgian waffle baker.* For an 8-inch square baker, pour 1⅓ cups batter onto grids (for a 6- to 7-inch round baker, pour ⅔ cup batter onto grids). Close lid quickly; do not open until done. Bake according to manufacturer's directions. When done, use a fork to lift waffle off grid. Repeat with remaining batter. Keep baked waffles warm in a 200°F oven.

4. Meanwhile, heat marmalade in a medium saucepan over medium-low heat until melted. Add berries; heat just until warmed, gently stirring occasionally. Spoon over warm waffles.

*Note Waffle bakers vary; this batter will work in any Belgian or regular waffle baker. Adjust the amount of batter added to the waffle baker depending on the size of the baker.

PER SERVING 251 cal., 11 g total fat (1 g sat. fat), 38 mg chol., 227 mg sodium, 34 g carbo., 5 g pro.

Granola

Of course, this granola is delicious for breakfast. Also try it sprinkled on ice cream, bag it as a portable snack, and give it as a healthful holiday gift.

PREP 15 minutes BAKE 35 minutes
OVEN 300°F MAKES 7½ cups

	Butter
4	cups regular rolled oats
1	cup nuts*
½	cup packed brown sugar
¼	cup cooking oil
¼	cup honey or maple-flavor syrup
½	teaspoon salt
½	teaspoon ground cinnamon
1	teaspoon vanilla
1	cup dried fruit**
½	cup other ingredients***

1. Preheat oven to 300°F. Line a large baking sheet with foil; butter the foil. Set aside. In a 15×10×1-inch baking pan combine oats and nuts. Set aside. In a small saucepan combine brown sugar, oil, honey, salt, and cinnamon. Heat and stir over medium heat until mixture is well combined and smooth. Stir in vanilla. Pour sugar mixture over oat mixture. Stir until well coated.

Cranberry-Almond Coffee Cake

2. Bake 35 to 40 minutes or until granola is golden brown, stirring carefully every 10 minutes. Stir in dried fruit. Spread granola onto buttered foil; cool completely. Stir in other ingredients. Store granola in an airtight container or large resealable plastic bag at room temperature up to 1 week or freeze up to 3 months.
*Nuts (whole, chopped, or sliced) Almonds, walnuts, pecans, pistachios, cashews, hazelnuts, sunflower seeds (½ cup), unsalted peanuts.
**Dried fruit (whole or snipped) Raisins, currants, tropical fruit bits, mixed fruit bits, banana chips, pineapple, mango, cherries, blueberries, cranberries, dates, apple.
***Other ingredients Flaked sweetened coconut (add with nuts in Step 1), chocolate baking pieces, butterscotch-flavor pieces, peanut butter-flavored pieces, cinnamon-flavor pieces, roasted pumpkin seeds (pepitas)
PER ½ CUP *250 cal., 11 g total fat (2 g sat. fat), 0 mg chol., 88 mg sodium, 37 g carbo., 4 g fiber, 5 g pro.*

Cranberry-Almond Coffee Cake
The fruit filling for this festive coffee cake is whole cranberry sauce. It's a sweet way use it other than as a side to Thanksgiving turkey.

PREP **30 minutes** BAKE **40 minutes**
COOL **30 minutes** OVEN **350°F** MAKES **12 servings**

1   tablespoon butter
2   tablespoons all-purpose flour
2   tablespoons sugar
1   teaspoon ground cinnamon
½   cup butter, softened
1   cup sugar
1   teaspoon baking powder
1   teaspoon baking soda
½   teaspoon salt
2   eggs
1   8-ounce carton sour cream
1   teaspoon almond extract
½   teaspoon vanilla
2   cups all-purpose flour
1   8-ounce can or ½ of a 16-ounce can whole cranberry sauce (¾ cup)
½   cup sliced almonds, toasted (see note, page 119)
¼   cup sliced almonds

1. Preheat oven to 350°F. Lightly grease a 9×9×2-inch baking pan; set aside. For crumb mixture, in a small microwave-safe bowl or custard cup heat 1 tablespoon butter on high for 20 to 30 seconds or until melted. Stir in 2 tablespoons flour, 2 tablespoons sugar, and cinnamon; set aside.
2. In a large mixing bowl stir together the softened butter, 1 cup sugar, baking powder, baking soda, and salt until combined. Stir in eggs, sour cream, almond extract, and vanilla until combined. Stir in 2 cups flour until moistened.
3. Spoon half the batter into prepared pan. Spoon cranberry sauce on batter in pan and spread evenly. Sprinkle with toasted almonds. Top with remaining batter, spreading evenly to cover. Sprinkle with crumb mixture and ¼ cup almonds.
4. Bake for 40 to 45 minutes or until a wooden toothpick inserted near the center comes out clean. Cool in pan on a wire rack about 30 minutes before serving. Serve warm.
PER SERVING *354 cal., 18 g total fat (9 g sat. fat), 66 mg chol., 315 mg sodium, 44 g carbo., 2 g fiber, 6 g pro.*

Fruit and Yogurt Parfaits

Fruit and Yogurt Parfaits

Tiny but mighty, these just-bigger-than-bite-size parfaits are perfect for parties where there's lots of food to sample.

START TO FINISH **15 minutes** MAKES **12 parfaits**

1   32-ounce carton vanilla or plain low-fat yogurt
2   cups fresh red raspberries, blackberries, and/or blueberries
½   cup low-fat granola
¼   cup sliced almonds, toasted (see note, page 119)
2   tablespoons honey

1. Spoon 3 tablespoons of the yogurt into each of twelve 2- to 3-ounce stemmed glasses, shot glasses, or dishes. Top with berries, granola, and almonds. Drizzle with honey.
PER PARFAIT *114 cal., 2 g total fat (1 g sat. fat), 4 mg chol., 69 mg sodium, 20 g carbo., 2 g fiber, 5 g pro.*

Pineapple Mimosas

Substitute other frozen fruit juice concentrates for the pineapple-orange-banana juice concentrate if you like. Just be sure to use a 12-ounce can.

PREP **10 minutes** CHILL **2 hours** MAKES **6 servings**

1   12-ounce can frozen pineapple-orange-banana juice concentrate, thawed
1   cup cold water
1   750-milliliter bottle pink champagne, champagne, and/or sparkling apple juice, chilled
    Ice cubes
    Fresh pineapple spears (optional)

1. In a large pitcher combine juice concentrate and the water. Cover and chill for 2 to 24 hours.
2. Before serving, carefully add champagne. Add ice to pitcher or to each glass before serving. If desired, garnish with a fresh pineapple wedge.
PER 8 OUNCES *147 cal., 0 g total fat, 0 mg chol., 4 mg sodium, 18 g carbo., 0 g fiber, 1 g pro.*

Apricot Green Tea

Fragrant and sweet, this spiced tea is a warming treat. And it's healthful!

START TO FINISH **15 minutes** MAKES **8 servings**

8	cups water
12	dried apricot halves
½	cup apricot nectar
¼	cup packed brown sugar or raw sugar
4	green tea bags
¼	teaspoon ground ginger
8	cinnamon sticks

1. In a 4-quart Dutch oven combine the water, apricot halves, apricot nectar, brown sugar, green tea bags, and ginger. Bring to boiling; reduce heat. Cover and simmer for 10 minutes.
2. Place a cinnamon stick in each mug. Strain tea mixture; pour into prepared mugs.
PER 8 OUNCES *64 cal., 0 g total fat, 0 mg chol., 10 mg sodium, 16 g carbo., 1 g fiber, 0 g pro.*

Bittersweet Hot Chocolate

Simmer this hot chocolate while you go sledding, snowman-building, or ice-skating so it is ready to warm you when you return home from your outdoor adventures.

PREP **5 minutes** COOK **5 to 6 hours (high) or 2½ to 3 hours (low)** MAKES **12 servings**

1	quart half-and-half or light cream (4 cups)
1	quart milk (4 cups)
2	3-inch-long cinnamon sticks
1	12-ounce package bittersweet chocolate pieces or two 6-ounce packages bittersweet chocolate, chopped
1	tablespoon vanilla
	Marshmallows (optional)

1. In a 3- to 4-quart slow cooker combine half-and-half, milk, and cinnamon sticks. Cover and cook on low-heat setting for 5 to 6 hours or on high-heat setting for 2½ to 3 hours. Discard cinnamon sticks. If necessary, skim and discard the skin that forms om the surface. Stir in chocolate pieces; whisk until chocolate is melted and smooth. Stir in vanilla. Serve immediately or cover and keep warm on warm setting or low-heat setting up to 2 hours. Serve warm.
2. If desired, float marshmallows on each serving.
PER 6 OUNCES *284 cal., 21 g total fat (13 g sat. fat), 36 mg chol., 68 mg sodium, 23 g carbo., 2 g fiber, 7 g pro.*

Bittersweet Hot Chocolate

61

bread
basket

Few aromas are as warm and welcoming as bread baking in the oven. As the holidays kick into high gear, try a new recipe from this selection of sweet and savory breads. Give a dried fruit-and-chocolate-studded loaf of quick bread as a gift, take a fabulous homemade coffee cake to work, or bake a batch of scones to serve at home.

Pecan Browned Butter Coffee Cake, page 64

Montmorency Cherry
Coffee Cake

Montmorency Cherry Coffee Cake

Montmorency cherries are a type of sour cherry grown in abundance in Michigan and in Door County, Wisconsin. They are the juicy, sweet-tart filling in this tender coffee cake.

PREP 35 minutes BAKE 1 hour COOL 40 minutes
OVEN 350°F MAKES 16 servings

Nonstick cooking spray
1   16-ounce carton sour cream
2   teaspoons baking soda
4   cups all-purpose flour
1   tablespoon baking powder
1   cup packed brown sugar
½   cup chopped walnuts
4½ teaspoons ground cinnamon
1   cup butter, softened
1½ cups granulated sugar
4   eggs
2   teaspoons vanilla
1   16-ounce package frozen unsweetened pitted tart red cherries, thawed and drained

1. Preheat oven to 350°F. Coat a 13×9×2-inch baking pan with cooking spray; set aside. In a small bowl combine sour cream and baking soda; set aside. In a medium bowl combine flour and baking powder; set aside.
2. For topping, in a small bowl combine brown sugar, walnuts, and cinnamon; set aside.
3. In a large mixing bowl beat butter with an electric mixer on medium to high for 30 seconds. Gradually add granulated sugar, about ¼ cup at a time, beating on medium after each addition until well combined (about 3 minutes). Scrape sides of bowl; continue beating on medium for 2 minutes more. Add eggs, 1 at a time, beating after each addition. Beat in vanilla. Alternately add flour mixture and sour cream mixture to butter mixture, beating on low after each addition just until combined. Beat on medium to high for 20 seconds more.
4. Spread half of the batter in the prepared pan. Evenly top with cherries. Sprinkle one-third topping on cherries. Spread remaining half of batter over topping. Sprinkle remaining two-thirds of topping on batter.
5. Bake for 60 to 75 minutes or until a toothpick inserted near the center comes out clean. Cool about 40 minutes; serve warm.
PER SERVING 460 cal., 22 g total fat (12 g sat. fat), 96 mg chol., 322 mg sodium, 62 g carbo., 2 g fiber, 7 g pro.

Pecan Browned Butter Coffee Cake

Browned butter has a rich, nutty flavor. The French call it *beurre noisette,* which refers to butter cooked to the light brown color of a hazelnut (noisette).

PREP 35 minutes CHILL 2 hours BAKE 50 minutes
COOL 55 minutes OVEN 325°F MAKES 12 servings

¾   cup butter
2   cups pecan halves or pieces, toasted and finely chopped (see note, page 119)
2   cups packed brown sugar
2   teaspoons all-purpose flour
3   cups all-purpose flour
1½ teaspoons baking powder
1½ teaspoons baking soda
¾   teaspoon salt
3   eggs
1   teaspoon vanilla
1½ cups plain yogurt
1   recipe Coffee Icing

1. In a medium saucepan melt butter over medium heat. Reduce heat to medium-low. Continue to cook, without stirring, for 5 to 6 minutes or until butter becomes brown and fragrant. Remove from heat; cool slightly. Transfer to a small bowl. Cover and chill for 2 hours or freeze for 30 minutes or until firm.
2. Preheat oven to 325°F. Grease and flour a 10-inch fluted tube pan or coat with *nonstick baking spray;* set aside. For filling, in a small bowl combine ¾ cup of the

pecans, ½ cup of the brown sugar, and the 2 teaspoons flour. Add 3 tablespoons of the browned butter and work in with fingers or a fork until mixture is crumbly; set aside. In a medium bowl stir together the 3 cups flour, baking powder, baking soda, and salt; set aside.

3. In a large mixing bowl beat remaining browned butter with an electric mixer on medium for 30 seconds. Add remaining 1½ cups brown sugar; beat until combined, scraping sides of bowl occasionally. Add eggs, 1 at a time, beating after each addition until combined. Stir in vanilla. Alternately add flour mixture and yogurt to butter mixture, beating on low after each addition just until combined. Stir in remaining 1¼ cups pecans.

4. Spoon half the batter into prepared pan, spreading evenly. Evenly sprinkle filling on batter in pan. Spoon remaining batter on filling; spread to cover.

5. Bake about 50 minutes or until a toothpick inserted near the center comes out clean. Cool in pan on a wire rack for 10 minutes. Remove from pan. Cool about 45 minutes. To serve, drizzle with Coffee Icing.

Coffee Icing In a small bowl stir together 4 teaspoons milk and 1 teaspoon instant coffee crystals until dissolved. Stir in 1 cup powdered sugar and enough additional milk to make a drizzling consistency.

PER SERVING *561 cal., 27 g total fat (9 g sat. fat), 85 mg chol., 481 mg sodium, 75 g carbo., 3 g fiber, 8 g pro.*

Overnight Blueberry Coffee Cake

Spelt flour, blueberries, and almonds make this coffee bread healthful food. Spelt is a high-protein cereal grain with a mellow, nutty flavor. Look for it at health food stores.

PREP **35 minutes** CHILL **8 hours**
BAKE **1 hour 5 minutes** STAND **15 minutes**
COOL **45 minutes** OVEN **350°F** MAKES **12 servings**

2   cups all-purpose flour
½   cup spelt flour or whole wheat flour
2   teaspoons baking powder
½   teaspoon baking soda
½   to 1 teaspoon ground nutmeg or cinnamon
½   teaspoon salt
¾   cup butter, softened
1   cup granulated sugar
2   eggs
1   8-ounce carton sour cream*
1   teaspoon finely shredded lemon peel
1¾ cups fresh or frozen blueberries
½   cup packed brown sugar
1   teaspoon ground cinnamon
½   cup coarsely chopped slivered almonds
3   tablespoons butter

1. Grease and flour a 9-inch springform pan; set aside. In a bowl combine 1½ cups of the all-purpose flour, spelt flour, baking powder, baking soda, nutmeg, and salt.

2. In a large mixing bowl beat ¾ cup butter with an electric mixer on medium to high 30 seconds. Add granulated sugar; beat well. Add eggs and sour cream; beat until combined. Add flour mixture; beat on low speed just until combined. Stir in lemon peel and 1 cup of the blueberries (batter will be thick). Spread batter into prepared pan. Cover and refrigerate overnight. Stir together remaining ½ cup all-purpose flour, brown sugar, cinnamon, and nuts. For topping, cut in 3 tablespoons butter until mixture resembles coarse crumbs. Place in a covered container and chill overnight.

3. Preheat oven to 350°F. About 15 minutes before baking, remove cake and topping from refrigerator. Sprinkle cake with remaining blueberries. Sprinkle with topping. Bake, uncovered, for 65 minutes or until toothpick inserted near center comes out clean. Cool in pan on a wire rack for 15 minutes. Remove sides of pan. Cool 30 minutes more. Serve warm.

*Note Do not use reduced-fat sour cream; this cake needs the extra fat to become tender.

PER SERVING *407 cal., 22 g total fat (12 g sat. fat), 83 mg chol., 342 mg sodium, 50 g carbo., 2 g fiber, 5 g pro.*

Overnight Blueberry Coffee Cake

Apricot, Pecan, and White Chocolate Bread

There are two types of dried apricots, sulphured and unsulphured. Sulphur helps retain the bright orange color and moist texture. Unsulphured apricots are dark brown and a little drier; the flavor is the same. Look for both in natural food sections of supermarkets or health food stores.

PREP **25 minutes** BAKE **1 hour** COOL **10 minutes**
STAND **overnight** OVEN **350°F** MAKES **16 servings**

½   cup snipped dried apricots
2   cups all-purpose flour
1   cup sugar
1   tablespoon baking powder
½   teaspoon salt
1   egg, lightly beaten
1   cup milk
¼   cup cooking oil
½   cup chopped ,toasted pecans (see note, page 119)
½   cup white baking pieces

1. In a small bowl combine dried apricots and enough boiling water to cover. Let stand for 15 minutes; drain.
2. Meanwhile, preheat oven to 350°F. Line a 9×5×3-inch loaf pan with foil, extending foil over edges of pan. Grease foil; set aside. In a large bowl stir together flour, sugar, baking powder, and salt. Make a well in center of flour mixture; set aside.
3. In a medium bowl combine egg, milk, and oil. Add egg mixture all at once to flour mixture. Stir just until moistened (batter should be lumpy). Fold in pecans,

baking pieces, and drained apricots. Spoon batter into the prepared pan.
4. Bake for 60 to 65 minutes or until a toothpick inserted near center comes out clean. Cool in pan on a wire rack for 10 minutes.
5. Use the foil to lift bread out of pan; remove foil. Cool bread completely on wire rack. Wrap and store overnight before slicing.

PER SERVING *222 cal., 9 g total fat (3 g sat. fat), 14 mg chol., 162 mg sodium, 33 g carbo., 1 g fiber, 3 g pro.*

No-Knead Chocolate and Coconut Rolls

Purchased chocolate-hazelnut spread makes an easy and indulgent filling for these sweet rolls.

PREP **30 minutes** RISE **1 hour 30 minutes**
BAKE **15 minutes** OVEN **350°F** MAKES **9 rolls**

4   cups all-purpose flour
1   package active dry yeast
1   cup milk
⅓   cup sugar
¼   cup butter
2   eggs
1   13-ounce jar chocolate-hazelnut spread
1   cup shredded coconut
1   recipe Chocolate-Hazelnut Icing

1. In large mixing bowl combine 2 cups of the flour and the yeast. In small saucepan heat and stir milk, sugar, butter, and ½ teaspoon *salt* just until warm (120°F to 130°F) and butter is almost melted. Add milk mixture and eggs to flour mixture. Beat with electric mixer on low to medium for 30 seconds, scraping bowl as needed. Beat on medium for 3 minutes. Stir in remaining flour. Cover; let rise in warm place until double in size (45 to 60 minutes).
2. Turn dough out onto a well-floured surface. Cover; let rest for 10 minutes. Lightly grease a large baking sheet; set aside. Roll dough into a 12×9-inch rectangle. Spread ⅔ cup hazelnut spread on dough, leaving a 1-inch edge along one of the long sides. Sprinkle coconut on hazelnut spread. Roll up rectangle, starting from the long side with filling spread to edge. Pinch dough to seal seams. Slice into 9 rolls. Arrange 2 inches apart on prepared baking sheet. Cover; let rise in a warm place until nearly double in size (about 45 minutes).
3. Preheat oven to 350°F. Bake rolls for 15 to 20 minutes or until golden. Cool about 5 minutes; transfer to wire rack. Drizzle with Chocolate-Hazelnut Icing.
Chocolate-Hazelnut Icing In a bowl stir together remaining chocolate-hazelnut spread and enough milk to make icing a drizzling consistency.

PER ROLL *590 cal., 24 g total fat (8 g sat. fat), 64 mg chol., 272 mg sodium, 83 g carbo., 3 g fiber, 12 g pro.*

Apricot, Pecan, and White Chocolate Bread

No-Knead Chocolate and Coconut Rolls

Coconut Banana Bread

Substitute chocolate baking pieces for the white baking pieces if you prefer.

PREP 25 minutes BAKE 35 minutes
COOL 10 minutes STAND overnight OVEN 350°F
MAKES 1 loaf (16 slices)

Nonstick cooking spray
¾   cup all-purpose flour
½   cup whole wheat flour
¼   cup toasted wheat germ
1¼ teaspoon baking powder
1   teaspoon ground cinnamon
½   teaspoon baking soda
⅛   teaspoon salt
1   cup mashed bananas
1   egg, slightly beaten
¼   cup reduced-fat creamy peanut butter
½   cup packed brown sugar
½   cup sweetened shredded coconut
½   cup white baking pieces

1. Preheat oven to 350°F. Spray a 9×5×3-inch loaf pan with cooking spray; set aside.
2. In a medium bowl combine flours, wheat germ, baking powder, cinnamon, baking soda, and salt; set aside. In a large bowl combine mashed bananas and egg. In a small microwavable bowl heat peanut butter on high for 15 to 20 seconds or until softened. Stir into banana mixture along with brown sugar just until combined. Stir in flour mixture just until combined. Fold in coconut and white baking pieces just until combined. Spread into prepared pan.
3. Bake for 35 to 40 minutes or until a wooden toothpick inserted near center comes out clean. Cool in pan on a wire rack for 10 minutes. Remove from pan. Cool completely on a wire rack. Wrap and store overnight before slicing.
PER SLICE *172 cal., 5 g total fat (3 g sat. fat), 13 mg chol., 137 mg sodium, 28 g carbo., 2 g fiber, 4 g pro.*

Quick Seed Bread

Healthful whole grain breads aren't necessarily slow-rising yeast breads. This quick bread offers whole grain goodness and hearty crunch. Let it stand overnight, however, for easy slicing.

PREP 20 minutes BAKE 45 minutes STAND overnight
COOL 10 minutes OVEN 350°F MAKES 1 loaf
(14 servings)

1½ cups all-purpose flour
½   cup whole wheat flour
¾   cup packed brown sugar
½   cup dry-roasted sunflower kernels
⅓   cup flaxseed meal
2   tablespoons sesame seed
2   tablespoons poppy seed
1   teaspoon baking powder
½   teaspoon baking soda
½   teaspoon salt
1   egg
1¼ cups buttermilk or sour milk*
¼   cup vegetable oil
4   teaspoons sesame seeds, poppy seeds and/or dry roasted sunflower kernels

1. Preheat oven to 350°F. Grease the bottom and ½ inch up sides of a 9×5×3-inch loaf pan; set aside.
2. In a large bowl stir together the flours, brown sugar, the ½ cup sunflower kernels, flaxseed meal, the 2 tablespoons sesame seeds, the 2 tablespoons poppy seeds, the baking powder, baking soda, and salt. Make a well in the center of flour mixture; set aside. In a medium bowl beat egg with a fork; stir in buttermilk and oil. Add egg mixture all at once to flour mixture. Stir just until moistened (batter should be lumpy). Spread batter into prepared pan. Sprinkle with the 4 teaspoons seeds.
3. Bake for 45 to 55 minutes or until a wooden toothpick inserted near center comes out clean. Cool

Coconut Banana Bread

in pan on a wire rack for 10 minutes. Remove from pan. Cool completely on wire rack. Wrap and store bread overnight before slicing.

*Note To make 1¼ cups sour milk, place 4 teaspoons lemon juice or vinegar in a glass measuring cup. Add enough milk to equal 1¼ cups total liquid; stir. Let stand for 5 minutes before using.

PER SERVING *216 cal., 10 g total fat (1 g sat. fat), 16 mg chol., 180 mg sodium, 28 g carbo., 2 g fiber, 5 g pro.*

Cherry and Golden Raisin Bread

This fruited quick bread is a lovely gift or a welcome addition to a holiday brunch buffet.

PREP **25 minutes** BAKE **1 hour** COOL **10 minutes**
STAND **overnight** OVEN **350°F**
MAKES **1 loaf (16 slices)**

Cherry and Golden Raisin Bread

2   cups all-purpose flour
1   cup sugar
2   teaspoons baking powder
½   teaspoon salt
¼   teaspoon baking soda
1   egg
1   cup milk
⅓   cup cooking oil or melted butter or margarine
1   teaspoon vanilla
½   cup coarsely chopped dried cherries or cranberries
½   cup golden raisins or coarsely chopped dried apricots
2   teaspoons finely shredded lemon peel
1   recipe Lemon Glaze

1. Preheat oven to 350°F. Grease the bottom and ½ inch up sides of an 8×4×2-inch loaf pan; set aside. In a large bowl stir together the flour, sugar, baking powder, salt, and baking soda; set aside.
2. In a medium bowl combine the egg, milk, oil, and vanilla. Stir in the cherries, golden raisins, and lemon peel. Add the egg mixture all at once to the flour mixture. Stir just until moistened (batter should be lumpy). Spoon the batter into the prepared pan.
3. Bake for 1 hour or until a wooden pick inserted near center comes out clean. Cool in pan on a wire rack for 10 minutes. Remove from pan. Cool completely on a wire rack. Wrap and store overnight at room temperature before serving.
4. Before serving, prepare Lemon Glaze. Drizzle the glaze over the loaf.
Lemon Glaze In a small bowl combine ½ cup sifted powdered sugar and 1 teaspoon finely shredded lemon peel. Stir in enough lemon juice (1 to 2 teaspoons) to make smooth and creamy glaze drizzling consistency.

PER SLICE *192 cal., 5 g total fat (1 g sat. fat), 15 mg chol., 155 mg sodium, 34 g carbo., 1 g fiber, 3 g pro.*

Maple Crunch Muffins

Although pure maple syrup is pricey, be sure to use it, not pancake syrup made primarily with corn syrup, in this recipe. The maple flavor is well worth it.

PREP 30 minutes BAKE 15 minutes OVEN 375°F
MAKES 18 muffins

2   cups all-purpose flour
1   cup whole wheat flour
½   cup granola with almonds
1   tablespoon baking powder
1   teaspoon salt
1   cup milk
1   cup pure maple syrup
½   cup canola oil
2   eggs, lightly beaten
1   recipe Maple Frosting
    Granola with almonds

1. Preheat oven to 375°F. Line eighteen 3½-inch muffin cups with 5×5-inch squares of parchment paper (pleat to fit) or paper bake cups. Combine flours, granola, baking powder, and 1 teaspoon salt. Combine milk, syrup, oil, and eggs; add to flour mixture. Stir until moistened (batter will be lumpy). Spoon into muffin cups, filling each two-thirds full.

2. Bake 15 minutes or until a wooden toothpick comes out clean. Cool in muffin cups on wire rack 5 minutes. Remove from cups. Spread Maple Frosting on muffins and sprinkle with granola.
Maple Frosting In a bowl beat 2 ounces softened cream cheese 30 seconds. Add 2 tablespoons powdered sugar and 1 tablespoon maple syrup; beat until smooth.
PER MUFFIN *247 cal., 10 g total fat (1 g sat. fat), 27 mg chol., 219 mg sodium, 36 g carbo., 2 g fiber, 5 g pro.*

Walnut-Filled Muffins

The unusual filling in these muffins consists of ground toasted walnuts, sugar, orange juice, and cinnamon.

PREP 35 minutes BAKE 20 minutes COOL 5 minutes
OVEN 350°F MAKES 12 muffins

1⅔ cups walnuts, toasted, (see note, page 119)
2   tablespoons sugar
½   teaspoon salt
½   teaspoon ground cinnamon
1   tablespoon orange juice
1¾ cups all-purpose flour
2   teaspoon baking powder
⅓   cup butter, softened
⅔   cup sugar
1   egg
½   cup orange juice
¼   cup milk
1   recipe Frosting

1. Preheat oven to 350°F. Line 12 muffin cups with bake cups or lightly coat with *nonstick cooking spray;* set aside. In a food processor finely grind nuts with 2 tablespoons sugar, ¼ teaspoon salt, and cinnamon. Add 1 tablespoon orange juice; process until combined. Using a rounded teaspoon, shape some of the nut mixture into 12 balls; set aside remaining mixture.
2. Combine flour, baking powder, and ¼ teaspoon *salt;* set aside. In a large mixing bowl beat butter with an electric mixer for 30 seconds; beat in ⅔ cup sugar. Beat in egg, orange juice, and milk on low until combined. Gradually add flour mixture; beat just until combined. Spoon half the batter into cups; top with walnut balls and press in lightly. Top with remaining batter.
3. Bake about 20 minutes or until tops spring back when lightly touched. Cool in pans 5 minutes. Remove and cool on rack. Spread muffins with Frosting; top with reserved nut mixture.
Frosting In a mixing bowl beat ⅓ cup softened butter, 1 tablespoon whipping cream, and ½ teaspoon finely shredded orange peel with mixer on low just until combined. Add 1½ cups powdered sugar. Beat on medium until smooth. Makes about 1 cup.
PER MUFFIN *391 cal., 22 g total fat (8 g sat. fat), 47 mg chol., 239 mg sodium, 46 g carbo., 2 g fiber, 5 g pro.*

Maple Crunch Muffins

Cinnamon Twists

These warmly spiced sweet breads have all the yummy flavor of cinnamon rolls in a twist rather than a spiral.

PREP 25 minutes RISE 2 hours 45 minutes
BAKE 12 minutes OVEN 375°F MAKES 20 twists

3½ to 4 cups all-purpose flour
1 package active dry yeast
¾ cup milk
½ cup granulated sugar
⅓ cup butter
¾ teaspoon salt
2 eggs
¼ cup butter
⅔ cup packed brown sugar
1 teaspoon ground cinnamon
1½ cups powdered sugar
¼ teaspoon vanilla
⅛ teaspoon ground cinnamon
   Milk

1. In a mixing bowl stir together 1½ cups of the flour and the yeast; set aside. In a saucepan heat and stir ¾ cup milk, granulated sugar, ⅓ cup butter, and salt just until warm (120°F to 130°F) and butter almost melts. Add to flour mixture along with eggs. Beat with an electric mixer on low to medium for 30 seconds, scraping bowl constantly. Beat on high for 3 minutes. Stir in as much of the remaining flour as you can.
2. Turn dough out onto a floured surface. Knead in enough remaining flour to make a moderately soft dough that is smooth and elastic (3 to 5 minutes total). Shape dough in a ball. Place in a lightly greased bowl, turning once to grease surface; cover. Let rise in a warm place until double in size (about 2 hours).
3. Punch dough down. Turn out onto a lightly floured surface; cover and let rest for 10 minutes. Line 2 large baking sheets with parchment paper or foil; set aside. Roll dough to a 20×16-inch rectangle.
4. In a small saucepan melt the ¼ cup butter over low heat. Add brown sugar and 1 teaspoon cinnamon; mix well. Cool slightly and spread sugar mixture evenly on dough. Cut dough crosswise into twenty 1-inch strips. Fold each strip in half, end to end; twist several times. Arrange twists 2 inches apart on prepared baking sheets. Cover and let rise in a warm place until nearly double in size (45 to 60 minutes).
5. Preheat oven to 375°F. Bake for 12 to 15 minutes or until golden brown. Cool slightly on a wire rack.
6. In a small bowl combine powdered sugar, vanilla, ⅛ teaspoon cinnamon, and enough milk (2 to 3 tablespoons) to make drizzling consistency. Whisk until smooth; drizzle on warm rolls. Cool completely on rack.

PER TWIST 223 cal., 6 g total fat (4 g sat. fat), 36 mg chol., 139 mg sodium, 39 g carbo., 1 g fiber, 3 g pro.

Cinnamon Twists

White Chocolate Peppermint Scones

1. Preheat oven to 400°F. Grease a large baking sheet.
2. In a large bowl combine flour, sugar, baking powder, and salt. Using a pastry blender, cut in butter until mixture resembles coarse crumbs. Stir in white and peppermint baking pieces. Make a well in center of the flour mixture; set aside. In a bowl combine egg, buttermilk, and vanilla. Add egg mixture to flour mixture. Using a fork, stir just until moistened.
3. Turn dough out onto a lightly floured surface. Knead dough by folding and gently pressing 10 to 12 strokes or until dough is nearly smooth. Divide dough in half. Pat or lightly roll each dough half into a 6-inch circle about ½ inch thick. Cut each circle into 6 wedges. Place wedges 2 inches apart on the prepared baking sheet.
4. Bake for 15 minutes or until lightly browned and a toothpick inserted into a crack comes out clean. Remove scones from baking sheet. If desired, serve warm with Devonshire Cream.
PER SCONE 281 cal., 13 g total fat (9 g sat. fat), 34 mg chol., 154 mg sodium, 35 g carbo., 1 g fiber, 4 g pro.
Devonshire Cream In a 1-cup glass measuring cup combine ¼ cup cold water and ½ teaspoon unflavored gelatin; let stand 2 minutes to soften. Place measuring cup in a small saucepan of boiling water. Cook and stir about 1 minute or until gelatin is completely dissolved. Carefully remove from saucepan and cool. In a chilled medium mixing bowl beat ½ cup whipping cream, 2 tablespoons sugar, and 1 teaspoon vanilla with an electric mixer on medium-low until soft peaks form. Do not overbeat. Combine cooled gelatin mixture and ½ cup sour cream; mix well. Fold together sour cream mixture and whipped cream. Chill for 30 to 45 minutes or until mixture thickens and will mound on a spoon. Stir before using.

White Chocolate Peppermint Scones

Devonshire Cream is a thick, pale creamy yellow clotted cream originally produced in the counties of Devon, Cornwall, and Somerset, England. If you can't find it in a specialty store, make the close approximation.

PREP 25 minutes BAKE 15 minutes
OVEN 400°F MAKES 12 scones

2   cups all-purpose flour
⅓   cup sugar
1   teaspoon baking powder
¼   teaspoon salt
6   tablespoons chilled butter, cut into small pieces
¾   cup white baking pieces
½   cup peppermint and white chocolate baking pieces
1   egg, lightly beaten
⅔   cup buttermilk
1   teaspoon vanilla
1   recipe Devonshire Cream or purchased Devonshire cream (optional)

Blue Cheese Walnut Scones

These blue-cheese-filled spirals are a delicious accompaniment to roast beef or a savory appetizer to nibble with a glass of hearty red wine.

PREP 25 minutes BAKE 18 minutes
OVEN 400°F MAKES 12 scones

2   cups all-purpose flour
1   tablespoon sugar
1   tablespoon baking powder
¼   teaspoon salt
5   tablespoons cold butter, cut into small bits
¾   cup milk
½   cup crumbled blue cheese
⅓   cup coarsely chopped walnuts, toasted
¼   cup cream cheese, softened
2   tablespoons milk
     Milk

1. Preheat oven to 400°F. Lightly grease a baking sheet; set aside. In a large bowl combine flour, sugar, baking powder, and salt. Using a pastry blender, cut in butter

until mixture resembles coarse crumbs. Make a well in the center of the flour mixture. Add ¾ cup milk all at once to flour mixture. Using a fork, stir just until mixture is moistened.

2. Turn dough out onto a lightly floured surface. Knead dough by folding and gently pressing dough for 10 to 12 strokes or just until dough holds together. Lightly roll dough into a 16×10-inch rectangle.

3. In a small bowl combine blue cheese, walnuts, cream cheese, and 2 tablespoons milk. Mix with a wooden spoon until smooth and spreadable. With a knife or metal spatula, spread blue cheese mixture evenly on dough.

4. From the short end, roll dough in a cylinder. Using a serrated knife, slice roll in 12 portions. Place rolls, just touching, on the prepared baking sheet. Lightly brush tops of rolls with additional milk. Bake for 18 to 20 minutes or until golden. Serve warm.

PER SCONE *190 cal., 11 g total fat (5 g sat. fat), 24 mg chol., 276 mg sodium, 19 g carbo., 1 g fiber, 5 g pro.*

Lemony Scones with Dried Fruit

These simple scones are dropped onto the baking sheet rather than shaped and cut in wedges. They are wonderful for breakfast or with a cup of afternoon tea.

PREP **25 minutes** BAKE **18 minutes**
OVEN **375°F** MAKES **16 to 18 scones**

2	cups all-purpose flour
2	teaspoons baking powder
½	teaspoon baking soda
½	cup butter
1	8-ounce carton sour cream
1	egg
¼	cup granulated sugar
1½	teaspoons finely shredded lemon peel
⅔	cup snipped dried apricots
⅔	cup dried figs or snipped pitted dried plums
½	cup powdered sugar
2	to 3 teaspoons lemon juice
¼	cup chopped, toasted walnuts (see note, page 119) (optional)

1. Preheat oven to 375°F. Lightly grease a large baking sheet. In bowl stir together flour, baking powder, soda, and ¼ teaspoon *salt*. Cut in butter to resemble coarse crumbs. In another bowl stir together sour cream, egg, granulated sugar, and 1 teaspoon peel; add to flour mixture. Combine just until moistened. Stir in apricots and dried plums. Drop dough onto baking sheet. Bake 18 to 20 minutes or until golden and toothpick inserted in centers comes out clean. Cool slightly on rack.

2. For glaze, stir together powdered sugar and ½ teaspoon of the lemon peel. Stir in enough lemon juice to make drizzling consistency; drizzle over scones. If desired, sprinkle with walnuts.

PER SCONE *200 cal., 9 g total fat (6 g sat. fat,), 35 mg chol., 175 mg sodium, 28 g carbo., 1 g fiber, 3 g pro.*

Lemony Scones with Dried Fruit

Gooey Ginger Coffee Rolls

Little Orange Caramel Rolls

The caramel sauce for these breakfast beauties is infused with fresh citrus flavor. Let the rolls rise in the refrigerator overnight to serve warm from the oven in the morning.

PREP 30 minutes STAND 1 hour 10 minutes
RISE 1 hour CHILL 2 hours RISE 1 hour
BAKE 25 minutes COOL 10 minutes OVEN 350°F
MAKES 24 rolls

5   to 5½ cups all-purpose flour
1   cup warm water or milk (105°F to 115°F)
⅔   cup sugar
2   packages active dry yeast
3   eggs
½   teaspoon salt
½   cup butter, cut into small pieces and softened
⅓   cup butter, softened
⅓   cup sugar
1   recipe Orange-Caramel Goo

1. In a large mixing bowl combine 1½ cups of the flour, the water, 1 tablespoon of the ⅔ cup sugar, and the yeast. Beat with electric mixer on medium for 2 minutes or until smooth.(Mixture will be thick and sticky.) Cover with plastic wrap. Let stand at room temperature about 30 minutes or until bubbly.
2. Add the eggs, salt, and remaining ⅔ cup sugar to the flour mixture. Beat on medium about 2 minutes or until smooth. Add the ½ cup butter, a few pieces at a time, and beat until well combined. Stir in as much remaining flour as you can.
3. Turn dough out onto a lightly floured surface. Knead in enough remaining flour to make a moderately soft dough that is smooth and elastic (3 to 5 minutes total).

Shape dough into a ball. Butter a large bowl. Place the dough into bowl, turning once. Cover; let rise in a warm place until dough doubles in size (about 1 hour).
4. Punch dough down. Divide in half. Turn out onto a lightly floured surface. Cover; let rest for 10 minutes. Meanwhile, lightly grease two 13×9×2-inch baking pans; set aside. Divide and evenly spread the slightly warm Orange-Caramel Goo in prepared pans.
5. Roll each dough half into a 12×8-inch rectangle. Divide and evenly spread the ⅓ cup softened butter on dough rectangles; sprinkle with the ⅓ cup sugar. Roll up each rectangle starting from a long side. Seal seams. Slice each roll into 12 pieces. Place, cut sides down, in prepared pans.
6. Cover dough loosely with plastic wrap, leaving room for rolls to rise. Chill for 2 to 24 hours. Uncover; let stand at room temperature for 30 minutes. (To bake rolls right away, do not chill dough. Cover dough loosely with plastic wrap; let rise in a warm place until nearly double in size, about 30 minutes.) Break any surface bubbles with a greased toothpick.
7. Preheat oven to 350°F. Bake for 25 to 30 minutes or until light brown (if necessary, cover rolls with foil the last 5 minutes to prevent overbrowning). Remove from oven. Let the rolls stand in the pans for 10 minutes. Carefully invert rolls onto serving trays. Serve warm.
Orange-Caramel Goo In a small saucepan combine 1¼ cups sugar, ⅓ cup butter, ⅓ cup whipping cream, 1 teaspoon finely shredded orange peel, 2 tablespoons orange juice, 1 teaspoon lemon juice, ¼ teaspoon orange extract, and ⅛ teaspoon salt. Cook and stir over medium-low heat for 5 minutes. Remove from heat.
PER ROLL *259 cal., 11 g total fat (7 g sat. fat), 55 mg chol., 167 mg sodium, 37 g carbo., 1 g fiber, 4 g pro.*

Gooey Ginger Coffee Rolls

Crystallized ginger is fresh ginger that has been cooked in sugar syrup then dried. It gives the coating on these rolls a deliciously spicy-sweet flavor.

PREP 20 minutes BAKE 35 minutes COOL 16 minutes
OVEN 350°F MAKES 10 servings (2 rolls each)

1¼   cups sugar
2   tablespoons finely chopped crystallized ginger
¼   teaspoon ground ginger
2   teaspoons finely shredded lemon or orange peel
⅓   cup orange juice
¼   cup butter, melted
2   10-to 12-ounce packages refrigerated biscuits (10 biscuits each)

1. Preheat oven to 350°F. Grease a 10-inch fluted tube pan. Set aside.
2. In a small bowl combine sugar, crystallized ginger, ground ginger, and lemon peel, breaking up any peel clumps. In another small bowl combine orange juice and melted butter. Separate biscuits. Dip each biscuit

into the orange juice-butter mixture and roll in sugar mixture to coat.

3. Arrange biscuits in a single layer, sides touching, in prepared pan. Pour remaining juice mixture on top; sprinkle with remaining sugar.

4. Bake for 35 minutes. If rolls brown too quickly, cover with foil the last 10 minutes of baking. Cool in pan on wire rack 1 minute. Invert pan onto serving plate. Remove pan. Spoon any remaining topping in pan on rolls. Cool 15 minutes. Serve warm.

PER SERVING *280 cal., 6 g total fat (3 g sat. fat), 12 mg chol., 512 mg sodium, 53 g carbo., 1 g fiber, 4 g pro.*

Chocolate-Pistachio Wreath Bread

This beautiful braided chocolate-pistachio bread is infused with the flavor of fresh orange. It makes a lovely addition to a holiday brunch buffet.

PREP **30 minutes** STAND **40 minutes**
RISE **1 hour 45 minutes** BAKE **25 minutes**
OVEN **375°F** MAKES **1 loaf (16 to 20 servings)**

3½ to 4½ cups all-purpose flour
1 cup warm milk (105°F to 115°F)
2 teaspoons sugar
1 package active dry yeast
2 eggs
½ cup sugar
⅓ cup unsweetened cocoa powder
⅓ cup finely chopped pistachio nuts or almonds
2 teaspoons finely shredded orange peel (optional)
¾ teaspoon salt
⅓ cup butter, cut into small pieces and softened
1 egg, lightly beaten
1 tablespoon milk
1 recipe Chocolate Icing
   Chopped pistachio nuts (optional)

1. In a mixing bowl combine 1 cup of the flour, 1 cup warm milk, 2 teaspoons sugar, and the yeast. Beat with an electric mixer on medium about 2 minutes or until smooth (mixture will be thick and sticky). Cover with plastic wrap. Let stand at room temperature for 30 minutes or until bubbly.

2. Add the 2 eggs, ½ cup sugar, cocoa powder, finely chopped pistachio nuts, orange peel (if using), and salt to flour mixture; stir in another ½ cup of the flour. Beat with an electric mixer on medium about 2 minutes or until smooth. Add butter, a few pieces at a time, beating until well combined. Using a wooden spoon, stir in as much of the remaining flour as you can.

3. Turn dough out onto a lightly floured surface. Knead in enough remaining flour to make a moderately stiff dough that is smooth and elastic (6 to 8 minutes total). Shape dough in a ball. Place dough in a lightly greased bowl, turning once to grease surface. Cover and let rise in a warm place until double in size (about 1 hour).

4. Punch down dough. Turn out onto lightly floured surface. Divide dough in 3 equal portions. Cover; let rest for 10 minutes.

5. Roll each portion of dough into a thick 20-inch-long rope. Line up the 3 ropes 1 inch apart on the lightly floured surface; braid. Join ends of braid to form a wreath. Carefully transfer wreath to a greased baking sheet; place a greased ball of foil in center to hold shape. Cover; let rise until nearly double in size (45 to 60 minutes).

6. Preheat oven to 375°F. Stir together the 1 egg and 1 tablespoon milk. Brush on top the wreath. Bake about 25 minutes or until bread sounds hollow when lightly tapped. Cover with foil the last 10 minutes, if necessary, to prevent overbrowning. Remove from baking sheet; cool slightly. Remove foil ball from center.

7. Spread bread with Chocolate Icing. If desired, sprinkle with additional pistachio nuts.

Chocolate Icing In a small saucepan melt ½ cup milk chocolate pieces and 2 tablespoons butter over low heat, stirring frequently. Remove from heat. Stir in 1 cup powdered sugar and 2 tablespoons hot water. If needed, stir in additional hot water to make a smooth and creamy icing spreading consistency. Makes ¾ cup icing.

PER SERVING *282 cal., 10 g total fat (5 g sat. fat), 56 mg chol., 178 mg sodium, 42 g carbo., 1 g fiber, 6 g pro.*

Chocolate-Pistachio Wreath Bread

Cheesy Garlic Rolls

Yes, that's 24 cloves of garlic divided among six dinner rolls. Don't be daunted—cooking the garlic in broth and wine before stuffing it into the rolls mellows it. The creamy garlic melts with the cheese when the rolls are warmed in the oven—yum!

PREP 25 minutes COOK 25 minutes BAKE 8 minutes
COOL 20 minutes OVEN 325°F MAKES 6 servings

⅓ cup peeled garlic cloves (24 cloves)
⅔ cup chicken broth
½ cup dry white wine
½ a 12-ounce package Hawaiian sweet rolls or dinner rolls (6 rolls)
½ cup shredded fontina cheese (2 ounces)
  Olive oil

1. In a heavy saucepan combine garlic, broth, and wine. Bring to boiling; reduce heat. Boil gently, uncovered, over medium heat about 25 minutes or until garlic is tender and ⅓ cup of the liquid remains. Set aside.
2. Preheat oven to 325°F. Place rolls (do not separate rolls) in a greased 8×8×2-inch baking pan. Cut an X about ½ inch deep in the top of each roll; spread open slightly. Spoon garlic cloves and shredded cheese into openings, pressing down lightly. Drizzle remaining broth mixture over rolls. Brush rolls with olive oil.

3. Bake for 8 to 10 minutes until heated through and cheese is melted. Serve warm.
PER SERVING 181 cal., 7 g total fat (3 g sat. fat), 21 mg chol., 275 mg sodium, 19 g carbo., 0 g fiber, 6 g pro.

Herbed Focaccia

This savory bread is wonderful as an accompaniment to dinner—or split the wedges and use it to make sandwiches.

PREP 30 minutes RISE 1 hour BAKE 20 minutes
STAND 2 hours FREEZE 2 hours OVEN 400°F
MAKES 2 focaccia rounds (12 servings)

3¾ to 4 cups all-purpose flour
½ cup warm water (105°F to 115°F)
1 teaspoon active dry yeast
1 cup warm water (105°F to 115°F)
2 teaspoons coarse salt
2 tablespoons snipped fresh basil
2 tablespoons snipped fresh chives
2 teaspoons snipped fresh thyme
1 clove garlic, minced
1 tablespoon olive oil
⅓ cup finely shredded Parmesan cheese
  Fresh rosemary leaves (optional)
  Coarse salt (optional)

1. For the sponge, in a large bowl combine ½ cup of the flour, the ½ cup warm water, and the yeast. Beat with a wooden spoon until smooth. Cover bowl loosely with plastic wrap. Let sponge stand at room temperature for 2 to 8 hours to ferment.
2. Gradually stir in the 1 cup warm water, 2 teaspoons salt, basil, chives, thyme, garlic, and just enough of the remaining flour to make a dough that pulls away from the sides of the bowl. Turn dough out onto a lightly floured surface. Knead in enough of the remaining flour to make a soft dough that is smooth and elastic (3 to 5 minutes total). Place dough in a lightly greased bowl, turning once. Cover; let rise in a warm place until double in size (about 1 hour).
3. Lightly grease two 12-inch pizza pans; set aside. Punch dough down. Let rest for 10 minutes. Divide dough in half. Place each half into a prepared pan. Gently press each half to edges of pan using oiled hands. Brush dough rounds with olive oil. Using the tips of your fingers, make ½-inch-deep indentations in the surface of each dough round. Cover with plastic wrap and let stand in a warm place for 30 minutes.
4. Preheat oven to 400°F. If necessary, press indentations in tops of dough rounds again. Sprinkle dough rounds with Parmesan cheese and, if desired, rosemary.
5. Bake for 20 to 25 minutes or until golden, checking after 8 minutes and popping any large air bubbles with a sharp knife. Use 2 large spatulas to transfer

Cheesy Garlic Rolls

each focaccia round to a wire rack; cool completely. If desired, sprinkle with additional coarse salt.

PER SERVING 163 cal., 2 g total fat (0 g sat. fat), 0 mg chol., 324 mg sodium, 32 g carbo., 1 g fiber, 5 g pro.

Pine Nut and Parsley Rolls

Pine nuts have a high oil content, which makes them susceptible to spoilage. Buy small amounts and store them in the refrigerator to retain freshness.

PREP 30 minutes   RISE 30 minutes   BAKE 15 minutes
COOL 20 minutes   OVEN 375°F   MAKES 12 rolls

1   16-ounce package hot roll mix
1   cup warm water (120°F to 130°F)
2   tablespoons butter
1   egg
½   cup finely chopped pine nuts or slivered almonds
⅓   cup grated Parmesan cheese
¼   cup snipped fresh parsley
2   tablespoons butter, melted
1   egg, lightly beaten
1   tablespoon water

1. Lightly grease an extra-large baking sheet; set aside. Prepare roll mix according to package directions using the warm water, 2 tablespoons butter, and egg. Knead dough and let rest according to package directions.
2. Combine pine nuts, cheese, and parsley. Roll dough on a lightly floured surface in an 18-inch square. Brush with 2 tablespoons melted butter; sprinkle with cheese mixture. Roll up dough in a spiral; moisten and seal seam. Cut roll crosswise into twelve 1½-inch slices.
3. Place slices, seam sides down, on prepared baking sheet. Let rest for 5 minutes. Using a wooden spoon handle, press down in center of each slice to make a deep lengthwise crease on top of roll. Let rise in a warm place until nearly double (30 to 35 minutes). Stir together lightly beaten egg and water; brush on rolls.
4. Preheat oven to 375°F. Bake for 15 minutes or until golden. Remove from baking sheet. Cool for 20 minutes on a wire rack. Serve warm.

PER ROLL 235 cal., 40 g total fat (4 g sat. fat), 49 mg chol., 325 mg sodium, 30 g carbo., 0 g fiber, 9 g pro.

Pull-Apart Cornmeal Dinner Rolls

Cornmeal adds a pleasing crunch to these dinner rolls. They're delicious paired with creamy vegetable soup.

PREP 25 minutes   RISE 1 hour 30 minutes
BAKE 12 minutes   STAND 10 minutes   OVEN 400°F
MAKES 32 rolls

1   cup milk
¼   cup sugar
¼   cup butter
¼   cup yellow cornmeal

Pull-Apart Cornmeal Dinner Rolls

1   teaspoon salt
1   package active dry yeast
¼   cup warm water (105° to 115°)
1   egg, lightly beaten
3½ to 4 cups all-purpose flour
    Butter, melted
    Yellow cornmeal (optional)

1. In small saucepan combine milk, sugar, ¼ cup butter, ¼ cup cornmeal, and salt; cook and stir until warm (105°F to 115°F).
2. In large bowl dissolve yeast in warm water. Add egg and milk mixture. Gradually stir in enough flour to make a soft dough. Turn out onto a lightly floured surface; knead gently 2 to 3 minutes to make a smooth ball. (Knead in just enough remaining flour until dough is no longer sticky.) Place in greased bowl; turn once to grease surface. Cover; let rise in warm place until double in size (1 hour). Punch dough down; turn out on lightly floured surface. Let dough rest for 10 minutes. Grease 15×10×1-inch baking pan.
3. To shape rolls, roll or pat dough to a 10×8-inch rectangle about ¾ inch thick. Cut into 2½×1-inch strips. Arrange strips in prepared pan, about leaving ½ inch between each. Cover and let rise until nearly doubled in size (about 30 minutes).
4. Preheat oven to 400°F. Brush with melted butter. If desired, sprinkle with additional cornmeal. Bake for 12 to 15 minutes or until golden and rolls sound hollow when lightly tapped. Remove from pan. Serve warm or at room temperature.

PER ROLL 82 cal., 2 g total fat (1 g sat. fat), 12 mg chol., 92 mg sodium, 13 g carbo., 0 g fiber, 2 g pro.

divine desserts

Save room! This selection of rich and creamy cheesecakes, fanciful cupcakes, towering layer cakes, old-fashioned fruit desserts, and decadent chocolate treats will tempt even when you think you can't eat one more bite. Most can be made ahead—and are even better when they are—making them ideal for holiday entertaining.

Hazelnut-Pumpkin Cheesecake, page 93

Dutch Mocha Chocolate Cake

1. Preheat oven to 350°F. In a medium bowl stir together the cocoa powder and the ¾ cup sugar. Gradually whisk in coffee until mixture is dissolved. Cool to room temperature.

2. Meanwhile, grease and lightly flour three 9×1½-inch round baking pans. Set aside. Sift together cake flour, baking soda, and salt; set aside.

3. In a large mixing bowl beat butter with an electric mixer for 30 seconds. Add 1 cup sugar and vanilla; beat well.

4. Whisk or stir the sour cream into the cooled cocoa mixture. Alternately add flour mixture with cocoa mixture to the creamed butter mixture, beating after each addition until just combined.

5. Using clean beaters, in a large mixing bowl beat egg whites on medium-high about 1 minute or until soft peaks form (tips curl). Gradually add 1 cup sugar and beat on high until stiff peaks form (tips stand straight). Gently fold about one-third of the egg white mixture into creamed mixture to lighten. Fold in remaining egg white mixture.

6. Divide batter among the 3 prepared pans. Bake for 25 to 30 minutes or until a toothpick inserted near centers comes out clean. Cool cake layers in pans on wire racks for 10 minutes. Remove the cake layers from pans and cool completely on wire racks.

7. Frost with Unforgettable White Chocolate Frosting. If desired, pipe frosting around top and bottom edges of the cake. Cover and refrigerate. Allow to stand at room temperature for 30 minutes before serving.

Unforgettable White Chocolate Frosting In a heavy saucepan melt 18 ounces chopped white chocolate baking squares or bars on low heat. Cool until slightly warm. In a large mixing bowl beat 1 softened 3-ounce package cream cheese with an electric mixer on medium-high until smooth. Cut 1½ cups butter into pieces. Add to cream cheese; beat until fluffy. Gradually add cooled chocolate; beat until well blended.

PER SERVING *725 cal., 44 g total fat (28 g sat. fat), 95 mg chol., 437 mg sodium, 76 g carbo., 2 g fiber, 7 g pro.*

Dutch Mocha Chocolate Cake

The fabulous frosting for this rich cake is called Unforgettable White Chocolate Frosting for a very good reason: It's made with melted white chocolate, cream cheese, and butter.

PREP **40 minutes** BAKE **25 minutes**
COOL **1 hour** OVEN **350°F** MAKES **16 servings**

¾	cup unsweetened cocoa powder
¾	cup sugar
1	cup very strong hot coffee
3	cups sifted cake flour
1	teaspoon baking soda
½	teaspoon salt
1	cup butter
1	cup sugar
2	teaspoons vanilla
1	8-ounce carton sour cream
5	egg whites
1	cup sugar
1	recipe Unforgettable White Chocolate Frosting

Walnut Cake with Caramel Whipped Cream

This nut-flavored sponge cake is split and filled with whipped cream that's stirred with finely chopped homemade caramel.

PREP **1 hour** BAKE **35 minutes**
OVEN **325°F** MAKES **12 servings**

1	cup walnut halves or pieces
¾	cup unbleached all-purpose flour
1	cup sugar
1	medium orange
7	eggs, separated
¼	teaspoon salt
½	teaspoon cream of tartar
1	recipe Caramel Whipped Cream
1	recipe Simple Caramel Sauce

1. Preheat oven to 325°F. In a food processor combine walnuts and flour. Cover and process with on/off pulses until nuts are finely ground; set aside. Set aside 2 tablespoons of the sugar. Finely shred peel from orange; squeeze juice from orange. In a large mixing bowl combine the remaining sugar, 1 teaspoon of the orange peel, ⅓ cup of the orange juice, the egg yolks, and salt. Beat with an electric mixer on high for 3 to 5 minutes or until very thick and pale.

2. Thoroughly wash beaters. In another large mixing bowl combine egg whites and cream of tartar. Beat on medium until soft peaks form (tips curl). Gradually add the reserved 2 tablespoons sugar, beating until stiff peaks form (tips stand straight). Spoon about one-fourth of the beaten egg whites over yolk mixture. Add nut mixture; fold in gently. Fold in the remaining beaten egg whites just until combined. Transfer batter to an ungreased 10-inch tube pan.

3. Bake for 35 to 40 minutes or until top is golden brown and springs back when lightly touched. Immediately invert cake; cool completely in pan. Loosen sides of cake from pan; remove cake from pan. Using a sharp serrated knife, cut cake in half horizontally. Place bottom cake layer on a serving plate. Spread with Caramel Whipped Cream. Replace top cake layer. Serve with Simple Caramel Sauce.

Caramel Whipped Cream Line a baking sheet with foil or parchment paper; set aside. Place ½ cup water in a 2-quart saucepan. Pour 1 cup sugar into center of pan to form a low mound. Don't stir; use your fingers to pat sugar mound down until completely moistened. (Any sugar touching side of pan should be below the water line.) Cook, covered, over medium heat, without stirring, until sugar is dissolved and syrup is clear. Cook, uncovered, without stirring until syrup begins to color slightly, swirling pan gently (rather than stirring) if syrup is coloring unevenly. Use a skewer to drop a bead of syrup onto a plate from time to time. When a drop looks pale amber, stir in 1⅓ cups coarsely chopped walnuts or pecans. Cook until a drop of syrup looks golden amber (about 30 minutes total), gently pushing nuts around if syrup is coloring unevenly. If syrup gets too dark, it will taste bitter. Immediately scrape mixture onto the prepared baking sheet and spread it out. While still warm but cool enough to handle, break into small pieces. When cool, transfer to a food processor. Cover and process with on/off pulses until finely chopped. In a large mixing bowl beat 1 cup whipping cream with an electric mixer on medium until soft peaks form (tips curl). Fold in chopped nut mixture. Makes 3 cups.

Simple Caramel Sauce In a small saucepan combine ¾ cup whipping cream and 2 tablespoons water. Heat until steaming. Remove from heat; set aside. Place ½ cup water in a 2-quart saucepan. Pour 1 cup sugar and ¼ teaspoon salt into center of pan to form a low mound. Don't stir; use your fingers to pat down sugar mound until completely moistened. (Any sugar touching side of pan should be below the water line.) Cook, covered, over medium heat, without stirring, until sugar is dissolved and syrup is clear. Cook, uncovered, without stirring until syrup begins to color slightly, swirling pan gently (rather than stirring) if syrup is coloring unevenly. Use a skewer to drop a bead of syrup onto a plate from time to time. When a drop looks amber (about 13 minutes), remove from heat. Holding pan away from you, gradually pour in hot cream mixture. Cook and stir over low heat until combined. Simmer for 1 to 2 minutes. Remove from heat; stir in 1 teaspoon vanilla. Cool until slightly thickened. Serve warm.

PER SERVING (WITH CARAMEL WHIPPED CREAM AND SAUCE) *541 cal., 31 g total fat (10 g sat. fat), 171 mg chol., 152 mg sodium, 62 g carbo., 2 g fiber, 9 g pro.*

Walnut Cake with Caramel Whipped Cream

Chocolate Chip-Banana Cake with Fudge Sauce

When you don't have buttermilk, you can make sour milk. To make ½ cup, place 1½ teaspoons lemon juice or vinegar in a glass measuring cup. Add enough milk to equal ½ cup total liquid; stir. Let stand for 5 minutes before using.

PREP **20 minutes**   BAKE **25 minutes**   COOL **30 minutes**
OVEN **350°F**   MAKES **9 servings**

1   cup all-purpose flour
¾   teaspoon baking powder
½   teaspoon baking soda
¼   teaspoon salt
¼   cup butter, softened
¾   cup sugar
1   egg
⅓   cups mashed ripe banana (1 medium)
½   teaspoon vanilla
⅓   cup buttermilk or sour milk
⅓   cup miniature semisweet chocolate pieces
        Purchased fudge or caramel ice cream topping
        (optional)
        Sliced bananas (optional)

1. Preheat oven to 350°F. Grease an 8×8×2-inch baking pan; set aside. In a small bowl combine the flour, baking powder, soda, and salt; set aside.
2. In a medium mixing bowl beat butter with an electric mixer on medium for 30 seconds. Add sugar, beating until combined. Beat in egg until well combined. Beat in banana and vanilla until combined. Alternately add flour mixture and buttermilk, beating on low after each addition just until combined. (Batter may appear slightly curdled.) Stir in chocolate pieces. Spread in prepared pan.
3. Bake for 25 to 30 minutes or until a wooden toothpick inserted near the center comes out clean. Cool in pan on wire rack for 30 minutes. If desired, serve with warm fudge topping and banana slices.
PER SERVING *232 cal., 8 g total fat (5 g sat. fat), 37 mg chol., 219 mg sodium, 37 g carbo., 1 g fiber, 3 g pro.*

Vanilla-Sparkling Wine Pound Cake

Any type of sparkling wine works in this cake—choose one that suits your taste: extra brut or extra dry; brut or dry; or a sweet spumante-style.

PREP **30 minutes**   BAKE **50 minutes**   COOL **15 minutes**
OVEN **350°F**   MAKES **16 servings**

3   cups unbleached all-purpose flour
1   teaspoon baking powder
¼   teaspoon salt
1   cup sparkling wine or milk
3   tablespoons sour cream
2   cups sugar
¾   cup unsalted butter, melted
¼   cup safflower or canola oil
5   cold eggs
2   tablespoons vanilla paste or vanilla extract
1   recipe Sparkling Wine Glaze

1. Preheat oven to 350°F. Grease and flour a 10-inch tube pan; set aside. In a large bowl mix together flour, baking powder, and salt. Sift mixture; set aside. In another bowl stir together sparkling wine and sour cream; set aside.
2. In a large mixing bowl beat sugar, melted butter, and oil with electric mixer until well combined. Add eggs, 1 at a time, beating well after each. Beat in vanilla paste. Beat on medium to high for 3 to 5 minutes or until thick and light in color. Add one-third of the flour mixture; beat on low just until combined, scraping sides of bowl as needed. Add half of the wine mixture; beat just until combined. Repeat with one-third of the flour mixture, the remaining wine mixture, and remaining flour mixture. With a rubber spatula scrape batter into prepared pan.

Warm Banana Cake with
Fudge Sauce

3. Bake 50 to 55 minutes or until a wooden pick inserted near center comes out clean. Cool in pan on wire rack for 15 minutes. Turn out on rack; cool completely. Drizzle with Sparkling Wine Glaze.
Sparkling Wine Glaze In a small bowl combine 1 cup powdered sugar and 1 tablespoon sparkling wine. Stir in additional wine, 1 teaspoon at a time, to reach drizzling consistency.

PER SERVING *361 cal., 14 g total fat (6 g sat. fat), 90 mg chol., 145 mg sodium, 51 g carbo., 1 g fiber, 5 g pro.*

Sweet Potato-Buttermilk Pound Cake

Serve slices of this moist pound cake with cranberry sauce or lingonberry preserves.

PREP **30 minutes** STAND **30 minutes**
BAKE **1 hour 5 minutes** COOL **2 hours** OVEN **350°F**
MAKES **12 servings**

3	eggs
½	cup buttermilk
2	cups all-purpose flour
1	teaspoon baking powder
1	teaspoon ground cinnamon
½	teaspoon baking soda
¼	teaspoon salt
¼	teaspoon ground allspice
¼	teaspoon ground nutmeg
¾	cup butter, cut into pieces
1	cup sugar
1	teaspoon vanilla
2	cups shredded, unpeeled sweet potato

1. Allow eggs and buttermilk to stand at room temperature for 30 minutes. Meanwhile, preheat oven to 350°F. Grease and lightly flour a 9×5×3-inch loaf pan; set aside. In a medium bowl stir together flour, baking powder, cinnamon, baking soda, salt, allspice, and nutmeg; set aside.
2. In a large microwave-safe bowl microwave butter on low for 1½ to 2½ minutes or until very soft but not melted, checking and turning bowl every 30 seconds. Whisk in sugar until combined. Add eggs, 1 at a time, whisking well after each addition. Whisk in buttermilk and vanilla (mixture might look curdled). Whisk in flour mixture until smooth. Fold in sweet potato. Pour batter into the prepared pan; spread evenly.
3. Bake for 65 to 70 minutes or until top springs back when lightly touched and crack looks dry. Cool in pan on a wire rack for 10 minutes. Remove from pan; cool completely.

PER SERVING *295 cal., 13 g total fat (8 g sat. fat), 84 mg chol., 245 mg sodium, 41 g carbo., 2 g fiber, 5 g pro.*

Sweet Potato-Buttermilk Pound Cake

Plum-Almond Kuchen Roll

Plum-Almond Kuchen Roll

Serve this fruit-filled, yeast-raised German cake for dessert or breakfast.

PREP 1 hour RISE 1 hour 30 minutes
BAKE 20 minutes COOL 45 minutes OVEN 375°F
MAKES 2 rolls (12 slices each)

4½ to 5 cups all-purpose flour
1 package active dry yeast
1 cup milk
½ cup granulated sugar
⅓ cup butter
½ teaspoon salt
2 eggs
1 cup packed brown sugar
⅓ cup all-purpose flour
⅓ cup butter
2 cups chopped pitted fresh plums or 1 cup pitted dried plums*
¼ teaspoon almond extract
1 recipe Butter Icing
2 tablespoons sliced almonds, toasted (see note, page 119)

1. In a large mixing bowl combine 2 cups of the flour and the yeast; set aside. In a small saucepan heat and stir milk, granulated sugar, ⅓ cup butter, and the salt just until warm (120°F to 130°F) and butter almost melts. Add milk mixture and eggs to flour mixture. Beat with an electric mixer on low to medium for 30 seconds, scraping sides of the bowl constantly. Beat on high for 3 minutes. Using a wooden spoon, stir in as much of the remaining 2½ to 3 cups flour as you can.
2. Turn dough out onto a floured surface. Knead in enough remaining flour to make a moderately soft dough that is smooth and elastic (3 to 5 minutes total). Shape dough into a ball. Place dough in a lightly greased bowl, turning once to grease surface of the dough. Cover and let rise in a warm place until double in size (1 to 1½ hours).
3. Punch dough down. Turn onto a lightly floured surface. Divide in half. Cover with a clean kitchen towel and let rest 10 minutes. Lightly grease a large baking sheet; set aside. For filling, in a medium bowl stir together brown sugar and ⅓ cup flour. Using a pastry blender, cut in ⅓ cup butter until mixture resembles coarse crumbs. Stir in plums and almond extract.
4. Roll each dough half into a 14×8-inch rectangle. Sprinkle filling on dough, leaving 1 inch unfilled along one long side. Roll up each rectangle, starting from the long filled side. Pinch dough to seal seams and ends. Place rolls on baking sheet. Cover and let rise in a warm place until nearly double in size (about 30 minutes).
5. Preheat oven to 375°F. Bake for 20 to 25 minutes or until golden and bread sounds hollow when lightly tapped. Cool on baking sheet on a wire rack for at least 45 minutes. Spread Butter Icing on each roll. If desired, sprinkle with almonds. Slice to serve.

Butter Icing In a small bowl combine 3 tablespoons softened butter and 1 teaspoon vanilla. Gradually stir in 2 cups powdered sugar. Stir in 1 to 2 tablespoons milk, 1 teaspoon at a time, until icing reaches spreading consistency. Makes about ¾ cup.

*Note If using dried plums, place in a small bowl; cover with boiling water. Let stand 5 minutes. Drain and chop.

PER SLICE *225 cal., 8 g total fat (4 g sat. fat), 36 mg chol., 109 mg sodium, 35 g carbo., 1 g fiber, 4 g pro.*

Gingerbread Roulade with Dulce de Leche Cream Filling

If the dulce de leche is too thick to spread, place it in a small microwave-safe bowl. Microwave on high for 10 seconds; stir. Repeat just until softened, stir every 10 seconds.

PREP **45 minutes** STAND **30 minutes** BAKE **12 minutes**
CHILL **2 hours** OVEN **350°F** MAKES **8 to 10 servings**

4	eggs
⅔	cup all-purpose flour
1	teaspoon ground ginger
1	teaspoon ground cinnamon
½	teaspoon baking powder
½	teaspoon ground allspice
¼	teaspoon salt
½	cup packed brown sugar
2	tablespoons butter, melted
2	tablespoons molasses
	Powdered sugar
1	7-ounce container créme fraîche (¾ cup)
¾	cup dulce de leche
¼	cup crystallized ginger, finely chopped
	Thin lemon slices
1	recipe Lemon Sauce

1. Separate eggs. Allow egg yolks and egg whites to stand at room temperature for 30 minutes. Meanwhile, grease a 15×10×1-inch baking pan. Line bottom of pan with waxed paper or parchment paper; grease and flour the paper. Set aside. In a small bowl combine flour, ginger, cinnamon, baking powder, allspice, and salt; set aside.
2. Preheat oven to 350°F. In a large mixing bowl combine egg yolks and brown sugar; beat with an electric mixer on high about 3 minutes or until thick and light in color. Stir in melted butter and molasses. Fold in flour mixture.
3. Thoroughly wash and dry beaters. In a medium mixing bowl beat egg whites with an electric mixer on medium to high until stiff peaks form (tips stand straight). Stir one-third of the beaten egg whites into egg yolk mixture to lighten. Fold in remaining egg whites. Gently and evenly spread batter in prepared pan.
4. Bake about 12 minutes or until top springs back when lightly touched. Meanwhile, lay a clean kitchen towel on a work surface. Sprinkle with powdered sugar. Immediately invert cake onto towel. Carefully peel

waxed paper from the cake. Starting from a long side, roll cake and towel together into a spiral. Place, seam side down, on a wire rack; cool.
5. When cool, carefully unroll cake. Spread cake with créme fraîche, leaving a 1-inch border. Spoon dulce de leche in mounds on the créme fraîche; gently swirl together with a table knife or thin metal spatula. Evenly sprinkle crystallized ginger on swirled mixture. Starting from a long side, roll up cake. Wrap in plastic wrap; chill for 2 to 48 hours.
6. When ready to serve, unwrap; garnish with lemon slices and sprinkle with powdered sugar. Using a serrated knife, cut into slices. Serve with Lemon Sauce.
Lemon Sauce In a small saucepan stir together ⅔ cup sugar and 4 teaspoons cornstarch. Stir in ¼ cup water, 2 teaspoons finely shredded Meyer lemon peel or regular lemon peel, and ¼ cup Meyer lemon juice or regular lemon juice. Cook and stir over medium heat until thickened and bubbly. Cook and stir for 1 minute more. In a small mixing bowl beat 2 egg yolks with a fork. Gradually stir some of the hot mixture into egg yolks. Return egg yolk mixture to remaining hot mixture in saucepan. Reduce heat to low. Cook and stir for 2 minutes more. Gradually whisk in 6 tablespoons butter, cut up, whisking until melted. Stir in ¼ cup half-and-half, light cream, or milk. Serve warm.
PER SERVING *518 cal., 25 g total fat (15 g sat. fat), 219 mg chol., 275 mg sodium, 68 g carbo., 1 g fiber, 8 g pro.*

Gingerbread Roulade with
Dulce de Leche Cream Filling

4. Bake about 12 minutes or until cake edges feel firm. Cool in ramekins on a wire rack for 2 to 3 minutes. Using a knife, loosen each cake from sides of ramekins. Invert onto dessert plates. Sift with powdered sugar and serve with fresh raspberries and mint leaves.

PER CAKE 544 cal., 45 g total fat (27 g sat. fat), 282 mg chol., 233 mg sodium, 36 g carbo., 4 g fiber, 7 g pro.

Grasshopper Cupcakes
If using white crème de menthe, add 1 or 2 drops of green food coloring to the batter along with the liqueur.

PREP 35 minutes STAND 30 minutes
BAKE 20 minutes COOL 5 minutes OVEN 350°F
MAKES 28 cupcakes

¾ cup butter
3 eggs
1¼ cups milk
4 ounces sweet baking chocolate, chopped
2 cups all-purpose flour
1 teaspoon baking soda
¾ teaspoon baking powder
½ teaspoon salt
1½ cups sugar
3 tablespoons green or white crème de menthe
1 teaspoon vanilla
1 recipe Grasshopper Frosting
   Milk chocolate kisses

1. Allow butter and eggs to stand at room temperature for 30 minutes. Meanwhile, in a small saucepan combine milk and chocolate. Cook and stir over medium-low heat until chocolate is melted; cool.
2. Preheat oven to 350°F. Grease and flour twenty-eight 2½-inch muffin cups or line with paper bake cups. In a medium bowl stir together flour, baking soda, baking powder, and salt; set aside.
3. In a large mixing bowl beat butter with an electric mixer on medium to high for 30 seconds. Gradually add sugar, beating on medium until combined. Beat for 2 minutes more, scraping side of bowl occasionally. Add eggs,1 at a time, beating well after each addition. Beat in crème de menthe and vanilla. Alternately add flour mixture and chocolate mixture, beating on low after each addition just until combined. Beat on medium to high for 20 seconds more. Spoon batter into the prepared cups, filling each about three-fourths full.
4. Bake 20 minutes or until tops spring back when lightly touched. Cool in pans on wire racks 5 minutes. Remove from pans; cool completely on racks.
5. Spread or pipe Grasshopper Frosting on tops of cupcakes. Top each with a chocolate kiss.
Grasshopper Frosting In a 1-cup glass measuring cup combine 2 tablespoons cold water and 1 teaspoon unflavored gelatin. Let stand for 2 minutes. Place measuring cup in a saucepan of boiling water. Cook and stir about 1 minute or until gelatin is completely

Molten Chocolate Lava Cakes
Serve these rich chocolate cakes still very warm. When they're cut into, the gooey "molten" chocolate flows out in the most tantalizing way.

PREP 15 minutes BAKE 12 minutes COOL 2 minutes
OVEN 425°F MAKES 6 cakes

2 tablespoons butter
8 ounces bittersweet chocolate, coarsely chopped
¾ cup butter
3 eggs
3 egg yolks
⅓ cup granulated sugar
1 teaspoon vanilla
1 tablespoon all-purpose flour
   Powdered sugar
   Fresh raspberries (optional)
   Fresh mint leaves (optional)

1. Preheat oven to 425°F. Using the 2 tablespoons butter, grease six 8- to 10-ounce ramekins, soufflé dishes, or custard cups. Place ramekins in a 15×10×1-inch baking pan; set aside.
2. In a small heavy saucepan combine chocolate and the ¾ cup butter. Cook and stir over low heat until chocolate is melted. Remove pan from heat; set aside.
3. In a large mixing bowl beat eggs, egg yolks, granulated sugar, and vanilla with an electric mixer on high for 8 to 10 minutes or until thick and lemon color. Fold one-third of the chocolate mixture into egg mixture. Fold remaining chocolate mixture and flour into egg mixture. Spoon about ⅔ cup batter into each prepared ramekin, dividing evenly.

dissolved. In a large mixing bowl combine 2 cups whipping cream, ¼ cup sugar, and 2 tablespoons green crème de menthe. Drizzle the warm gelatin mixture over cream mixture while beating constantly with an electric mixer on medium. Continue beating on medium to high until stiff peaks form (tips stand straight).

PER CUPCAKE 258 cal., 15 g total fat (9 g sat. fat), 61 mg chol., 154 mg sodium, 27 g carbo., 1 g fiber, 3 g pro.

Hazelnut-Crème Brûlée Cupcakes

Hazelnuts, also called filberts, are sweet and rich grape-size nuts that grow in clusters on hazel trees. Remove their bitter brown skin before use. (See note with this recipe.)

PREP 45 minutes BAKE 15 minutes STAND 30 minutes
COOL 5 minutes OVEN 350°F MAKES 24 cupcakes

¾ cup butter
3 eggs
2½ cups all-purpose flour
2 teaspoons baking powder
½ teaspoon salt
1¾ cups sugar
2 tablespoons hazelnut liqueur
2 teaspoons vanilla
1 cup milk
½ cup finely chopped, toasted hazelnuts (filberts)*
1 recipe Vanilla-Hazelnut Buttercream
1 recipe Caramelized Sugar Drizzle

1. Allow butter and eggs to stand at room temperature for 30 minutes. Meanwhile, preheat oven to 350°F. Grease and flour twenty-four 2½-inch muffin cups or line with paper bake cups. In a medium bowl stir together flour, baking powder, and salt; set aside.
2. In a mixing bowl beat butter with an electric mixer on medium for 30 seconds. Gradually add sugar until combined. Beat for 2 minutes. Add eggs, 1 at a time, beating well after each addition. Beat in liqueur and vanilla. Alternately add flour mixture and milk, beating on low after each addition just until combined. Fold in nuts. Spoon batter into cups, filling each about three-fourths full.
3. Bake for 15 to 18 minutes or until tops spring back when lightly touched. Cool in pans on wire racks for 5 minutes. Remove from pans; cool completely on racks.
4. Spread Vanilla-Hazelnut Buttercream on tops of cupcakes. Drizzle with Caramelized Sugar Drizzle.
Vanilla-Hazelnut Buttercream In a large mixing bowl beat ⅓ cup softened butter with an electric mixer on medium until smooth. Gradually add 1 cup powdered sugar, beating well. Beat in 2 tablespoons milk, 1 tablespoon hazelnut liqueur, and 1 teaspoon vanilla. Gradually beat in 3 cups additional powdered sugar. Beat in enough additional milk (3 to 4 teaspoons) to make a frosting of spreading consistency.

Caramelized Sugar Drizzle In a large skillet cook ⅓ cup sugar over medium-high heat until sugar starts to melt, shaking skillet occasionally. Do not stir. When sugar starts to melt, reduce heat to low and cook about 5 minutes or until all of the sugar is melted, stirring as needed with a wooden spoon. Remove from heat. Immediately drizzle over frosted cupcakes.
***Note** To toast hazelnuts, spread in a single layer on a rimmed baking sheet. Bake in a 350°F oven for 7 to 9 minutes, stirring once, until golden and the skins start to split. When the nuts have cooled slightly, put them on a clean kitchen towel and rub vigorously to remove as much of the skins as you can.

PER CUPCAKE 306 cal., 11 g total fat (6 g sat. fat), 49 mg chol., 152 mg sodium, 49 g carbo., 1 g fiber, 3 g pro.

Hazelnut-Crème Brûlée Cupcakes

White Chocolate Bread Pudding with Hard Sauce

Be sure the vanilla bean you use is soft and pliable before you add it to the milk mixture. If the pod is dried out, it will be difficult to split to get at the intensely flavored seeds inside.

PREP 30 minutes CHILL 1 hour BAKE 1 hour
COOL 30 minutes OVEN 350°F MAKES 12 servings

2   cups whole milk, half-and-half, or light cream
10 ounces white baking chocolate with cocoa butter
1   4-inch vanilla bean or 1½ teaspoons vanilla
5   eggs
⅔   cup sugar
½   teaspoon ground cinnamon
6   cups dry French bread cubes*
⅓   cup dried tart cherries, cranberries or raisins
1   recipe Hard Sauce

1. In a medium saucepan heat and stir milk, half the white chocolate, and the vanilla bean (if using) over low heat just until simmering and chocolate is melted. Remove from heat. Remove vanilla bean. Using a sharp paring knife, split vanilla bean lengthwise. Using the knife tip, scrape out seeds. Stir seeds (or 1½ teaspoons vanilla if using) into the milk mixture.
2. In a large mixing bowl beat together eggs, sugar, and cinnamon just until combined. Gradually add milk mixture to egg mixture, stirring constantly.
3. In an ungreased 2-quart square baking dish toss together bread cubes, remaining white chocolate, and dried cherries. Pour milk mixture evenly over bread mixture. Press mixture lightly with back of a large spoon. Cover baking dish with foil and refrigerate for at least 1 hour.

4. Preheat oven to 350°F. Place baking dish in larger pan. Pour hot water into large pan to reach 1 inch up side of dish. Bake, covered, about 60 minutes or until top appears evenly set. Cool slightly on a wire rack. Serve warm with Hard Sauce.
*Note To dry bread cubes, place them in a large shallow baking pan and bake in a 350°F oven for 10 minutes, stirring twice.

Hard Sauce In a bowl lightly beat 4 egg yolks. In a small heavy saucepan cook and stir 1 cup butter and ½ cup sugar over medium heat until the butter is melted and the mixture is bubbly. Remove from heat. Gradually whisk mixture into yolks; return to saucepan. Cook and stir over medium-low heat about 15 minutes or until mixture reaches 170°F when tested with an instant-read thermometer. Remove from heat. Stir in ¼ cup whiskey or milk. If necessary, stir in hot water, 1 teaspoon at a time, to make sauce the desired consistency. Serve immediately or cover and let stand at room temperature up to 1 hour.

PER SERVING *703 cal., 39 g total fat (20 g sat. fat), 277 mg chol., 485 mg sodium, 69 g carbo., 1 g fiber, 12 g pro.*

Coffee-Nut Torte

A torte is a type of cake that usually has very little, if any, fat in the form of butter and that almost always contains finely ground nuts. Some torte recipes don't call for any flour at all—just ground nuts.

PREP 30 minutes STAND 30 minutes
BAKE 20 minutes COOL 10 minutes OVEN 350°F
MAKES 12 to 14 servings

6   eggs
2   cups all-purpose flour
1   tablespoon baking powder
1½   cups sugar
½   cup strong brewed coffee or espresso, room
     temperature
1   cup ground walnuts or pecans
1   recipe Creamy Butter Frosting
     Coarsely chopped nuts (optional)

1. Preheat oven to 350°F. Separate eggs. Allow egg yolks and egg whites to stand at room temperature for 30 minutes. Grease the bottoms of three 9×1½-inch round cake pans. Line pans with waxed paper; grease waxed paper. Set pans aside. In a medium bowl stir together flour and baking powder; set aside.
2. In a large mixing bowl beat egg yolks, sugar, and coffee with an electric mixer on low until combined. Beat on high about 5 minutes or until smooth. Add flour mixture and beat until combined; stir in nuts. Set aside.
3. Thoroughly wash beaters. In a very large mixing bowl beat egg whites on medium until stiff peaks form (tips stand straight). Gradually fold flour-egg yolk mixture into beaten egg whites until combined. Pour batter into prepared baking pans.

Coffee-Nut Torte

4. Bake for 20 to 25 minutes or until cake tops spring back when lightly touched (centers may dip slightly). Cool cake layers on wire racks for 10 minutes. Remove cake layers from pans; remove waxed paper. Cool thoroughly on wire racks. Spread ½ cup Creamy Butter Frosting on each layer; stack layers. Frost sides of cake with remaining frosting. If you like, garnish with chopped nuts. Loosely cover and chill cake up to 3 days.

Creamy Butter Frosting In a small saucepan whisk ½ cup milk into 2 teaspoons cornstarch. Cook and stir over medium heat until thickened and bubbly. Reduce heat; cook and stir for 2 minutes more. Stir in 1 tablespoon rum or ½ teaspoon rum extract. Cover surface with plastic wrap. Cool to room temperature (do not stir). In a large mixing bowl beat ¾ cup softened butter for 30 seconds. Add 2 cups powdered sugar, 2 tablespoons unsweetened cocoa powder, and 1 teaspoon vanilla. Beat with electric mixer on medium until light and fluffy. Add cooled milk mixture to butter mixture, half at a time, beating on low after each addition until smooth. Beat in 5 to 6 cups additional powdered sugar until spreading consistency. Makes about 3¼ cups.

PER SERVING *655 cal., 21 g total fat (9 g sat. fat), 137 mg chol., 183 mg sodium, 113 g carbo., 1 g fiber, 7 g pro.*

Chile-Chocolate Torte

Chocolate and chile create an exhilarating taste combination. Chile heightens the richness of the chocolate flavor and makes the lips and tongue tingle.

PREP **40 minutes** BAKE **40 minutes** COOL **1 hour**
CHILL **4 hours** OVEN **325°F** MAKES **12 to 16 servings**

	Nonstick cooking spray
	All-purpose flour
1	cup whole blanched almonds
2	tablespoons granulated sugar
2	tablespoons all-purpose flour
1	pound Mexican chocolate, such as Ibarra brand, or 1 pound semisweet chocolate, coarsely chopped
3	ounces semisweet chocolate, coarsely chopped
1	cup butter
6	egg yolks
¼	cup strong brewed coffee, cooled
1	teaspoon vanilla
¼	teaspoon almond extract
⅛	teaspoon salt
½	teaspoon chipotle chile powder or ¼ teaspoon cayenne pepper
¼	teaspoon ground cinnamon
6	egg whites
¼	cup granulated sugar
1	cup whipping cream
¼	cup powdered sugar
¼	teaspoon ground cinnamon
	Whole or sliced almonds (optional)
	Unsweetened cocoa powder (optional)

Chile-Chocolate Torte

1. Preheat oven to 325°F. Line the bottom of a 9-inch springform pan with parchment paper. Lightly coat the paper and side of pan with cooking spray. Lightly coat bottom and side of pan with flour, shaking out excess; set aside.

2. In a food processor combine 1 cup almonds, 2 tablespoons granulated sugar, and 2 tablespoons flour. Cover; process until ground, about 30 seconds.

3. In a large heavy saucepan combine Mexican chocolate, the 3 ounces semisweet chocolate, and butter. Cook over low heat, stirring occasionally, until chocolate and butter are melted; cool 5 minutes.

4. Meanwhile, in an extra-large bowl whisk together the egg yolks, coffee, vanilla, almond extract, and salt. Stir in ground almond mixture, chocolate mixture, chile powder, and ¼ teaspoon cinnamon. In a large mixing bowl beat egg whites with an electric mixer on high until soft peaks form (tips curl). Gradually add ¼ cup granulated sugar, beating for 2 to 3 minutes or until stiff peaks form (tips stand straight). Stir some of the whites into chocolate mixture to lighten. Fold remaining egg whites into chocolate mixture. Pour into prepared springform pan.

5. Bake for 40 to 45 minutes or until top appears set when lightly shaken. (Torte puffs during baking.) Transfer pan to wire rack; cool for 1 hour. (Center sinks as cake cools.) Cover and chill at least 4 hours or overnight.

6. To unmold cake, use a small sharp knife to loosen cake from side of pan; remove side of pan. Invert cake onto plate and remove pan bottom and parchment paper. Invert cake again onto platter.

7. In a chilled mixing bowl combine whipping cream, ¼ cup powdered sugar, and ¼ teaspoon cinnamon. Beat until soft peaks form (tips curl). Top torte with whipped cream. If desired, sprinkle with almonds and unsweetened cocoa powder.

PER SERVING *553 cal., 40 g total fat (19 g sat. fat,), 173 mg chol., 184 mg sodium, 46 g carbo., 3 g fiber, 8 g pro.*

Chocolate-Espresso Tiramisu

Chocolate-Espresso Tiramisu

If you don't have an espresso machine, make the coffee from instant espresso powder.

PREP **50 minutes** BAKE **15 minutes** COOL **1 hour**
CHILL **6 hours** OVEN **350°F** MAKES **12 servings**

24   ladyfingers, split
¼   cup freshly brewed strong espresso coffee
2   tablespoons coffee liqueur (optional)
3   ounces bittersweet chocolate, chopped
1   8-ounce carton mascarpone cheese
1   cup whipping or heavy cream
¼   cup powdered sugar
1   teaspoon vanilla
2   tablespoons coffee liqueur or freshly brewed
      strong espresso
      Bittersweet or semisweet chocolate, melted
      (optional)
      Chocolate-covered coffee beans, whole or
      chopped (optional)

1. Layer half the ladyfingers in a 2-quart baking dish, cutting ladyfingers to fit. Drizzle 2 tablespoons of the espresso and, if desired, 1 tablespoon of the coffee liqueur over the lady fingers. Set aside.
2. Place bittersweet chocolate in a small microwave-safe bowl. Microwave, uncovered, on medium about 1 minute or until chocolate is melted and smooth, stirring every 15 seconds. Set aside to cool.
3. In a large mixing bowl beat the mascarpone cheese, whipping cream, powdered sugar, and vanilla with an electric mixer on medium until soft peaks form (tips curl). Beat in the 2 tablespoons coffee liqueur and cooled chocolate just until combined.
4. Spoon half the mascarpone mixture on ladyfingers in baking dish, spreading evenly. Top with the remaining ladyfingers, cutting to fit as necessary. Drizzle with the remaining espresso and, if desired, the remaining coffee liqueur. Top with the remaining mascarpone mixture, spreading evenly.
5. Cover and chill for 6 to 24 hours. If desired, garnish with melted chocolate and chocolate-covered coffee beans.
PER SERVING *345 cal., 22 g total fat (13 g sat. fat), 93 mg chol., 127 mg sodium, 35 g carbo., 1 g fiber, 7 g pro.*

Apple Tart with Cheddar Cheese Crust

A wedge of apple pie with a slice of cheese is good. A wedge of apple pie with cheese baked into the crust is superb.

PREP 40 minutes BAKE 1 hour CHILL 1 hour
OVEN 350°F MAKES 8 servings

2⅔ cups all-purpose flour
¼ cup sugar
¾ teaspoon salt
¾ cup butter
4 ounces sharp cheddar cheese, shredded (1 cup)
½ to ¾ cup cold water
2½ pounds apples, such as Rome, Granny Smith, and/or Gala, peeled if desired, cored, and cut into ½-inch wedges
¼ cup sugar
2 tablespoons lemon juice
2 tablespoons all-purpose flour
½ teaspoon ground cinnamon
1 egg, lightly beaten
1 to 2 tablespoons sanding sugar or coarse decorating sugar
¼ cup apple jelly
Vanilla ice cream (optional)

1. For pastry, in a large bowl stir together the 2⅔ cups flour, ¼ cup sugar, and salt. Using a pastry blender, cut in butter until pieces are pea size. Stir in cheese. Sprinkle 1 tablespoon of the water over part of the flour mixture; toss with a fork. Push moistened pastry to side of bowl. Repeat moistening flour mixture, using 1 tablespoon of water at a time, until the flour mixture is moistened. Form pastry into a flat disk and wrap in plastic wrap. Chill for 1 hour or overnight until firm (if chilling overnight, let stand at room temperature 10 minutes before rolling).
2. Preheat oven to 350°F. On a lightly floured surface roll pastry into a circle about 16 inches in diameter. Carefully transfer to a 10- or 11-inch ovenproof skillet or a 9½- or 10-inch deep-dish pie plate.
3. For filling, in a large bowl toss apples with ¼ cup sugar, lemon juice, 2 tablespoons flour, and cinnamon until well combined.
4. Mound filling in pastry-lined skillet or pie plate and bring up edges of pastry toward center, pleating pastry flat against the filling. Brush top of pastry with egg and sprinkle with sanding sugar. Cover apples with foil. Bake for 30 minutes. Remove foil. Bake about 30 to 35 minutes more or until apples are tender and crust is golden brown.
5. In a small saucepan melt jelly over medium-low heat; brush over apples. Cool slightly. To serve, cut tart into wedges. If desired, serve with vanilla ice cream.
PER SERVING 528 cal., 23 g total fat (14 g sat. fat), 87 mg chol., 443 mg sodium, 73 g carbo., 4 g fiber, 9 g pro.

Pumpkin Trifle

These pumpkin-and-caramel trifles are a festive finish to a holiday dinner.

PREP 30 minutes MAKES 8 servings

1 cup whipping cream
2 tablespoons sugar
8 ½-inch-thick slices pumpkin bread, halved crosswise
1 10-ounce jar pumpkin butter
1 12.25-ounce jar caramel ice cream topping
1 4-serving size package vanilla instant pudding and pie filling mix, prepared according to package directions
½ cup chopped walnuts or pecans, toasted (see note, page 119)

1. In a medium mixing bowl combine whipping cream and sugar. With an electric mixer, beat on medium to high speed until stiff peaks form (tips stand straight).
2. Divide one-third of the whipped cream (about 1 rounded tablespoon) among eight 12-ounce glasses. Top with a piece of pumpkin bread, half the pumpkin butter, half the caramel, and half the pudding. Repeat layers. Top with nuts and remaining whipped cream.
PER SERVING 614 cal., 24 g total fat (9 g sat. fat), 73 mg chol., 570 mg sodium, 95 g carbo., 2 g fiber, 7 g pro.

Pumpkin Trifle

Cranberry-Orange Cheesecake

Using reduced-fat cream cheese makes this a bit lighter than the average cheesecake, just 275 calories per slice.

PREP **25 minutes**   BAKE **35 minutes**   COOL **2 hours**
CHILL **4 hours**   OVEN **375°F**   MAKES **12 to 16 servings**

- ⅔   cup crushed chocolate wafer cookies (12 to 13 cookies)
- 1½   teaspoons finely shredded orange peel
- 2   tablespoons butter, melted
- 3   8-ounce packages reduced-fat cream cheese (Neufchâtel), softened
- ¾   cup sugar
- 2   tablespoons all-purpose flour
- 3   eggs, lightly beaten
- ⅓   cup snipped dried cranberries
- ¼   cup low-calorie cranberry juice or fat-free milk
- ½   cup fresh cranberries, coarsely chopped

1. Preheat oven to 375°F. For crust, in a bowl combine crushed cookies and 1 teaspoon of the orange peel. Stir in butter. Press crust in bottom of a 9-inch springform pan; set aside.

2. In a mixing bowl beat cream cheese, sugar, and flour with electric mixer on medium for 5 minutes. Mix in eggs and remaining ½ teaspoon orange peel until combined. Fold in dried cranberries and juice. Pour into crust-lined pan. Sprinkle with fresh cranberries.

3. Bake for 35 to 40 minutes or until a 2½-inch area around edges appears set when gently shaken. Cool on a wire rack for 15 minutes. Using a small sharp knife, loosen edges from sides of pan. Cool for 30 minutes. Remove sides of pan. Cool completely. Cover and refrigerate at least 4 hours before serving.

PER SERVING *275 cal., 17 g total fat (10 g sat. fat), 101 mg chol., 293 mg sodium, 23 g carbo., 1 g fiber, 8 g pro.*

Cranberry-Orange Cheesecake

Hazelnut-Pumpkin Cheesecake

This festive cheesecake features a spicy gingersnap crust.

PREP 30 minutes BAKE 48 minutes COOL 2 hours
CHILL 12 hours STAND 20 minutes OVEN 350°F
MAKES 12 servings

24   gingersnaps
2   tablespoons granulated sugar
¼   cup unsalted butter, melted
2   8-ounce packages cream cheese, softened
5   eggs
1   15-ounce can pumpkin
¾   cup packed brown sugar
½   cup hazelnut liqueur
1   teaspoon ground cinnamon
1   teaspoon vanilla
½   teaspoon ground ginger
¼   teaspoon grated whole nutmeg
¼   teaspoon ground cloves
1   16-ounce carton sour cream
¼   cup granulated sugar
¼   cup hazelnut liqueur
½   cup hazelnuts (filberts), toasted and coarsely
     chopped (see note, page 87)

1. For crust, in a food processor combine gingersnaps
and 2 tablespoons granulated sugar. Cover and process
to form fine crumbs. With processor running slowly,
add melted butter, processing until combined. Press
mixture evenly onto the bottom of a 9-inch springform
pan. Chill until firm.
2. Meanwhile, preheat oven to 350°F. For filling, place
cream cheese in food processor. Cover and process until
smooth. Add eggs, pumpkin, brown sugar, ½ cup liqueur,
cinnamon, vanilla, ginger, nutmeg, and cloves. Cover and
process until smooth, stopping once to scrape down side
of bowl. Pour filling into crust, spreading evenly.
3. Place springform pan in a shallow baking pan. Bake for
40 to 45 minutes or until edge is firm and center appears
nearly set when gently shaken.
4. Meanwhile, for topping, in a medium bowl combine
sour cream, ¼ cup granulated sugar, and ¼ cup liqueur.
Transfer to a measuring cup with a lip. Without
removing cheesecake from oven, pour topping over
cheesecake, spreading evenly. Bake for 8 to 10 minutes
more or until edge of topping just starts to bubble. Cool
completely in pan on a wire rack. Cover loosely and
chill for at least 12 hours.
5. To serve, loosen edge of cheesecake from side of pan;
remove side of pan. Cut cheesecake while it is chilled
and firm. Let stand at room temperature for
20 minutes before serving. Sprinkle with hazelnuts.
PER SERVING *491 cal., 31 g total fat (15 g sat. fat),*
160 mg chol., 279 mg sodium, 42 g carbo., 2 g fiber, 8 g pro.

Crimson Cranberry-Apple Crisp

Crimson Cranberry-Apple Crisp

To prevent the topping from burning before baking
time is done, allow the fruit to partially cook before
the topping is sprinkled.

PREP 25 minutes BAKE 40 minutes OVEN 375°F
MAKES 6 servings

¼   to ⅓ cup granulated sugar
1   teaspoon ground cinnamon
3   cups sliced, peeled cooking apples
2   cups cranberries
½   cup quick-cooking or regular rolled oats
¼   cup packed brown sugar
2   tablespoons all-purpose flour
¼   teaspoon ground nutmeg or ground ginger
3   tablespoons butter
2   tablespoons chopped coconut or chopped nuts
     (optional)
     Vanilla ice cream (optional)

1. Preheat oven to 375°F. In a small bowl combine
granulated sugar and cinnamon. Place the apples
and cranberries in an ungreased 1½-quart casserole.
Sprinkle sugar-cinnamon mixture over fruit. Toss
gently to coat. Bake, covered, for 25 minutes.
2. For topping, in a small bowl combine oats, brown
sugar, flour, and nutmeg. With a pastry blender, cut
in butter until mixture resembles coarse crumbs. If
desired, stir in coconut. Sprinkle topping over partially
cooked fruit mixture.
3. Return to oven and bake for 15 to 20 minutes more or
until fruit is tender and topping is golden. Transfer to a
cooling rack; cool slightly. Serve warm. If desired, serve
with ice cream.
PER SERVING *205 cal., 7 g total fat (4 g sat. fat), 16 mg*
chol., 66 mg sodium, 36 g carbo., 4 g fiber, 2 g pro.

Vanilla Flan with Butterscotch Sauce

You can use vanilla extract in this silky Mexican custard, but if you can get your hands on vanilla bean, use it. There really is no substitute for the amazing flavor, fragrance, and beautiful speckle that vanilla bean imparts.

PREP 25 minutes STAND 15 minutes
BAKE 35 minutes COOL 30 minutes
CHILL 6 hours OVEN 350°F MAKES 8 servings

3   cups half-and-half
1   vanilla bean or 2 teaspoons vanilla extract
½   cup packed dark brown sugar
½   teaspoon salt
5   eggs
½   cup granulated sugar

1. In a medium saucepan heat half-and-half and vanilla bean over medium heat until steaming (140°F to 145°F), about 3 minutes (too hot to insert a finger for more than a moment). Remove from heat; cover. Steep for 15 minutes.
2. Position rack in lower third of oven. Preheat oven to 350°F. In a small bowl combine brown sugar and ¼ teaspoon of the salt, pinching and mashing to eliminate lumps. Spoon sugar mixture into a 9-inch deep-dish pie plate. Pack in firm, even layer.
3. Remove bean from half-and-half; cut bean lengthwise. With point of small knife, scrape seeds from bean and add to half-and-half. Briefly reheat mixture for 1 to 2 minutes, just to steaming.
4. In a large bowl whisk eggs, granulated sugar, and remaining ¼ teaspoon salt. Gradually whisk in warm half-and-half until well combined.
5. Slowly pour egg mixture into a pie plate over brown sugar. Some sugar may float up but will settle to bottom eventually.
6. Place pie plate in a deep roasting pan. Place pan in oven. Pour boiling water in roasting pan to halfway up side of pie plate. Bake 35 to 40 minutes or until a knife inserted in center comes out clean.
7. Carefully remove pie plate from roasting pan. Cool on wire rack 30 minutes. Cover and refrigerate at least 6 hours or overnight. To serve, gently run a thin metal spatula or knife around edge of flan. Invert onto serving plate.

PER SERVING *282 cal., 13 g total fat (7 g sat. fat), 165 mg chol., 231 mg sodium, 35 g carbo., 0 g fiber, 7 g pro.*

Gooey Chocolate-Caramel Fantasy

Gooey Chocolate-Caramel Fantasy

A layer of pecan-studded caramel is sandwiched between the chocolate crust and chocolate-drizzled topping in this decadent dessert.

PREP 20 minutes BAKE 10 minutes CHILL 2 hours
OVEN 350°F MAKES 12 servings

2	cups chocolate wafer crumbs (about 38 wafers)
⅓	cup butter, melted
30	vanilla caramels
½	cup caramel ice cream topping
¼	cup whipping cream
2	cups chopped pecans, toasted (see note, page 119)
¾	cup semisweet chocolate pieces
¼	cup whipping cream
	Pecan halves (optional)

1. Preheat oven to 350°F. In a medium bowl stir together chocolate wafer crumbs and melted butter. Press onto the bottom of a 9-inch springform pan. Bake for 10 minutes. Cool slightly on a wire rack.
2. In a medium-size heavy saucepan melt caramels in caramel ice cream topping over low heat, stirring often. Stir in ¼ cup whipping cream. Remove from heat; stir in the chopped nuts. Spread on crust. Chill 1 hour.
3. For topping, in a small heavy saucepan melt chocolate over low heat. Remove from heat; stir in ¼ cup whipping cream. Drizzle or spread over caramel-pecan mixture. Cover and chill at least 1 hour. If desired, top with additional pecan halves.
PER SERVING 464 cal., 29 g total fat (11 g sat. fat,), 27 mg chol., 251 mg sodium, 49 g carbo., 4 g fiber, 5 g pro.

Gianduja Cream Puffs

Gianduja [zhahn-DOO-yah] is a Swiss chocolate, either milk chocolate or bittersweet, flavored with hazelnut.

PREP 35 minutes COOL 10 minutes BAKE 30 minutes
OVEN 400°F MAKES 12 cream puffs

1	cup water
½	cup butter
¼	teaspoon salt
1	cup all-purpose flour
4	eggs
1½	cups whipping cream
¾	cup chocolate-hazelnut spread
	Powdered sugar (optional)
	Cocoa powder (optional)

Gianduja Cream Puffs

1. Preheat oven to 400°F. Grease a large baking sheet; set aside.
2. In a medium saucepan combine the water, butter, and salt. Bring to boiling. Add flour all at once, stirring vigorously. Cook and stir until mixture forms a ball that doesn't separate. Remove from heat. Cool for 10 minutes. Add eggs, one at a time, beating well with a wooden spoon after each addition.
3. Pipe dough with a decorating bag fitted with a large star tip or drop 12 mounds of dough onto the prepared baking sheet. Using a moistened finger, smooth any rough peaks in the tops of the cream puffs.
4. Bake for 30 to 35 minutes or until golden brown and firm; cool. Cut tops from cream puffs; remove soft dough from insides.
5. For filling, in a large mixing bowl beat whipping cream with an electric mixer on medium until soft peaks form (tips curl). Beat in chocolate-hazelnut spread.
6. Before serving, pipe or spoon filling into cream puffs. Replace tops. If desired, sprinkle puffs with powdered sugar and cocoa powder.
PER CREAM PUFF 313 cal., 25 g total fat (12 g sat. fat), 132 mg chol., 154 mg sodium, 18 g carbo., 0 g fiber, 5 g pro.

tempting cookies

Perhaps more than any other goodie, cookies are synonymous with Christmas. Rolled and cut, sliced, shaped, dropped, or molded, these sweet treats are as fun to make as they are to share. Keep a cookie tray filled with this collection of festive cookies—or package them prettily to give as gifts.

Red Velvet Shortbread Cookies, 102

Soft Maple Sugar Cookies

vanilla until combined. Beat in as much of the flour as you can with the mixer. Using a wooden spoon, stir in any remaining flour.

2. Shape dough in 1-inch balls. Place 2 inches apart on an ungreased cookie sheet.

3. Bake for 12 to 14 minutes or until edges are lightly browned. Cool on cookie sheet for 2 minutes. Transfer to a wire rack; cool. Centers will dip as cookies cool. Drizzle with Maple Icing.

Maple Icing In a medium bowl stir together ¼ cup whipping cream or milk, ¼ cup melted butter, and 3 tablespoons pure maple syrup. Whisk in 3 to 4 cups powdered sugar to make icing of drizzling consistency.

PER COOKIE *134 cal., 6 g total fat (3 g sat. fat), 22 mg chol., 54 mg sodium, 20 g carbo., 0 g fiber, 1 g pro.*

Chocolate-Cherry-Walnut Thumbprints

Fans of chocolate-covered cherries will love their favorite flavors in cookie form.

PREP **40 minutes** BAKE **8 minutes per batch**
OVEN **350°F** MAKES **36 to 40 cookies**

1¼ cups semisweet chocolate pieces
2 tablespoons shortening
½ cup unsalted butter, softened
¾ cup sugar
1 egg
1 tablespoon milk
1 teaspoon vanilla
2 cups all-purpose flour
1 tablespoon unsweetened cocoa powder
1 teaspoon baking powder
¼ teaspoon salt
¼ teaspoon instant espresso coffee powder
½ cup finely chopped, toasted walnuts (see note, page 119)
¾ cup cherry pie filling (with 36 to 40 cherries)

1. Preheat oven to 350°F. Line a baking sheet with parchment paper; set aside. In a small saucepan combine ½ cup of the chocolate pieces and 1 tablespoon of the shortening. Cook and stir over low heat until chocolate is melted. Set aside to cool.

2. In a large mixing bowl beat butter and sugar with an electric mixer on medium until fluffy. Beat in cooled chocolate mixture. Add egg, milk, and vanilla. Beat until combined. Add flour, cocoa powder, baking powder, salt, and espresso powder. Beat on low just until combined.

3. Shape dough in 1-inch balls. Roll the balls in chopped walnuts. Place balls 1 inch apart on prepared cookie sheet. Using your thumb, make an indentation in the center of each cookie.

4. Bake for 8 to 10 minutes or until edges are firm. Transfer cookies to a wire rack; let cool. Spoon a cherry with some of the sauce into each cookie center. In

Soft Maple Sugar Cookies

If you can find it, sprinkle a little maple sugar on the just-glazed cookies for an additional shot of maple flavor.

PREP **30 minutes** BAKE **12 minutes per batch**
OVEN **300°F** MAKES **48 cookies**

½ cup butter, softened
½ cup shortening
1½ cups granulated sugar
¼ cup packed brown sugar
¼ cup pure maple syrup
1 teaspoon baking soda
1 teaspoon cream of tartar
⅛ teaspoon salt
3 egg yolks
½ teaspoon vanilla
1¾ cups all-purpose flour
1 recipe Maple Icing

1. Preheat oven to 300°F. In a large mixing bowl combine butter and shortening. Beat with an electric mixer on medium to high for 30 seconds. Add granulated sugar, brown sugar, maple syrup, baking soda, cream of tartar, and salt. Beat until combined, scraping bowl occasionally. Beat in egg yolks and

a small saucepan heat and stir remaining chocolate pieces and shortening over low heat until chocolate is melted and mixture is smooth. Cool slightly. Drizzle chocolate mixture over tops of cookies. Let stand until chocolate is set.

PER COOKIE *119 cal., 6 g total fat (3 g sat. fat), 13 mg chol., 30 mg sodium, 15 g carbo., 1 g fiber, 1 g pro.*

Caramel Corn Cookies

The corn in these cookies is actually cornmeal, which gives them a pleasing crunch.

PREP **35 minutes** BAKE **8 minutes per batch**
OVEN **350°F** MAKES **48 cookies**

½   cup shortening
¼   cup butter, softened
½   cup granulated sugar
½   cup packed brown sugar
½   cup yellow cornmeal
1   teaspoon baking soda
½   teaspoon salt
1   egg
¼   cup honey
1   tablespoon vanilla
1¾ cups all-purpose flour
1   cup miniature round caramel bits or
     butterscotch-flavor pieces
½   cup chopped honey-roasted peanuts
     Coarse sugar or turbinado sugar

1. Preheat oven to 350°F. Line a cookie sheet with parchment paper or lightly grease a cookie sheet; set aside.
2. In a large mixing bowl combine shortening and butter. Beat with an electric mixer on medium to high for 30 seconds. Add granulated sugar, brown sugar, cornmeal, baking soda, and salt. Beat until combined, scraping bowl occasionally. Beat in egg, honey, and vanilla until combined. Beat in as much of the flour as you can with the mixer. Using a wooden spoon, stir in any remaining flour, the caramel bits, and peanuts.
3. Place coarse sugar in a small bowl. Shape dough in 1¼-inch balls. Roll balls in coarse sugar to coat. Place 2 inches apart on the prepared cookie sheet.
4. Bake for 8 to 10 minutes or until tops are golden and edges are firm. Cool on cookie sheet for 2 minutes. Transfer cookies to a wire rack; cool.

PER COOKIE *98 cal., 4 g total fat (1 g sat. fat), 7 mg chol., 74 mg sodium, 15 g carbo., 0 g fiber, 1 g pro.*

Chocolate-Cherry-Walnut Thumbprints

Pistachio-Cream Cheese Sugar Cookies

Get a jump-start on holiday baking with these classic icebox cookies. Make them through Step 2 (eliminate the chilling time), wrap the logs tightly in plastic wrap, seal in a plastic bag, then freeze them up to 2 months before baking.

PREP 35 minutes CHILL 1 hour BAKE 7 minutes per batch OVEN 375°F MAKES 44 cookies

½   cup butter, softened
1   3-ounce package cream cheese, softened
1   cup powdered sugar
½   teaspoon baking powder
¼   teaspoon salt
1   egg
1   teaspoon vanilla
2½ cups all-purpose flour
2   teaspoons finely shredded orange or lemon peel (optional)
½   cup finely chopped lightly salted pistachio nuts

1. In a large mixing bowl combine butter and cream cheese. Beat with an electric mixer on medium to high for 30 seconds. Add powdered sugar, baking powder, and salt. Beat until combined, scraping bowl occasionally. Beat in egg and vanilla until combined. Beat in as much of the flour as you can with the mixer. Using a wooden spoon, stir in any remaining flour. If desired, stir in orange peel.
2. Divide dough in half. Shape each half in a 7½-inch-long roll (about 1½ inches in diameter). Roll each roll in pistachio nuts. Wrap each roll in plastic wrap or waxed paper. Chill about 1 hour or until dough is firm enough to slice.
3. Preheat oven to 375°F. Cut rolls into ¼-inch slices. Place 1 inch apart on an ungreased cookie sheet.
4. Bake for 7 to 9 minutes or until edges are lightly browned. Transfer to a wire rack; cool.
PER COOKIE *72 cal., 4 g total fat (2 g sat. fat), 12 mg chol., 46 mg sodium, 9 g carbo., 0 g fiber, 1 g pro.*

Pistachio-Cream Cheese Sugar Cookies

Black-and-White Cookies

Dress up purchased cookies in formal black and white, and they're ready for any gathering.

START TO FINISH 35 minutes MAKES 8 to 10 cookies

2   cups powdered sugar
2   tablespoons light-color corn syrup
1   to 2 tablespoons milk
½   to 1 teaspoon vanilla
1   tablespoon unsweetened cocoa powder
1   to 1½ teaspoons milk (optional)
8   to ten 3-inch packaged sugar, chocolate chip, molasses, or other flat soft cookies

1. For white icing, in a medium mixing bowl combine powdered sugar, corn syrup, 1 tablespoon of the milk, and vanilla. Beat with an electric mixer on low until combined. Stir in more milk, 1 teaspoon at a time, to make an icing piping consistency. Place half the white icing in a small bowl.
2. For cocoa icing, stir cocoa powder into the remaining white icing. If necessary, add enough of the milk to make icing piping consistency.
3. Place cookies on a wire rack set over waxed paper. Spoon the white icing into a decorating bag fitted with a small round tip. (Or fill a resealable plastic bag; snip off 1 small corner.) For each cookie, pipe icing in a very thin line along the center of a cookie; pipe icing to outline half. Let stand until outlines are slightly firm.
4. Pipe white icing into the center of the white icing outline; use a thin metal spatula and/or a toothpick to spread icing to edges. Repeat piping process with cocoa icing on the other half of each cookie. Let stand until firm.
PER COOKIE *226 cal., 3 g total fat (1 g sat. fat), 4 mg chol., 157 mg sodium, 49 g carbo., 1 g fiber, 1 g pro.*

Coconut Macaroons

Coconut Macaroons

After they've baked and cooled, a drizzle of melted chocolate is a nice addition to these chewy cookies. But they're delicious unadorned as well. If you drizzle them with chocolate, omit the powdered sugar.

PREP 25 minutes BAKE 20 minutes per batch
OVEN 325°F MAKES about 30 cookies

2   cups flaked coconut
¾   cup coarsely chopped macadamia nuts
⅔   cup sugar
⅓   cup all-purpose flour
¼   teaspoon salt
3   egg whites, lightly beaten
1   teaspoon finely shredded lemon peel
1   tablespoon lemon juice
     Powdered sugar (optional)

1. Preheat oven to 325°F. Line a large cookie sheet with parchment paper; set aside.
2. In a large bowl combine coconut, macadamia nuts, sugar, flour, and salt. Add egg whites, lemon peel, and lemon juice, stirring until combined. Drop dough by rounded teaspoons 2 inches apart onto the prepared cookie sheet.
3. Bake for 20 to 25 minutes or until edges are lightly browned. Transfer cookies to a wire rack; cool. If desired, sprinkle with powdered sugar.
PER COOKIE *85 cal., 5 g total fat (3 g sat. fat), 0 mg chol., 55 mg sodium, 9 g carbo., 1 g fiber, 1 g pro.*

Mint-Chocolate Cookies

The favorite flavor combination—chocolate and mint—teams up in these cookies. Serve a couple cookies in a pretty dessert dish with a scoop of vanilla ice cream drizzled with chocolate sauce and garnished with a fresh mint leaf.

PREP 35 minutes BAKE 8 minutes per batch
OVEN 350°F MAKES 42 cookies

2   cups crème de menthe baking pieces or chopped
     layered chocolate-mint candies
3   tablespoons shortening
1   cup packed brown sugar
1   egg
¼   cup light-color corn syrup
1   tablespoon water
2   teaspoons vanilla
1¾   cups all-purpose flour
⅔   cup powdered sugar
⅓   cup unsweetened cocoa powder
2   teaspoons baking powder
¼   teaspoon salt

1. Preheat oven to 350°F. Line cookie sheets with parchment paper; set aside.
2. In a small saucepan combine 1 cup of the crème de menthe pieces and the shortening. Cook and stir over low heat until melted. Cool for 5 minutes. Transfer mixture to a large bowl. Stir in brown sugar, egg, corn syrup, the water, and vanilla.
3. In a medium bowl stir together flour, powdered sugar, cocoa powder, baking powder, and salt. Stir flour mixture into egg mixture (mixture will be stiff). Stir in the remaining 1 cup crème de menthe pieces. Roll dough in 1¼-inch balls. Arrange 2 inches apart on the prepared cookie sheets. Flatten slightly with hands.
4. Bake for 8 minutes or until cookies are set and tops are dry. Cool on cookie sheet for 5 minutes. Transfer cookies to a wire rack; cool.
PER COOKIE *114 cal., 5 g total fat (3 g sat. fat), 5 mg chol., 39 mg sodium, 19 g carbo., 0 g fiber, 1 g pro.*

Toasted Coconut Wafers

Toasted Coconut Wafers

To toast coconut, spread it in a shallow rimmed baking pan. Bake in a 350°F oven for 5 to 10 minutes, shaking pan once or twice.

PREP 25 minutes BAKE 10 minutes per batch
CHILL 4 hours OVEN 375°F MAKES 60 cookies

1   cup butter, softened
1¼ cups powdered sugar
½   teaspoon almond extract or vanilla
⅛   teaspoon salt
1   egg yolk
2¼ cups all-purpose flour
1   cup shredded coconut, toasted
1   egg white, lightly beaten
1   cup shredded coconut

1. In a mixing bowl beat butter with an electric mixer on medium for 30 seconds. Add powdered sugar, almond extract, and salt. Beat until combined, scraping side of bowl occasionally. Beat in egg yolk until combined. Beat in as much of the flour as you can. Stir in remaining flour and the 1 cup toasted coconut.
2. Divide dough in half. Shape each half in an 8-inch roll. Brush rolls with egg white, then roll in the 1 cup shredded coconut to coat. Wrap each roll in plastic wrap or waxed paper. Chill for 4 to 24 hours or until dough is firm enough to slice.
3. Preheat oven to 375°F. Cut rolls into ¼-inch slices. Place slices 1 inch apart on an ungreased cookie sheet. Bake for 10 to 12 minutes or until edges are light brown. Cool on cookie sheet for 1 minute. Transfer cookies to a wire rack; cool.

PER COOKIE *68 cal., 4 g total fat (2 g sat. fat), 12 mg chol., 14 mg sodium, 7 g carbo., 0 g fiber, 1 g pro.*

Red Velvet Shortbread Cookies

The flavor and festive crimson color of Red Velvet Cake translates to rich butter cookies.

PREP 30 minutes BAKE 20 minutes
OVEN 325°F MAKES 24 cookies

1¼ cups all-purpose flour
⅓   cup sugar
2   tablespoons unsweetened cocoa powder
¼   teaspoon salt
½   cup butter, cut up
1   tablespoon red food coloring
3   ounces white chocolate (with cocoa butter), coarsely chopped
1½ teaspoons shortening
     Finely chopped pistachios or rainbow nonpareils (optional)

1. Preheat oven to 325°F. In a food processor combine flour, sugar, cocoa powder, and salt. Cover and process with on/off turns until combined. Add butter and red food coloring. Process with on/off turns until mixture resembles fine crumbs. Process just until mixture forms a ball.

2. On a lightly floured surface knead dough lightly until nearly smooth. Roll or pat dough to a ½-inch thickness. Using a floured 1½-inch round crinkle cutter, cut out dough. Place cutouts 1 inch apart on an ungreased cookie sheet. Press scraps together and reroll.

3. Bake for 20 to 25 minutes or until centers are set. Transfer cookies to a wire rack; let cool.

4. In a small heavy saucepan melt white chocolate and shortening over low heat, stirring constantly. Dip half of each cookie into melted chocolate. If desired, sprinkle with pistachios or nonpareils.

PER COOKIE *80 cal., 5 g total fat (3 g sat. fat), 9 mg chol., 47 mg sodium, 9 g carbo., 0 g fiber, 1 g pro.*

Caramel Brittle and Shortbread Thumbprints

The well in each of these buttery, crunchy cookies holds creamy melted caramel.

PREP **30 minutes** BAKE **10 minutes per batch**
OVEN **375°F** MAKES **about 42 cookies**

22 vanilla caramels, unwrapped
3 tablespoons whipping cream
1 cup butter, softened
⅔ cup packed brown sugar
½ teaspoon vanilla
2¾ cups all-purpose flour
¼ cup whipping cream
⅔ cup crushed purchased peanut brittle
½ cup semisweet chocolate pieces
2 teaspoons shortening

1. Preheat oven to 375°F. In a small saucepan heat and stir caramels and 3 tablespoons whipping cream over low heat until mixture is melted and smooth. Set aside.

2. In a large mixing bowl beat butter with electric mixer on medium for 1 minute. Add brown sugar and vanilla. Beat until mixture is combined. Add half the flour and the ¼ cup cream. Beat in remaining flour on low until combined. Stir in ⅓ cup of crushed peanut brittle.

3. Shape the dough into 1¼-inch balls. Place 2 inches apart on ungreased cookie sheets. Make an indentation in the center of each cookie with your thumb.

4. Bake for 10 minutes or until edges are set. Press the cookie centers with the bowl of a measuring teaspoon. Spoon 1 teaspoon melted caramel mixture into each cookie center. Transfer cookies to wire racks. Sprinkle cookies with remaining ⅓ cup peanut brittle. Let cool.

5. In another saucepan heat and stir chocolate pieces and shortening over low heat until chocolate mixture is melted; cool slightly. Drizzle over tops of cookies.

PER COOKIE *136 cal., 7 g total fat (4 g sat. fat), 15 mg chol., 58 mg sodium, 17 g carbo., 0 g fiber, 2 g pro.*

Lemon on Lemon Shortbread Cookies

This buttery, lemony shortbread
icing. Enjoy a cookie with a cup of

PREP **20 minutes** BAKE **25 minutes**
COOL **5 minutes** OVEN **350°F** MAKES **16 cookies**

1¼ cups all-purpose flour
3 tablespoons sugar
1½ teaspoons finely shredded lemon peel
½ cup butter
1 recipe Lemon Icing

1. Preheat oven to 325°F. In a large bowl combine flour, sugar, and lemon peel. Using a pastry blender, cut in butter until mixture resembles fine crumbs. Knead gently until dough forms a ball.

2. To make wedges, on an ungreased cookie sheet pat dough into an 8-inch circle. Make a scalloped edge. Cut circle into 16 wedges. Leave wedges in circle.

3. Bake for 25 minutes or until edges start to brown and center is set. Recut circle into wedges while warm. Cool 5 minutes. Remove and cool on wire rack.

4. Prepare Lemon Icing. Drizzle over wedges.

Lemon Icing In a small bowl combine 1 cup powdered sugar and 1 tablespoon lemon juice. Stir in additional lemon juice, 1 teaspoon at a time, until icing reaches a drizzling consistency.

PER COOKIE *125 cal., 6 g total fat (4 g sat. fat), 15 mg chol., 41 mg sodium, 17 g carbo., 0 g fiber, 1 g pro.*

Caramel Brittle and
Shortbread Thumbprints

Almond-Hazelnut-Chocolate Crescents

Use either Dutch-process or natural cocoa powder in this recipe. Natural cocoa powder imparts more intense chocolate flavor than Dutch-process cocoa, which is treated with alkali. The process neutralizes acidity and mellows the cocoa slightly and gives it a reddish hue.

PREP 30 minutes CHILL 2 hours BAKE 15 minutes per batch OVEN 350°F MAKES 48 cookies

1¾ cups all-purpose flour
1¼ cups finely ground almonds
½   cup finely ground, toasted hazelnuts (filberts)
       (see note, page 87)
½   cup unsweetened cocoa powder
1 ¼ cups butter, softened
1   cup powdered sugar
1   teaspoon vanilla
6   ounces semisweet chocolate, melted

1. In a medium bowl combine flour, almonds, hazelnuts, and cocoa powder; set aside. In a large mixing bowl beat butter with an electric mixer on medium for 30 seconds. Add sugar and vanilla. Beat until combined, scraping bowl occasionally. Add the flour mixture,

beating on low just until combined. Cover and chill for 2 hours or until dough is easy to handle.
2. Preheat oven to 350°F. Shape dough into 1-inch balls. To shape crescents, roll each ball into a short log with tapered ends. Curve log slightly in a crescent shape and place crescents 1 inch apart on an ungreased cookie sheet. Bake for 15 to 17 minutes or until edges are set. Transfer cookies to a wire rack; let cool.
3. Drizzle melted chocolate over cooled cookies. Let stand until chocolate sets.
PER COOKIE *113 cal., 8 g total fat (4 g sat. fat), 13 mg chol., 34 mg sodium, 9 g carbo., 1 g fiber, 2 g pro.*

Kringla

Each Scandinavian country has its own version of this Nordic pretzel. As much pastry as cookie, these Kringla (the Swedish variety) are not overly sweet.

PREP 45 minutes CHILL 5 hours
BAKE 5 to 7 minutes per batch OVEN 425°F
MAKES 40 cookies

3   cups all-purpose flour
2½   teaspoons baking powder
1   teaspoon baking soda
½   teaspoon salt
¼   teaspoon ground nutmeg or cardamom (optional)
½   cup butter, softened (1 stick)
1   cup sugar
1   egg
1   teaspoon vanilla
1   cup buttermilk or sour milk*

1. In a medium bowl stir together flour, baking powder, baking soda, salt, and, if desired, nutmeg or cardamom.
2. In a large mixing bowl beat butter with an electric mixer on medium to high for 30 seconds. Add sugar and beat until fluffy. Add egg and vanilla and beat well. Alternately add flour mixture and buttermilk, beating until well mixed. (Dough will be soft and sticky.) Cover and chill 5 hours or overnight or freeze for 3 hours.
3. Preheat oven to 425°F. Divide dough in half; return half to the refrigerator. On a well-floured surface roll into a 10×5-inch rectangle. With a sharp knife, cut rectangle in twenty 5×½-inch strips. Place half the strips on a baking sheet in the refrigerator while shaping and baking the first 10 strips. Roll each strip into a 10-inch-long rope. Shape each rope in a loop, crossing 1½ inches from ends. Twist rope at crossing point. Lift loop over to touch ends and seal, forming a pretzel shape. (Or fold each 10-inch-long rope in half and twist 3 times; seal ends.) Place cookies 2 inches apart on ungreased cookie sheets.
4. Bake for 5 to 7 minutes or until cookie bottoms are light brown (tops will be pale). Remove from cookie sheets and cool slightly on wire racks. Repeat with remaining dough strips and dough. Serve warm or cool.

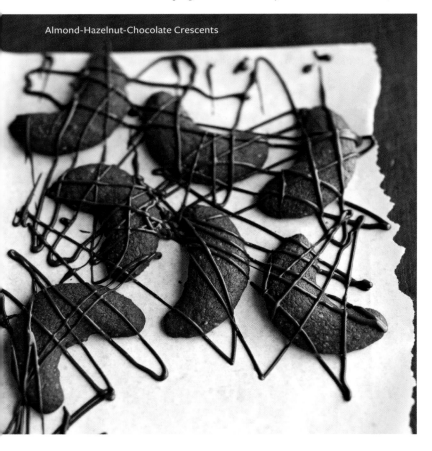
Almond-Hazelnut-Chocolate Crescents

Eggnog Spritz

*Note To make 1 cup sour milk, place 1 tablespoon lemon juice or vinegar in a glass measuring cup. Add enough milk to equal 1 cup total liquid; stir. Let stand for 5 minutes before using.

PER COOKIE *79 cal., 3 g total fat (2 g sat. fat), 12 mg chol., 100 mg sodium, 13 g carbo., 0 g fiber, 1 g pro.*

Eggnog Spritz

A cookie press (also called a spritz gun) allows you to vary cookie designs and shapes.

PREP 30 minutes BAKE 7 minutes per batch
OVEN 375°F MAKES 42 cookies

¾ cup butter, softened
½ cup sugar
1 teaspoon baking powder
¼ teaspoon salt
¼ teaspoon ground nutmeg
1 egg
1 teaspoon rum extract
1¾ cups all-purpose flour
4 ounces white baking chocolate with cocoa butter, chopped
2 teaspoons shortening
   Freshly grated or ground nutmeg (optional)

1. Preheat oven to 375°F. In a mixing bowl beat butter with an electric mixer on medium for 30 seconds. Add sugar, baking powder, salt, and ¼ teaspoon ground nutmeg. Beat until combined. Beat in egg and rum extract until combined. Beat in as much of the flour as you can with the mixer. Using a wooden spoon, stir in any remaining flour.
2. Place dough in a cookie press. Pipe dough in shapes about 1 inch apart on an ungreased cookie sheet.
3. Bake for 7 to 9 minutes or until edges are firm but not brown. Transfer cookies to a wire rack; cool.
4. In a small saucepan combine white chocolate and shortening. Cook and stir over low heat until melted. Drizzle melted white chocolate over cookies or dip cookie tops in melted white chocolate. If desired, sprinkle with nutmeg. Let stand until chocolate is set.
PER COOKIE *134 cal., 8 g total fat (5 g sat. fat), 25 mg chol., 83 mg sodium, 14 g carbo., 0 g fiber, 2 g pro.*

Painted Cookies

Painted Cookies

Kids love doing this edible craft project—the perfect activity for a children's holiday party. There's fun in creating and everyone goes home with a bag or plate of beautifully decorated cookies!

PREP **1 hour** CHILL **3 hours**
BAKE **8 minutes per batch** STAND **1 hour**
OVEN **375°F** MAKES **30 cookies**

⅓	cup butter, softened
⅓	cup shortening
¾	cup sugar
1	teaspoon baking powder
⅛	teaspoon salt
1	egg
1½	teaspoons vanilla
½	teaspoon almond extract
2	cups all-purpose flour
1	recipe Royal Icing
	Red and green paste food coloring
	Vodka or gin

1. In a large mixing bowl combine butter and shortening. Beat with an electric mixer on medium to high for 30 seconds. Add sugar, baking powder, and salt. Beat until combined, scraping bowl occasionally. Beat in egg, vanilla, and almond extract until combined. Beat in as much of the flour as you can with the mixer. Using a wooden spoon, stir in any remaining flour. Divide dough in half. Cover and chill about 3 hours or until easy to handle.

2. Preheat oven to 375°F. On a lightly floured surface roll half the dough at a time to ¼-inch thickness. Cut dough using a 3- to 4-inch fluted round cookie cutter, cane-shape cutter, or other shape cutter. Place cutouts on an ungreased cookie sheet. Bake in the preheated oven for 8 to 10 minutes or until edges are firm and bottoms are very lightly browned. Cool on cookie sheet for 1 minute. Transfer cookies to a wire rack; let cool.

3. Ice cookies with a thin layer of Royal Icing. Transfer cookies to a work surface covered with waxed paper to dry.

4. In very small bowls or custard cups combine a small amount of the red or green paste food coloring and 2 to 3 teaspoons vodka or gin. Use a small brush to paint cookies with the thinned coloring.

Royal Icing In a large mixing owl stir together 4 cups powdered sugar, 3 tablespoons meringue powder, and ½ teaspoon cream of tartar. Add ½ cup warm water. Beat with an electric mixer on low until combined, then on high for 7 to 10 minutes or until very stiff. Add 2 to 4 tablespoons additional water, 1 teaspoon at a time, to make icing desired consistency.

PER COOKIE *153 cal., 4 g total fat (2 g sat. fat), 12 mg chol., 39 mg sodium, 27 g carbo., 0 g fiber, 1 g pro.*

Linzer Pinwheels

These pretty whorled cookies feature raspberry preserves, the star ingredient of the classic Austrian dessert, Linzertorte, in a smaller scale than the original tart.

PREP **35 minutes** CHILL **5 hours** BAKE **10 minutes** per batch OVEN **375°F** MAKES **72 cookies**

1	cup butter, softened
1½	cups sugar
½	teaspoon baking powder
½	teaspoon salt
2	eggs
1	teaspoon finely shredded lemon peel
3 /4	cups all-purpose flour
⅔	cup seedless raspberry preserves

1. In a large mixing bowl beat butter with an electric mixer on medium to high for 30 seconds. Add sugar, baking powder, and salt. Beat until combined, scraping bowl occasionally. Beat in eggs and lemon peel until combined. Beat in as much of the flour as you can with the mixer. Using a wooden spoon, sir in any remaining flour. Divide dough in half. Cover and chill dough about 1 hour or until easy to handle.

2. Place each portion of dough between 2 sheets of waxed paper; roll each portion in a 10-inch square. Spread preserves on dough to within ½ inch of the edges. Roll dough in a spiral. Moisten edges; pinch to seal. Wrap each roll in waxed paper or plastic wrap. Chill dough for 4 to 24 hours or until firm enough to slice.

3. Preheat oven to 375°F. Line a large cookie sheet with parchment paper. Quickly cut rolls in ¼-inch slices, rotating rolls often to keep them round. (If rolls become too soft during cutting, place them in the freezer for 10 minutes or until they firm up.) Place slices 2 inches apart on the prepared cookie sheet.

4. Bake for 10 to 12 minutes or until edges are firm and bottoms are lightly browned. Cool on cookie sheet for 1 minute. Transfer cookies to a wire rack; cool.

PER COOKIE *70 cal., 3 g total fat (2 g sat. fat), 13 mg chol., 40 mg sodium, 11 g carbo., 0 g fiber, 1 g pro.*

Linzer Pinwheels

Peppermint Cream Bites

Peppermint Cream Bites

To push the cookie cutter through the baked and iced bars, press down on the top of the cookie cutter with the bottom of a measuring cup.

PREP 20 minutes BAKE 8 minutes
FREEZE 45 minutes OVEN 350°F MAKES 30 cookies

1½ cups crushed chocolate sandwich cookies with white filling (about 15 cookies)
3 tablespoons butter, melted
2 cups powdered sugar
2 tablespoons butter, softened
2 tablespoons milk
1 teaspoon peppermint extract
6 ounces bittersweet chocolate baking bar, chopped
2 teaspoons shortening

1. Preheat oven to 350°F. Line an 8×8×2-inch baking pan with foil, extending foil over pan edges.
2. In a medium bowl combine crushed cookies and melted butter. Press crumb mixture into the bottom of pan. Bake for 8 minutes. Cool slightly in pan on a wire rack.
3. Meanwhile, combine powdered sugar and softened butter in a food processor. Cover and process until butter is evenly distributed. With processor running, add milk and peppermint extract to make a paste. Spread peppermint mixture evenly on the prepared crust. Freeze for 45 minutes.
4. In a medium microwave-safe bowl, combine chopped chocolate and shortening. Microwave on high for

1 minute or until chocolate is melted, stirring once. Let chocolate cool 15 minutes. Pour chocolate over mint layer and spread evenly. Using the edges of the foil, lift the uncut bars out of the pan. Use a 1½-inch round cookie cutter to cut into rounds.
PER COOKIE *107 cal., 6 g total fat (3 g sat. fat), 5 mg chol., 46 mg sodium, 15 g carbo., 1 g fiber, 1 g pro.*

French Filled Macaroons

French macaroons are quite different than their chewy coconut drop-cookie American cousins. The Gallic version consists of flavored ganache sandwiched between whisper-light cookies made with ground nuts. They are charming and very impressive!

PREP 45 minutes STAND 30 minutes
BAKE 10 minutes per batch OVEN 325°F
MAKES 36 macaroons

1¼ cups powdered sugar
1 cup finely ground almonds or pistachio nuts
3 egg whites
½ teaspoon vanilla
   Dash salt
¼ cup granulated sugar
1 to 2 drops red or green food coloring*
   Cherry Filling or Chocolate Filling*
   White baking chocolate or semisweet chocolate, melted* (optional)

1. Line 3 large cookie sheets with parchment paper; set aside. In a medium bowl stir together powdered sugar and nuts; set aside.
2. In a large mixing bowl combine egg whites, vanilla, and salt. Beat with an electric mixer on medium until soft peaks form (tips curl). Gradually add granulated sugar, about 1 tablespoon at a time, beating on high just until stiff peaks form (tips stand straight). Stir in nut mixture and food coloring.
3. Spoon macaroon mixture into a large decorating bag fitted with a large (about ½-inch) round tip.** Pipe 1½-inch circles 1 inch apart onto the prepared cookie sheets. Let stand for 30 minutes before baking.
4. Preheat oven to 325°F. Bake for 10 minutes or just until set. Cool on cookie sheets on wire racks. Peel cookies off parchment paper.
5. Spread about 1 teaspoon of the Cherry Filling or Chocolate Filling on bottoms of half the cookies. Top with remaining cookies, bottom sides down. If desired, drizzle cookies with melted chocolate.
Cherry Filling In a mixing bowl beat 3 tablespoons softened butter with an electric mixer on medium for 30 seconds. Add 1 cup powdered sugar, 1 tablespoon maraschino cherry juice, and ½ teaspoon vanilla; beat until combined. Beat in 1 cup additional powdered sugar. If necessary, beat in additional maraschino cherry juice to make filling spreading consistency. Tint bright pink with red food coloring.

Chocolate Filling In a medium mixing bowl beat 3 tablespoons softened butter with an electric mixer on medium to high for 30 seconds. Add 1 cup powdered sugar, 2 tablespoons unsweetened cocoa powder, 1 tablespoon milk, and ½ teaspoon vanilla; beat until combined. Beat in 1 cup additional powdered sugar. If necessary, beat in additional milk (2 to 3 teaspoons) to make a filling of spreading consistency.

*Note If making macaroons with almonds, use red food coloring, Cherry Filling, and, if desired, melted white chocolate. If making macaroons with pistachios, use green food coloring, Chocolate Filling, and, if desired, melted semisweet chocolate.

**Note If you don't own a decorating bag, spoon mixture into a large resealable plastic bag and snip a ½-inch hole in 1 corner of the bag.

PER MACAROON 74 cal., 2 g total fat (1 g sat. fat), 3 mg chol., 16 mg sodium, 13 g carbo., 0 g fiber, 1 g pro.

Giant Crème de Menthe Whoopie Pies

Individually wrap up these generous size whoopies in cellophane, tie them with a ribbon, and give them as gifts.

PREP 35 minutes BAKE 15 minutes per batch OVEN 350°F MAKES 32 sandwich cookies

- ¾ cup butter, softened
- ½ cup granulated sugar
- ½ cup packed brown sugar
- 1 teaspoon baking soda
- ⅛ teaspoon salt
- 2 eggs
- 1 teaspoon vanilla
- 2 cups all-purpose flour
- ½ cup unsweetened cocoa powder
- 1 cup milk
- 1 recipe Crème de Menthe Filling
  Layered chocolate-mint candies, chopped

1. Preheat oven to 350°F. Line 2 very large cookie sheets with parchment paper. Draw two 6-inch circles on each parchment paper, leaving 3 inches between circles. Turn paper over so the marks are on the underside of the paper; set aside.

2. In a large mixing bowl beat butter with an electric mixer on medium to high for 30 seconds. Add granulated sugar, brown sugar, baking soda, and salt. Beat until well combined, scraping bowl occasionally. Beat in eggs and vanilla until combined. In a medium bowl stir together flour and cocoa powder. Alternately add flour mixture and milk to butter mixture, beating on low after each addition just until combined.

3. Spoon dough evenly on circles on prepared cookie sheets. Spread dough evenly in each circle. Bake for 15 minutes or until cookies are set. Cool completely on sheets on wire racks.

4. Using a large spatula, invert 1 cookie onto a serving platter. Spread with half the Crème de Menthe Filling. Top with another cookie, flat side down. Repeat with remaining cookies and filling. With a serrated knife, cut each whoopie pie in 16 wedges. If desired, top wedges with chopped candies.

Crème de Menthe Filling In a medium mixing bowl beat ½ cup softened butter with an electric mixer on medium to high for 30 seconds. Gradually beat in 1 cup powdered sugar. Beat in 2 tablespoon crème de menthe* (or 2 tablespoons milk, ½ teaspoon mint extract, and several drops green food coloring) and 1 tablespoon milk. Gradually beat in 5 cups powdered sugar. Beat in 3 to 4 tablespoons additional milk to make filling spreading consistency.

*Note If using clear crème de menthe, add several drops green food coloring to the filling.

PER COOKIE 221 cal., 8 g total fat (5 g sat. fat), 33 mg chol., 109 mg sodium, 37 g carbo., 1 g fiber, 2 g pro.

Giant Crème de Menthe Whoopie Pies

Double-Chocolate Peppermint Biscotti

medium to high for 30 seconds. Add sugar, cocoa powder, baking powder, and salt. Beat until combined, scraping bowl occasionally. Beat in eggs and peppermint extract until combined. Beat in as much of the flour as you can with the mixer. Using a wooden spoon, stir in any remaining flour and the bittersweet chocolate.

2. Divide dough into 4 portions. Wrap each portion in plastic wrap. Chill for 30 to 60 minutes or until dough is easy to handle.

3. Preheat oven to 375°F. Unwrap each dough portion and shape in a 7-inch loaf. Place loaves 4 inches apart on the prepared cookie sheets; flatten each loaf slightly to about 2 inches wide.

4. Bake, 1 sheet at a time, for 14 to 16 minutes or until a toothpick inserted near centers comes out clean. Cool on cookie sheets on wire racks for 1 hour.

5. Reduce heat to 325°F. Using a serrated knife, cut loaves diagonally into ½-inch slices. Place slices, cut side down, on cookie sheets. Bake for 5 minutes. Turn slices over; bake for 5 to 7 minutes more or until crisp and dry. Transfer biscotti to wire racks; cool.

6. Dip 1 long side of each cookie into melted candy coating. Place cookies on waxed paper. Sprinkle with crushed candies while coating is wet. Let stand until coating is set.

PER BISCOTTI *105 cal., 5 g total fat (4 g sat. fat), 16 mg chol., 59 mg sodium, 13 g carbo., 0 g fiber, 1 g pro.*

Lemon Meringue Tassies

For a head start on these cookies, make the tarts and store them, tightly covered, at room temperature up to 3 days. The Lemon Butter Cream frosting may be made 1 day ahead and stored, covered, in the refrigerator. Only the Meringue Frosting needs to be made the day you serve the cookies.

PREP 40 minutes   BAKE 10 minutes
OVEN 375°F   MAKES 24 tassies

½   cup butter, softened
1   3-ounce package cream cheese, softened
1   cup all-purpose flour
1   recipe Lemon Filling
1   recipe Meringue or Lemon Butter Cream Frosting

1. Preheat oven to 375°F. For pastry, in a mixing bowl beat the butter and cream cheese until combined. Stir in the flour. Press a rounded teaspoon of pastry evenly into the bottom and up the sides of 24 ungreased 1¾-inch muffin cups.

2. Bake 10 to 15 minutes or until lightly browned. Cool in pans on a wire rack for 5 minutes. Transfer to racks to cool completely. Fill with Lemon Filling. Pipe or spoon Meringue Frosting or Lemon Butter Cream Frosting on the filling. Serve immediately.

Lemon Filling In a medium saucepan combine ¾ cup sugar, 2 tablespoons all-purpose flour, 1 to 2 teaspoons finely shredded lemon peel, ¼ cup lemon juice, ¼ cup

Double-Chocolate Peppermint Biscotti

To crush the peppermint candies, place whole candies in a plastic bag and roll over the bag with a rolling pin.

PREP 45 minutes   CHILL 30 minutes
BAKE 24 minutes per batch   COOL 1 hour
OVEN 375°F/325°F   MAKES about 42 biscotti

½   cup butter, softened
⅔   cup sugar
¼   cup unsweetened cocoa powder
2   teaspoons baking powder
½   teaspoon salt
2   eggs
1   teaspoon peppermint extract
1¾   cups all-purpose flour
4   ounces bittersweet chocolate, chopped
8   ounces vanilla-flavor candy coating, melted
¼   cup crushed peppermint candies

1. Lightly grease 2 cookie sheets; set aside. In a large mixing bowl beat butter with an electric mixer on

water and ⅛ teaspoon salt. Whisk in 1 slightly beaten egg. Cook and stir over medium heat until thickened. Cool completely.

Meringue Frosting In a mixing bowl combine ¼ cup sugar, 2 tablespoons water, 1 tablespoon pasteurized liquid egg whites or 1 teaspoon meringue powder, ½ teaspoon vanilla, and ⅛ teaspoon cream of tartar. Beat on high until soft peaks form (tips curl).

Lemon Butter Cream Frosting In a large mixing bowl beat ¼ cup butter with an electric mixer on medium for 30 seconds. Gradually add 1½ cups powdered sugar, beating well. Add 2 tablespoons milk and 1 teaspoon lemon juice. Gradually beat in additional 1½ cups powdered sugar and enough milk (1 to 2 tablespoons) to reach spreading consistency.

PER TASSIE *104 cal., 5 g total fat (3 g sat. fat), 23 mg chol., 55 mg sodium, 13 g carbo., 0 g fiber, 1 g pro.*

Ooey, Gooey, Chewy S'mores Bars

To easily spread the crust mixture in the pan, dip a large spoon in water and use the back of it to press and smooth the crust without sticking.

PREP 25 minutes BAKE 35 minutes
OVEN 350°F MAKES 24 bars

¾ cup butter, softened
1½ cups packed brown sugar
2 eggs
2 teaspoons vanilla
1 cup all-purpose flour
1½ cups quick-cooking rolled oats
1 cup graham cracker crumbs
2½ cups tiny marshmallows
1¼ cups semisweet chocolate baking chunks or milk chocolate baking pieces

1. Preheat oven to 350°F. Line a 13×9×2-inch baking pan with heavy foil, extending foil over pan edges. Lightly grease foil. Set pan aside. In a large mixing bowl beat butter with an electric mixer on medium to high for 30 seconds. Beat in brown sugar until combined, scraping bowl occasionally. Beat in eggs and vanilla until combined. Beat in flour. Stir in oats and graham cracker crumbs.
2. Reserve 1 cup of the oat mixture. Spread remaining oat mixture into prepared pan. Bake for 15 minutes or until lightly browned. Sprinkle marshmallows evenly over warm crust. Top with chocolate chunks. Dot remaining oat mixture on chocolate and marshmallows.
3. Bake for 20 minutes or until top is lightly browned. Cool completely in pan on a wire rack. Using the edges of the foil, lift the uncut bars out of the pan. Cut into bars.
PER BAR *224 cal., 9 g total fat (5 g sat. fat), 33 mg chol., 92 mg sodium, 34 g carbo., 1 g fiber, 3 g pro.*

Star Mint Meringues

The simple trick of brushing the inside with red paste food coloring before pipi pretty visual effect of candy stripes.

PREP 20 minutes BAKE 90 minutes
OVEN 200°F MAKES 24 cookies

3 egg whites
¼ teaspoon cream of tartar
¼ teaspoon peppermint extract
⅛ teaspoon salt
¾ cup sugar
Red paste food coloring

1. Preheat oven to 200°F. Line a cookie sheet with parchment paper; set aside. In a large mixing bowl combine egg whites, cream of tartar, peppermint extract, and salt. Beat with an electric mixer on medium until soft peaks form (tips curl). Gradually add sugar, 1 tablespoon at a time, beating on high until stiff peaks form (tips stand straight).
2. With a small clean paintbrush, brush stripes of red paste food coloring on the inside of a pastry bag fitted with a ½-inch open star tip. Carefully transfer meringue into the bag. Pipe 2-inch stars 1 inch apart onto prepared cookie sheet.
3. Bake for 90 minutes or until meringues appear dry and are firm when lightly touched. Transfer cookies to a wire rack; let cool.
PER COOKIE *270 cal., 0 g total fat, 0 mg chol., 19 mg sodium, 6 g carbo., 0 g fiber, 0 g pro.*

Star Mint Meringues

Triple-Chocolate and Espresso Brownies

baking pan with heavy foil, extending foil over pan edges. Grease foil; set pan aside.

2. Stir the sugar into the cooled chocolate mixture. Add the eggs, one at a time, beating with a wooden spoon just until combined. Stir in espresso powder and vanilla. In a small bowl stir together the flour, baking soda, and salt. Add flour mixture to chocolate mixture; stir just until combined. Stir in chocolate pieces. Spread the batter evenly in the prepared pan.

3. Bake for 30 minutes. Cool in pan on a wire rack. Spread Chocolate Cream Cheese Frosting on cooled brownies. Using the edges of the foil, lift the uncut brownies out of the pan. Place on cutting board; cut in squares. If desired, sprinkle with chocolate-covered espresso beans.

Chocolate Cream Cheese Frosting In a saucepan heat and stir ½ cup semisweet chocolate pieces over low heat until smooth. Remove from heat; let cool. In a medium bowl stir together one 3-ounce package softened cream cheese and ¼ cup powdered sugar. Stir in melted chocolate until smooth.

PER BROWNIE *258 cal., 16 g total fat (9 g sat. fat), 38 mg chol., 85 mg sodium, 30 g carbo., 2 g fiber, 3 g pro.*

Raspberry French Silk Bars

Bar cookies are generally casual fare, but these unusually elegant chocolate and raspberry bars are sweetly suited to the fanciest occasions.

PREP **40 minutes** BAKE **10 minutes**
CHILL **2 hours** OVEN **375°F** MAKES **32 bars**

1   recipe Chocolate Crumb Crust
1   cup whipping cream
½   cup chopped semisweet chocolate (3 ounces)
½   cup chopped bittersweet chocolate (3 ounces)
⅓   cup sugar
⅓   cup butter
2   egg yolks, beaten
3   tablespoons crème de cacao or whipping cream
½   cup raspberry preserves or seedless raspberry jam
1   recipe Raspberry Ganache
    Fresh raspberries (optional)

1. Preheat oven to 375°F. Line a 13×9×2-inch baking pan with foil, extending the foil over the pan edges. Press Chocolate Crumb Crust onto the bottom and slightly up the sides of the pan. Bake 10 minutes or until crust is set. Cool completely in pan on a wire rack.

2. Meanwhile, for filling, in a medium heavy saucepan combine whipping cream, chocolates, sugar, and butter. Cook and stir over low heat about 10 minutes or until chocolates are melted and smooth. Remove from heat. Gradually stir half the hot mixture into beaten egg yolks. Add egg yolk mixture to chocolate mixture in saucepan. Cook and stir over medium-low heat 5 minutes or until mixture is slightly thickened and bubbly.

Triple-Chocolate and Espresso Brownies

With three chocolates, espresso powder, and a chocolate-covered espresso bean topping, these super-rich brownies will keep the party hopping!

PREP **30 minutes** BAKE **30 minutes**
COOL **45 minutes** OVEN **350°F** MAKES **20 brownies**

½   cup butter
4   ounces bittersweet chocolate, coarsely chopped
3   ounces unsweetened chocolate, coarsely chopped
1   cup sugar
2   eggs
1   tablespoon espresso powder
1   teaspoon vanilla
⅔   cup all-purpose flour
¼   teaspoon baking soda
⅛   teaspoon salt
1   cup miniature semisweet chocolate pieces
1   recipe Chocolate Cream Cheese Frosting
    Chocolate-covered espresso beans, chopped (optional)

1. In a medium saucepan combine butter, bittersweet chocolate, and unsweetened chocolate. Cook and stir over low heat until melted and smooth. Remove from heat; cool. Preheat oven to 350°F. Line an 8×8×2-inch

3. Remove from heat. (Mixture may appear slightly curdled.) Stir in the crème de cacao. Place the saucepan in a bowl of ice water. Stir occasionally for about 20 minutes or until the mixture stiffens and becomes difficult to stir. Transfer the filling to a medium bowl.

4. Spread raspberry preserves on cooled Chocolate Crumb Crust. Beat filling with an electric mixer on medium to high for 2 to 3 minutes or until light and fluffy. Spread filling on preserves. Cover and refrigerate for 1 to 2 hours or until firm. Prepare Raspberry Ganache.

5. Remove bars from refrigerator. Spoon Raspberry Ganache over top, gently spreading evenly across the top. Cover and refrigerate for 1 to 2 hours or until firm. Using the edges of the foil, lift the uncut bars out of the pan. Cut into bars. If desired, garnish with fresh raspberries.

Chocolate Crumb Crust In a medium bowl combine 2 cups finely crushed chocolate wafers, chocolate graham crackers, or other crisp chocolate cookies (about 38 cookies); ¼ cup all-purpose flour; and 2 tablespoons granulated sugar. Add ½ cup melted butter and stir until well combined.

Raspberry Ganache In a large glass measuring cup combine 1 cup chopped semisweet chocolate or chocolate pieces, ⅓ cup whipping cream, and 1 tablespoon seedless raspberry jam. Microwave on high about 1 minute or until chocolate is melted, stirring every 30 seconds. Let stand about 1 hour or until slightly thickened.

PER BAR *200 cal., 13 g total fat (8 g sat. fat), 41 mg chol., 96 mg sodium, 21 g carbo., 1 g fiber, 2 g pro.*

Macadamia-Eggnog Bars

Lining the baking pan with greased foil makes removing these bars from the pan (and cleanup) a snap. It's a good trick when making any bar cookies or brownies.

PREP **25 minutes** BAKE **25 minutes**
OVEN **350°F** MAKES **36 bars**

2   cups granulated sugar
⅔   cup butter
2   eggs
1   teaspoon vanilla
2   cups all-purpose flour
1   teaspoon baking powder
½   teaspoon ground nutmeg
1   cup chopped macadamia nuts
1   recipe Eggnog Drizzle

1. Preheat oven to 350°F. Line a 13×9×2-inch baking pan with foil; grease foil and set aside. In a medium saucepan cook and stir sugar and butter over medium heat until butter is melted. Remove from heat. Cool slightly.

2. Stir eggs and vanilla into sugar mixture. Stir in flour, baking powder, and nutmeg. Stir in nuts.

3. Spread mixture evenly into prepared pan. Bake for 25 to 30 minutes or until edges begin to pull way from the sides of the pan. Cool in pan on a wire rack. Use foil to remove bars from pan; place on cutting board. Cut into diamonds. Drizzle with Eggnog Drizzle.

Eggnog Drizzle In a small bowl combine 1 cup powdered sugar, ¼ teaspoon vanilla, and 1 tablespoon eggnog. Stir in additional eggnog, 1 teaspoon at a time, until icing reaches drizzling consistency Drizzle icing over bars.

PER BAR *144 cal., 7 g total fat (3 g sat. fat), 21 mg chol., 39 mg sodium, 21 g carbo., 1 g fiber, 1 g pro.*

Macadamia-Eggnog Bars

melt-in-your-mouth candies

Turn your kitchen into the best confectionary in town. Candymaking is an art and science made simple with these foolproof recipes for truffles, fudge, crisp and buttery brittle, homemade marshmallows, chewy caramels, and toffee. Box them up beautifully and no one will believe you made them yourself.

Caramelized Peanut Brittle, page 121

Candy Bar Fudge

Candy Bar Fudge

Use your microwave to make this simple and delicious from-scratch fudge that tastes like a Snickers bar.

PREP 15 minutes CHILL 2 hours
MAKES 2¾ pounds (64 pieces)

½   cup butter
⅓   cup unsweetened cocoa powder
¼   cup packed brown sugar
¼   cup milk
3½ cups powdered sugar
1   teaspoon vanilla
30 vanilla caramels, unwrapped
1   tablespoon water
2   cups peanuts
½   cup semisweet chocolate pieces
½   cup milk chocolate pieces

1. Line a 9×9×2-inch or 11×7×1½-inch baking pan with foil, extending foil over the edges of pan. Butter the foil; set pan aside.
2. In a microwave-safe bowl microwave the butter, uncovered, on high for 1 to 1½ minutes or until melted. Stir in cocoa powder, brown sugar, and milk. Microwave, uncovered, on high for 1 to 1½ minutes or until mixture boils, stirring once. Stir again; microwave for 30 seconds more. Stir in powdered sugar and vanilla until smooth. Spread fudge evenly in the prepared pan.
3. In another microwave-safe bowl combine caramels and water. Microwave, uncovered, on medium for 2 to 2½ minutes or until caramels are melted, stirring once. Stir in peanuts. Microwave, uncovered, on medium for 45 to 60 seconds more or until mixture is softened.

Gently and quickly spread caramel mixture on fudge layer in pan.
4. In a 2-cup microwave-safe glass measuring cup or bowl combine semisweet and milk chocolate pieces. Heat, uncovered, on medium for 2 to 2½ minutes or until melted, stirring once or twice. Spread on caramel layer. Cover and chill for 2 to 3 hours or until firm. Use foil to lift fudge from pan. Peel off foil and cut fudge into squares. Arrange fudge in gift container; cover with plastic wrap.

PER PIECE *102 cal., 5 g total fat (2 g sat. fat), 5 mg chol., 24 mg sodium, 14 g carbo., 1 g fiber, 2 g pro.*

Rocky Route Fudge

For a wonderfully soft texture, this marshmallow-and-pecan-studded fudge is made from cooked sugar, cream, and cocoa powder that has air beaten into it as it cools.

PREP 30 minutes COOK 10 minutes COOL 1 hour
MAKES 64 pieces

4   cups sugar
1¼   cups whipping cream
⅓   cup unsweetened cocoa powder
⅓   cup light-color corn syrup
¼   teaspoon salt
1   tablespoon vanilla
1   cup snipped tiny marshmallows
1   cup chopped pecans, toasted (see note, page 119)

1. Line an 8×8×2-inch baking pan with foil, extending the foil over edges of pan. Butter foil; set pan aside.
2. Butter the sides of a heavy 3-quart saucepan. In the saucepan combine sugar, cream, cocoa powder, corn

syrup, and salt. Cook and stir over medium heat until mixture is boiling. Clip a candy thermometer to the side of the pan. Reduce heat to medium-low; continue boiling at a moderate, steady rate, stirring occasionally, until thermometer registers 236°F, soft-ball stage (about 10 minutes). (Adjust heat as necessary to maintain a steady boil.)

3. Remove saucepan from heat. Add vanilla but do not stir. Cool, without stirring, to 110°F (1 to 1¼ hours). Remove thermometer from saucepan. Beat mixture vigorously with a clean wooden spoon just until candy starts to thicken. Add marshmallows and pecans. Continue beating just until fudge starts to lose its gloss (6 to 8 minutes total).

4. Immediately spread fudge evenly in the prepared pan. Score fudge into squares while warm. Let fudge cool to room temperature. When fudge is firm, use the edges of the foil to lift fudge from pan. Cut into squares.

To store Layer fudge between sheets of waxed paper in an airtight container; cover. Store in the refrigerator up to 1 week.

PER PIECE *84 cal., 3 g total fat (1 g sat. fat), 6 mg chol., 13 mg sodium, 15 g carbo., 0 g fiber, 0 g pro.*

Pumpkin-Spiced Gingersnap Truffles

Crushed gingersnaps create a nicely spiced coating on these made-in-the-microwave truffles.

PREP **30 minutes** STAND **5 minutes**
CHILL **2 hours 30 minutes** MAKES **20 to 25 truffles**

1¼ cups semisweet chocolate pieces
¼ teaspoon pumpkin pie spice
¼ teaspoon vanilla
½ cup whipping cream
¾ cup chopped gingersnaps (about 10 cookies)
⅓ cup finely crushed gingersnaps (about 7 cookies) and/or ¼ cup unsweetened cocoa powder

1. In a medium bowl combine chocolate pieces, pumpkin pie spice, and vanilla.

2. In a medium microwave-safe bowl place whipping cream. Microwave on high for 70 seconds or until boiling (or place cream in a saucepan and bring just to boiling). Pour cream over chocolate mixture. Let stand 5 minutes. Whisk until smooth. Stir in chopped gingersnaps. Cover; refrigerate 1½ to 2 hours or until firm but soft enough to form into balls.

3. Place crushed gingersnaps and/or cocoa powder in small bowl(s). Using a small spoon, scoop 1-tablespoon portions of truffle mixture and shape into balls. Roll in crushed gingersnaps or cocoa powder to coat. Refrigerate 1 hour or until firm. Store, covered, in refrigerator up to 3 days.

PER TRUFFLE *97 cal., 6 g total fat (3 g sat. fat), 8 mg chol., 42 mg sodium, 12 g carbo., 1 g fiber, 1 g pro.*

Sweet Cherry Truffles

These regal-looking sweets are beautiful enough to be gift-wrapped and put under the tree—but don't. They should be stored in the refrigerator.

PREP **1 hour** CHILL **1 hour** MAKES **about 24 truffles**

1 12-ounce package semisweet chocolate pieces
⅓ cup whipping cream
4 teaspoons cherry brandy (optional)
2 tablespoons finely chopped candied cherries
Unsweetened cocoa powder
Finely chopped walnuts, toasted (see note, page 119)
Powdered sugar

1. Line a baking sheet with waxed paper; set aside. In a heavy medium-size saucepan combine chocolate pieces and whipping cream. Cook and stir constantly over low heat until chocolate is melted. Remove saucepan from heat; cool slightly. Stir in cherry brandy. Beat chocolate mixture with an electric mixer on low until smooth. Stir in cherries. Chill about 1 hour or until firm.

2. Shape chilled chocolate mixture into ¾- to 1-inch balls. Roll balls in cocoa powder, finely chopped walnuts, and/or powdered sugar.

PER TRUFFLE *85 cal., 5 g total fat (3 g sat. fat), 4 mg chol., 3 mg sodium, 11 g carbo., 1 g fiber, 1 g pro.*

Sweet Cherry Truffles
Pumpkin-Spiced Gingersnap Truffles

Sandwich Cookie Pops

This big-batch recipe makes 50 pops—perfect for a school or office treat—filled with yummy Raspberry Buttercream and coated in white chocolate.

PREP **1 hour** CHILL **4 hours** BAKE **6 minutes** OVEN **375°F** MAKES **50 lollipop cookies**

1¼ cups all-purpose flour
1   teaspoon cream of tartar
½   teaspoon baking soda
½   teaspoon salt
½   cup butter, softened
¾   cup sugar
1   tablespoon Chambord or milk
1   teaspoon vanilla
1   recipe Raspberry Buttercream
1½   pounds white chocolate or white candy coating, chopped
     Red nonpareils

1. In a medium bowl whisk together flour, cream of tartar, baking soda, and salt; set aside.
2. In a large mixing bowl beat butter with an electric mixer on medium for 30 seconds. Add sugar and beat until creamy and smooth. Beat in Chambord and vanilla. Beat in flour mixture.

3. If dough is too sticky, cover and chill for 30 minutes or until easy to handle. Divide dough into 2 equal portions. Shape each portion into a 12-inch-long roll about 1 inch in diameter. Wrap and chill in the refrigerator for 4 to 24 hours.
4. Preheat oven to 375°F. Cut the rolls into slices about ⅛ inch thick. Place 50 lollipop craft sticks 1½ inches apart on ungreased cookie sheets. Place 1 dough slice on 1 end of each stick. Bake for 6 to 7 minutes or until edges are lightly browned. Bake remaining cookie slices without sticks. Cool on cookie sheets 1 minute. Transfer to wire racks to cool.
5. Spread a slightly rounded teaspoon of Raspberry Buttercream on the flat sides of the cookies with sticks. Top with remaining cookies, flat sides down.
6. Place white chocolate in a microwave-safe bowl. Microwave on high for 3 minutes until just melted, stirring after each minute; cool slightly. Hold pop by the stick and carefully dip and spoon melted chocolate over to coat; let excess chocolate drip off before placing on waxed or parchment paper. Sprinkle with nonpareils; cool.

Raspberry Buttercream In a large mixing bowl beat ½ cup softened butter for 30 seconds. Beat in 1 cup powdered sugar, 1 tablespoon Chambord or milk, and 2 tablespoon seedless raspberry preserves. Beat in 1½ cups additional powdered sugar.

PER COOKIE *163 cal., 8 g total fat (5 g sat. fat), 12 mg chol., 77 mg sodium, 20 g carbo., 0 g fiber, 1 g pro.*

Caramels

Salted caramel is all the rage these days. If you like a nip of salt with your sweets, sprinkle ½ teaspoon sea salt on caramel mixture after you've poured it into the pan and it has cooled for about 10 minutes. If you sprinkle too soon, it will dissolve and it won't adhere to the caramel.

PREP **20 minutes** COOK **45 minutes** STAND **2 hours** MAKES **64 pieces**

1   cup chopped walnuts, toasted if desired* (optional)
1   cup butter
1   16-ounce package (2¼ cups packed) brown sugar
2   cups half-and-half or light cream
1   cup light-color corn syrup
1   teaspoon vanilla

1. Line an 8×8×2-inch or 9×9×2-inch baking pan with foil, extending foil over edges of pan. Butter the foil. If desired, sprinkle walnuts in pan. Set pan aside.
2. In a heavy 3-quart saucepan melt butter over low heat. Add brown sugar, half-and-half, and corn syrup; mix well. Cook and stir over medium-high heat until mixture boils. Clip a candy thermometer to the side of the pan. Reduce heat to medium; continue boiling at a moderate, steady rate, stirring frequently, until the thermometer registers 248°F (firm-ball stage),

Sandwich Cookie Pops

45 to 60 minutes. Adjust heat as necessary to maintain a steady boil and watch temperature carefully during the last 10 to 15 minutes of cooking as temperature can increase quickly at the end.

3. Remove saucepan from heat; remove thermometer. Stir in vanilla. Quickly pour candy mixture into prepared pan. Let stand about 2 hours or until firm. When firm, use foil to lift it out of pan. Use a buttered knife to cut into 1-inch squares. Wrap each piece in waxed paper or plastic wrap. Store at room temperature up to 2 weeks.
*Note To toast nuts and coconut, spread whole nuts or large pieces in a shallow pan. Toast in a 350°F oven for 5 to 10 minutes, shaking the pan once or twice. Toast coconut in the same way, but watch very closely to avoid burning it. Toast finely chopped or ground nuts or sesame seeds in a dry skillet over medium heat. Stir often so they don't burn.

PER PIECE *73 cal., 4 g total fat (2 g sat. fat), 10 mg chol., 27 mg sodium, 10 g carbo., 0 g fiber, 0 g pro.*

Butter Mint Buttons

Chocolate Bonbon Pops

Arrange a "bouquet" of these chocolate pops in a vase on a holiday buffet table or wrap them individually and hand them out as party favors.

PREP 20 minutes FREEZE 30 minutes
CHILL 1 hour MAKES about 20 pops

18 chocolate sandwich cookies with cream filling
¾ cup pecans, toasted (see note, above)
3 tablespoons orange liqueur or orange juice
2 tablespoons unsweetened cocoa powder
2 tablespoons light-color corn syrup
20 lollipop sticks
1 cup milk chocolate pieces, white baking pieces, or semisweet chocolate pieces
1 teaspoon shortening
   Toasted coconut (see note, above), nonpareils, and/or finely chopped pecans (optional)

1. In large food processor combine cookies and the ¾ cup pecans. Cover and process with on/off turns until cookies are crushed. Add orange liqueur, cocoa powder, and corn syrup. Cover and process until combined.
2. Line a large baking sheet with parchment paper. Shape cookie mixture into 1-inch balls. Place balls on prepared baking sheet; insert a lollipop stick into each ball. Freeze for 30 minutes.
3. In a small saucepan stir chocolate pieces and shortening over medium-low heat just until mixture is melted and smooth. Remove from heat. Spoon the melted chocolate over cookies. If desired, sprinkle with toasted coconut, nonpareils, and/or finely chopped pecans. Loosely cover and chill about 1 hour or until chocolate is set. If pops contain orange liqueur, the flavor will mellow in a few days.

PER POP *208 cal., 14 g total fat (4 g sat. fat), 4 mg chol., 71 mg sodium, 20 g carbo., 2 g fiber, 3 g pro.*

Butter Mint Buttons

These buttery cookies feature butter mints, those old-fashioned melt-in-your-mouth candies.

PREP 30 minutes BAKE 14 minutes per batch
OVEN 325°F MAKES about 30 cookies

¾ cup butter, softened
½ cup powdered sugar
2 teaspoons vanilla
¼ teaspoon salt
2 cups all-purpose flour
¾ cup crushed butter mint candies
   Powdered sugar

1. Preheat oven to 325°F. In a large mixing bowl beat butter with an electric mixer on medium to high for 30 seconds. Add the ½ cup powdered sugar, the vanilla, and salt. Beat until combined, scraping bowl occasionally. Beat in as much of the flour as you can with the mixer. Using a wooden spoon, stir in any remaining flour and the crushed butter mint candies.
2. Shape dough into 1-inch balls. Place 1 inch apart on an ungreased cookie sheet.
3. Bake for 14 to 16 minutes or until edges are lightly browned. Cool on cookie sheet for 2 minutes. Transfer to a wire rack; cool for 5 minutes.
4. Place additional powdered sugar in a shallow bowl. While cookies are warm, roll in powdered sugar to coat. Cool completely. Roll cookies again in powdered sugar just before serving.

PER COOKIE *98 cal., 5 g total fat (3 g sat. fat), 12 mg chol., 52 mg sodium, 13 g carbo., 0 g fiber, 1 g pro.*

Eggnog Marshmallows

Eggnog Marshmallows

Homemade marshmallows are a special treat and almost magical to make. These light, ethereal, and fluffy marshmallows taste just like the decadent holiday drink. Eat them out of hand as a confection or drop one in a cup of homemade hot cocoa.

PREP 30 minutes   COOK 12 minutes
STAND 1 hour   MAKES 20 large marshmallows

	Nonstick cooking spray
2	envelopes unflavored gelatin (4¼ teaspoons)
¾	cup cold water
2	cups granulated sugar
⅔	cup light-color corn syrup
⅓	cup refrigerated egg white product or 2 pasteurized egg whites
¼	teaspoon salt
1	teaspoon rum extract
¼	teaspoon ground nutmeg
⅔	cup powdered sugar
3	tablespoons cornstarch
4	ounces vanilla-flavor candy coating, chopped, or white baking chocolate with cocoa butter White nonpareils

1. Lightly coat an 8×8×2-inch baking pan with cooking spray. Line pan with plastic wrap or line bottom of pan with waxed paper or parchment paper. Coat the plastic or paper with cooking spray; set pan aside.

2. In a large metal or heatproof bowl sprinkle gelatin over ½ cup of the cold water; set aside.

3. In a heavy 2-quart saucepan stir together remaining ¼ cup water, 1¾ cups of the sugar, and the corn syrup until combined. Bring to boiling over medium-high heat. Clip a candy thermometer to the side of the saucepan. Cook, without stirring, over medium-high heat until thermometer registers 260°F (hard-ball stage), 12 to 15 minutes total. Remove from heat; pour over gelatin mixture in bowl and stir well to combine (mixture will foam).

4. Meanwhile, in a large clean mixing bowl beat the egg whites and salt with an electric mixer on high until foamy. Gradually add remaining ¼ cup sugar, 1 tablespoon at a time, until stiff peaks form (tips stand straight). Beat in rum extract and nutmeg until combined. With mixer on high, gradually add gelatin mixture to egg white mixture, beating about 7 minutes or until thick (the consistency of thick, pourable cake batter). Quickly pour marshmallow mixture into prepared pan, spreading to edges of pan. Lightly coat another piece of plastic wrap with cooking spray; place, coated side down, on marshmallow mixture. Let stand at room temperature for 1 to 2 hours until firm.

5. Remove plastic wrap from top of marshmallows. In a small bowl combine powdered sugar and cornstarch; sprinkle about one-fourth of the mixture evenly onto a large cutting board. Loosen sides of marshmallows if necessary and carefully invert onto the cutting board. Remove plastic wrap or paper. Sprinkle top with some of the remaining powdered sugar mixture. Using a knife that has been dipped in warm water, cut 20 marshmallow squares. Place squares, a few at a time, in a large resealable plastic bag. Add remaining powdered sugar mixture; seal bag and toss to coat all sides of marshmallows with powdered sugar mixture.

6. In a small saucepan cook and stir white chocolate just until melted. Let stand 5 to 10 minutes or until cooled but not set. Spread in a thin, even layer on marshmallow tops. Top with nonpareils. Store marshmallows between sheets of waxed paper or parchment paper in an airtight container in the refrigerator up to 1 week or freeze up to 1 month. Bring to room temperature 30 minutes before serving.

PER MARSHMALLOW *158 cal., 2 g total fat (2 g sat. fat), 0 mg chol., 40 mg sodium, 35 g carbo., 0 g fiber, 1 g pro.*

Coconut Marshmallows Prepare as above, except sprinkle 1½ cups toasted flaked coconut (see note, page 119)in the 13×9×2-inch pan after coating with cooking spray. Add ¼ teaspoon coconut flavoring to the egg whites with the vanilla. Sprinkle marshmallow tops with an additional 1½ cups toasted flaked coconut. Cover and chill as directed above. Omit powdered sugar and cornstarch. Invert marshmallows onto a large cutting board. Cut into squares. Place squares, about one-third at a time, in a large resealable plastic bag. Add 1¼ cups toasted flaked coconut. Seal bag and shake to coat all sides of marshmallows with coconut.

Caramelized Peanut Brittle

Essentially two ingredients—sugar and peanuts—are transformed by heat into an irresistible treat. Be careful when cooking the sugar to avoid spattering. Melted sugar is extremely hot!

START TO FINISH **20 minutes**
MAKES **1¼ pounds (48 servings)**

1   tablespoon butter
1   cup chopped peanuts
2   cups sugar

1. Line a large baking sheet with foil; butter foil and set the baking sheet aside. In a small saucepan melt the 1 tablespoon butter over low heat. Stir in chopped peanuts; keep the peanuts warm over low heat.
2. To caramelize the sugar, place sugar in a heavy large skillet; heat over medium-high heat until sugar begins to melt, shaking skillet occasionally to heat sugar evenly. Reduce heat to medium-low; cook until sugar is melted and golden, stirring only as necessary after sugar begins to melt (12 to 15 minutes).
3. Remove the skillet from the heat; quickly stir in warm chopped peanuts. Immediately pour the mixture onto the prepared baking sheet, allowing syrup to flow and keeping nuts evenly distributed.
4. Cool brittle completely, then break into pieces. Store in a tightly covered container in a cool, dry place up to 1 month.
PER SERVING *51 cal., 2 g total fat (0 g sat. fat), 1 mg chol., 27 mg sodium, 9 g carbo., 0 g fiber, 1 g pro.*

Cranberry-Pistachio Toffee

Red and green, the classic colors of Christmas, are delivered in this sweet package of cranberries and pistachios.

PREP **20 minutes** COOK **12 minutes**
CHILL **20 minutes** MAKES **1¾ pounds (30 servings)**

1   cup butter
¾   cup granulated sugar
¼   cup packed brown sugar
¼   cup water
1   tablespoon light-color corn syrup
¾   cup pistachios, chopped
6   ounces white chocolate, coarsely chopped
¾   cup snipped dried cranberries and/or dried cherries

1. Line a 15×10×1-inch baking pan with foil; butter foil and set aside.

2. In a heavy medium saucepan combine butter, sugars, water, and corn syrup. Cook and stir over medium-high heat until mixture boils. Clip a candy thermometer to side of pan. Reduce heat to medium; continue boiling at a moderate, steady rate, stirring frequently, until thermometer registers 290°F (soft-crack stage) about 12 minutes. Adjust heat as necessary to maintain a steady boil. Remove saucepan from heat; remove thermometer. Stir in chopped pistachios. Pour into the prepared pan, spreading quickly to an even ¼-inch thickness. (Toffee will not cover entire surface of prepared pan.) Cool completely.
3. Place white chocolate in a small heavy saucepan; cook and stir over low heat just until melted. Spread on toffee; sprinkle with dried cranberries and/or cherries, pressing lightly. Chill in refrigerator about 20 minutes or until chocolate is firm.
4. Use foil to lift toffee out of pan; break candy into 2-inch pieces.
PER SERVING *140 cal., 9 g total fat (5 g sat. fat), 18 mg chol., 51 mg sodium, 14 g carbo., 0 g fiber, 1 g pro.*

Cranberry-Pistachio Toffee

heartwarming
gifts

A batch of spiced nuts or savory cheese biscuits— or anything you make yourself— is the sweetest of gifts. This collection of recipes ranges from classic layered cookie mixes in a jar and to party snack mixes to sophisticated savory pastries for nibbling as an appetizer. Together with imaginative packaging, each of them will be a perfect present.

Seeded Cheddar Biscotti, page 124

Curried Cashews

3. In a large saucepan combine the water, butter, and the remaining 1 tablespoon brown sugar. Bring to boiling, stirring constantly. Add cashews, stirring to coat. Cook and stir about 2 minutes or until liquid is evaporated. Remove from heat. Add curry mixture; toss gently to coat.
4. Spread nuts in an even layer in the same baking pan. Bake for 12 to 15 minutes or until golden brown, stirring once. Cool in pan on a wire rack.

PER ¼ CUP *188 cal., 14 g total fat (3 g sat. fat), 2 mg chol., 287 mg sodium, 13 g carbo., 1 g fiber, 5 g pro.*

Seeded Cheddar Biscotti
Crunchy and flavorful, these savory biscotti are meant to be served with before-dinner drinks.

PREP **30 minutes** BAKE **40 minutes** COOL **1 hour**
OVEN **375°F/325°F** MAKES **about 50 biscotti**

2¼ cups all-purpose flour
⅓ cup yellow cornmeal
1½ teaspoons sugar
1½ teaspoons salt
1½ teaspoons baking powder
½ teaspoon baking soda
½ teaspoon dry mustard
½ teaspoon coarsely ground black pepper
  Dash cayenne pepper
¾ cup shredded sharp cheddar cheese (3 ounces)
7 teaspoons assorted seeds (such as poppy seeds, dill seeds, celery seeds, sesame seeds, and/or flaxseeds) or purchased bread topping seed mix
2 eggs, lightly beaten
½ cup buttermilk
2 tablespoons butter, melted

1. Preheat oven to 375°F. Line a very large baking sheet with parchment paper or foil; set aside. In a bowl combine flour, cornmeal, sugar, salt, baking powder, baking soda, dry mustard, black pepper, and cayenne pepper. Stir in cheese and seeds.
2. In another bowl combine eggs, buttermilk, and melted butter. Add egg mixture to flour mixture; stir to form a crumbly dough.
3. Turn dough out onto a lightly floured surface. Gently knead until dough clings together. Divide dough into thirds. Shape into three 10-inch-long loaves. Place loaves on the prepared baking sheet; flatten slightly.
4. Bake about 20 minutes or until a toothpick inserted near the centers comes out clean. Turn off oven. Cool on baking sheet for 1 hour.
5. Preheat oven to 325°F. Using a serrated knife, cut loaves into ¼-inch slices. Place slices on an ungreased baking sheet. Bake for 10 minutes. Turn slices over; bake for 10 to 12 minutes more or until crisp and dry (do not overbake). Transfer slices to wire racks and let cool.

PER BISCOTTI *39 cal., 1 g total fat (1 g sat. fat), 12 mg chol., 109 mg sodium, 5 g carbo., 0 g fiber, 1 g pro.*

Curried Cashews
Sweet, salty, and spicy, these Indian-spiced nuts are delicious with a cold beer or mango-infused cocktail.

PREP **10 minutes** BAKE **22 minutes**
OVEN **350°F** MAKES **3 cups**

3 cups raw cashews (about 1 pound)
3 tablespoons packed brown sugar
2 teaspoons kosher salt
2 teaspoons curry powder
½ teaspoon ground cumin
¼ teaspoon cayenne pepper
¼ cup water
1 tablespoon butter

1. Preheat oven to 350°F. Line a 15×10×1-inch baking pan with parchment paper or foil. Spread cashews in an even layer in the prepared baking pan. Bake about 10 minutes or until lightly browned.
2. Meanwhile, in a small bowl combine 2 tablespoons of the brown sugar, the salt, curry powder, cumin, and cayenne pepper; set aside.

Sweet Mingle Mix

Ribbon-wrapped cellophane bags of this sweet snack mix make fun take-home favors for a children's holiday party.

PREP 15 minutes COOK 2 minutes
COOL 1 hour MAKES 12 cups

4   cups bite-size square rice or corn cereal
4   cups round toasted oat cereal
3   cups pretzel sticks, broken
2   cups peanuts, almonds, or mixed nuts
1¼   pounds vanilla-flavored candy coating, chopped
2   cups candy-coated chocolate pieces

1. Line a large baking sheet with waxed paper; set aside. In a bowl combine cereals, pretzels, and nuts; set aside.
2. In a heavy medium-size saucepan heat candy coating over low heat until melted and smooth, stirring frequently. (Or place candy coating in a microwave-safe bowl. Microwave, uncovered, on high for 1½ to 2 minutes or until coating is melted, stirring every 30 seconds.)
3. Pour the melted coating over cereal mixture. Using a wooden spoon, stir mixture to coat. Add candy-coated chocolate pieces; toss to mix. Quickly pour mixture onto the prepared baking sheet and spread in an even layer. Cool completely. Break into pieces.
Tooty Fruity Sweet Mingle Mix Prepare as above, except stir in 1⅓ cups golden raisins and 1⅓ cups dried cranberries in place of the candy-coated chocolate pieces.
To Make-Ahead Place snack mix in an airtight container; cover. Store at room temperature up to 1 week.
PER ½ CUP *327 cal., 17 g total fat (9 g sat. fat), 1 mg chol., 236 mg sodium, 39 g carbo., 2 g fiber, 5 g pro.*

Good Cheer Holiday Crunch

If you can't find cashew butter at a supermarket, look for it at natural food stores.

START TO FINISH 20 minutes MAKES about 14 cups

1½   cups powdered sugar
½   teaspoon ground nutmeg
8   cups bite-size corn or rice square cereal
1   cup white baking pieces
½   cup cashew butter or smooth peanut butter
¼   cup butter, cut up
¼   teaspoon vanilla
1½   cups lightly salted cashews
1⅓   cups dried cherries or cranberries and/or chopped dried apricots (about 6 ounces)

1. In a very large plastic bag combine powdered sugar and nutmeg; set aside. Place cereal in a very large bowl; set aside.
2. In a medium saucepan combine white baking pieces, cashew butter, and butter. Stir over low heat until baking pieces and butter are melted. Remove from heat. Stir in vanilla.
3. Pour butter mixture over cereal mixture; carefully stir until cereal is evenly coated. Cool slightly. Add cereal mixture, half at a time, to powdered sugar mixture in bag and shake to coat. Add nuts and fruit. Shake just until combined. Pour into a shallow baking pan lined with waxed paper to cool. Spoon into tall plastic containers; cover.
Chocolate-Peanut Holiday Crunch Prepare as directed, except substitute ¼ cup unsweetened cocoa powder for the nutmeg, peanuts for the cashews, dried fruit bits for the dried cherries, and peanut butter for the cashew butter.
To Make-Ahead Store in airtight containers for up to 2 days.
PER ½ CUP *186 cal., 9 g total fat (3 g sat. fat), 6 mg chol., 140 mg sodium, 24 g carbo., 1 g fiber, 3 g pro.*

Good Cheer Holiday Crunch

Caraway-Cheese Crisps

Frozen puffed pastry makes these flaky crisps as simple as can be to make—just cut it into strips, sprinkle with cheese and caraway seeds, and bake.

PREP 10 minutes BAKE 10 minutes
OVEN 400°F MAKES 27 crisps

½ of a 17.3-ounce package frozen puff pastry (1 sheet)
1 egg white, slightly beaten
1 tablespoon water
½ cup shredded Swiss cheese (2 ounces)
2 teaspoons caraway seeds, crushed

1. Thaw pastry according to package directions. Preheat oven to 400°F. Grease a large baking sheet; set aside.
2. On a lightly floured surface unfold pastry sheet. In a bowl stir together egg white and the water. Brush pastry with egg white mixture. Sprinkle with Swiss cheese and caraway seeds. Cut pastry crosswise into nine 1-inch strips. Cut pastry lengthwise into thirds, making a total of twenty-seven 3×1-inch strips. Place on prepared baking sheet.
3. Bake for 10 to 12 minutes or until puffed and golden. Cool on wire racks.

Caraway-Cheese Crisps

To Make-Ahead Place crisps in layers separated by waxed paper in an airtight container; cover and freeze for up to 1 month. Thaw crisps at room temperature for 30 minutes. Preheat oven to 400°F. Place crisps on a baking sheet lined with parchment paper. Bake about 5 minutes or until crisp.
PER CRISP *93 cal., 6 g total fat (2 g sat. fat), 2 mg chol., 45 mg sodium, 7 g carbo., 0 g fiber, 2 g pro.*

White Cheddar Cheese Ball

Placed on a pretty plate and tightly wrapped, this savory cheese spread makes a welcome hostess gift.

PREP 25 minutes STAND 45 minutes CHILL 4 hours
FREEZE 15 minutes MAKES 16 servings

1 8-ounce package cream cheese
4 ounces aged white cheddar cheese, shredded
¼ cup butter
1 tablespoon half-and-half, light cream, or milk
1½ teaspoons finely shredded orange peel
⅓ cup finely chopped pecans, toasted (see note, page 119)
¼ cup finely chopped green onions (2)
⅔ cup chopped fresh parsley, chopped toasted pecans, and/or finely chopped green onions
    Assorted crackers

1. Allow cream cheese, cheddar cheese, and butter to stand at room temperature for 30 minutes. In a food processor combine cream cheese, cheddar cheese, butter, half-and-half, and orange peel. Cover and process until mixture is combined but still slightly chunky. Transfer mixture to a bowl.
2. Stir the ⅓ cup chopped pecans and the ¼ cup chopped green onions into the cheese mixture. Cover; freeze for 15 to 20 minutes or until mixture is easy to handle. Shape mixture into a ball. Wrap with plastic wrap and chill for at least 4 hours.
3. Let cheese ball stand at room temperature for 15 minutes. Roll cheese ball in the ⅔ cup parsley. Wrap in plastic wrap. Store in the refrigerator.
To Make-Ahead Prepare cheese ball through Step 2. Wrap in plastic wrap. Store in the refrigerator for up to 24 hours or place in airtight container and freeze for up to 3 months. If frozen, thaw in refrigerator overnight and continue with Step 3.
PER SERVING *121 cal., 12 g total fat (6 g sat. fat), 31 mg chol., 112 mg sodium, 1 g carbo., 0 g fiber, 3 g pro.*

Cheddar Cornmeal Sticks

These spicy, tangy cheese pastries are wonderful to nibble with a glass of wine.

PREP 20 minutes BAKE 15 minutes STAND 1 hour
OVEN 350°F MAKES 48 crackers

2   cups finely shredded sharp cheddar cheese
     (8 ounces)
½   cup butter
1¼   cups all-purpose flour
¼   cup yellow cornmeal
¼   teaspoon salt
¼   teaspoon cayenne pepper
¼   teaspoon ground nutmeg

1. Preheat oven to 350°F. Lightly grease baking sheets; set aside. In a bowl combine cheese and butter; allow to stand at room temperature for 1 hour. Beat with an electric mixer on medium until well mixed. Stir in flour, cornmeal, salt, cayenne pepper, and nutmeg. Divide dough in half.
2. On a lightly floured surface roll each dough half into a 12×4-inch rectangle. Using a sharp knife, slice dough into 4×½-inch pieces. Place dough pieces ½ inch apart on prepared baking sheets.
3. Bake about 15 minutes or until bottoms are lightly browned. Transfer to a wire rack and let cool.
Make-Ahead Directions Place cooled crackers in layers separated by waxed paper in an airtight container; cover. Store at room temperature for up to 3 days or freeze for up to 3 months.
PER CRACKER *51 cal., 4 g total fat (2 g sat. fat), 10 mg chol., 55 mg sodium, 3 g carbo., 0 g fiber, 2 g pro.*

Triple-Treat Pretzels

Layers of caramel, vanilla, chocolate, and chopped mix nuts coat pretzel rods for a sweet and salty treat.

PREP 30 minutes COOK 10 minutes
STAND 1 hour MAKES 18 pretzels

1½   cups chopped mixed nuts
1   14-ounce package (about 50) vanilla caramels,
     unwrapped
2   tablespoons whipping cream, half-and-half, or
     light cream
18   large pretzel rods
2   ounces vanilla-flavor candy coating
1   teaspoon shortening
2   ounces chocolate-flavored candy coating

1. Butter a large baking sheet; set aside. Spread nuts in an even layer on a plate; set aside.
2. In a heavy medium saucepan heat and stir caramels and whipping cream over medium-low heat just until caramels are melted. Reduce heat to low.

Triple-Treat Pretzels

3. Hold each pretzel rod by 1 end over the pan and spoon hot caramel mixture evenly over three-fourths of the pretzel; shake off excess. Roll coated part of pretzel in nuts, turning to coat all sides. Place pretzels on prepared baking sheet and let stand about 30 minutes or until caramel is set.
4. In a small heavy saucepan melt vanilla-flavor candy coating and ½ teaspoon of the shortening. In another small heavy saucepan melt the chocolate-flavor candy coating and the remaining ½ teaspoon shortening. Carefully spoon each candy coating mixture into a heavy resealable plastic bag. Snip off a corner of each bag.
5. Transfer pretzel rods to a sheet of waxed paper. Drizzle some of each mixture over the caramel and nuts on each pretzel, turning pretzel to coat all sides. Return pretzels to baking sheet and let stand about 30 minutes or until firm.
To Make-Ahead Place pretzels in a single layer in an airtight container; cover. Store at room temperature for up to 3 days.
PER PRETZEL *239 cal., 12 g total fat (5 g sat. fat), 2 mg chol., 254 mg sodium, 30 g carbo., 1 g fiber, 4 g pro.*

Coconut Crunch Cookie Mix

1. In a quart jar layer granulated sugar, nuts, coconut, crushed cornflakes, brown sugar, and oats. In a bowl combine flour, baking soda, baking powder, and salt. Add flour mixture to jar. Fasten lid; attach directions for making cookies to jar.

To Make-Ahead Store in a cool, dry place for up to 1 month.

To Make Cookies Preheat oven to 350°F. In a mixing bowl stir together the contents of the jar. Add ½ cup softened butter, 1 lightly beaten egg, and 1 teaspoon vanilla. Mix until well combined. Shape dough into 1-inch balls. Place balls 2 inches apart on an ungreased cookie sheet. Bake for 10 to 12 minutes or until edges are light brown. Cool for 2 minutes on cookie sheet. Transfer cookies to a wire rack and let cool. Makes 36 cookies.

PER COOKIE *112 cal., 5 g total fat (3 g sat. fat), 13 mg chol., 112 mg sodium, 15 g carbo., 1 g fiber, 1 g pro.*

Toffee Blondies in a Jar

All the recipient of this sweet gift needs to contribute is a little melted butter, eggs, and vanilla. Viola! Blondies!

START TO FINISH **15 minutes** MAKES **1 gift jar**

1	cup packed brown sugar
½	cup miniature semisweet chocolate pieces
1	cup all-purpose flour
1	teaspoon baking powder
¼	teaspoon salt
¾	cup coarsely chopped pecans or walnuts
½	cup toffee pieces or butterscotch-flavor pieces

1. In a 1-quart glass jar layer brown sugar, chocolate pieces, flour, baking powder, salt, nuts, and toffee pieces, tapping jar gently on the counter to settle each layer before adding the next. Cover jar.

2. Store at room temperature up to 1 month. Or attach baking directions and give as a gift.

To Make-Ahead Store at room temperature for up to 1 month.

To Make Blondies Preheat oven to 350°F. Grease an 8×8×2-inch baking pan. In a bowl combine ¼ cup melted butter, 2 lightly beaten eggs, and 1 teaspoon vanilla. Stir in contents of the jar. Spread batter into prepared pan. Bake for 25 to 30 minutes or until set and golden brown and edges just begin to pull away from pan. Cool in pan on a wire rack. Cut into bars. Makes 16 bars.

PER BAR *202 cal., 10 g total fat (3 g sat. fat), 36 mg chol., 108 mg sodium, 27 g carbo., 1 g fiber, 3 g pro.*

Coconut Crunch Cookie Mix

The crunch in these cookies comes from crushed cornflakes or wheat cereal flakes.

START TO FINISH **20 minutes**
MAKES **1 gift jar**

½	cup granulated sugar
½	cup chopped pecans or hazelnuts
1¼	cups flaked coconut
1	cup crushed cornflakes or wheat cereal flakes
¾	cup packed brown sugar
½	cup quick-cooking rolled oats
1¼	cups all-purpose flour
1	teaspoon baking soda
1	teaspoon baking powder
¼	teaspoon salt

Hot Peppermint-Cocoa Mix

Crushed peppermint candies quickly dissolve when the dry mix is combined with hot water, infusing the cocoa with sweet peppermint flavor.

START TO FINISH **10 minutes**
MAKES **5 gift bags**

3   cups nonfat dry milk powder
1½ cups unsweetened cocoa powder
¾   cup sugar
½   cup crushed peppermint candies (3 ounces)

1. In a bowl stir together milk powder, cocoa powder, and sugar. Divide among 5 clear gift canisters. Top with crushed candies. Tie bags closed with string and place in tins. Attach serving directions to tins.

To Make-Ahead Store cocoa mix in a tightly covered container at room temperature up to 3 months.

To Serve Shake contents of the container. For each serving, place 3 tablespoons of the mix in a 10-ounce mug and add 1 cup boiling water; stir until mix is well incorporated (crushed candies will dissolve in about 2 minutes as the mixture stands).

PER SERVING *139 cal., 1 g total fat (0 g sat. fat), 4 mg chol., 99 mg sodium, 24 g carbo., 0 g fiber, 8 g pro.*

Mocha Hot Cocoa Mix Prepare as above, except omit the peppermint candies and add ¼ cup instant coffee crystals or instant espresso coffee powder.

Hot Peppermint-Cocoa Mix

Toffee Butter Crunch

1. Line a 13×9×2-inch baking pan with foil, extending the foil over edges of pan; set pan aside.
2. In a heavy 2-quart saucepan melt butter over low heat. Stir in sugar, water, and corn syrup. Bring to boiling over medium-high heat, stirring until sugar is dissolved. Avoid splashing side of saucepan. Clip a candy thermometer to side of pan. Cook over medium heat, stirring frequently, until thermometer registers 290°F (soft-crack stage), about 12 minutes. Sugar mixture should boil at a moderate, steady rate with bubbles over entire surface. (Adjust heat as necessary to maintain a steady boil and watch temperature carefully during the last 5 minutes of cooking as temperature can increase quickly at the end.) Remove from heat; remove thermometer.
3. Carefully pour hot mixture into prepared pan; spread evenly. Cool for 4 to 5 minutes or just until top is set. Sprinkle evenly with chocolate pieces; let stand for 2 minutes. Spread softened chocolate into an even layer over toffee layer. Sprinkle with nuts; lightly press into chocolate. Let stand at room temperature several hours or until chocolate is set. Use foil to lift candy out of pan; break into pieces.
Make-Ahead Directions Place toffee pieces in layers separated by waxed paper in an airtight container; cover. Store at room temperature up to 2 weeks.
PER PIECE *141 cal., 10 g total fat (6 g sat. fat), 22 mg chol., 59 mg sodium, 12 g carbo., 0 g fiber, 1 g pro.*

Spiced Pumpkin Butter

Spread this warmly spiced fruit butter on toasted raisin bread or fresh-from-the-oven bran muffins.

PREP **15 minutes** COOK **25 minutes**
MAKES **4 half-pints**

4   cups pumpkin puree or two 15-ounce cans pumpkin
1¼ cups pure maple syrup
½   cup apple juice
2   tablespoons lemon juice
1   teaspoon ground ginger
½   teaspoon ground cinnamon
½   teaspoon ground nutmeg
¼   teaspoon salt

1. In a heavy 5-quart Dutch oven combine pumpkin puree, maple syrup, apple juice, lemon juice, ginger, cinnamon, nutmeg, and salt. Bring to boiling; reduce heat. Cook, uncovered, over medium heat, stirring frequently, about 25 minutes or until thick. Remove from heat; cool.
2. Ladle pumpkin butter into clean half-pint or pint freezer containers or jars, leaving a ½-inch headspace; seal. Store in the refrigerator.
PER 2 TABLESPOONS *35 cal., 0 g total fat, 0 mg chol., 17 mg sodium, 9 g carbo., 0 g fiber, 0 g pro.*

Toffee Butter Crunch

Package this buttery toffee in festive disposable drinking glasses lined with parchment paper.

PREP **25 minutes** COOK **12 minutes**
STAND **3 hours** MAKES **24 pieces**

1   cup butter
1   cup sugar
3   tablespoons water
1   tablespoon light-color corn syrup
¾   cup milk chocolate pieces or semisweet chocolate pieces
½   to ¾ cup chopped nuts such as almonds, pecans, walnuts, and/or cashews, toasted (see note, page 110)

Caramel-Rum Sauce

Pair a jar of this sauce with one of the hot fudge sauce variations (below) for a double treat.

PREP 15 minutes STAND: 45 minutes
MAKES 4 half-pints

2   cups packed brown sugar
¼   cup cornstarch
1⅓ cups half-and-half or light cream
1   cup water
½   cup light-color corn syrup
¼   cup butter
¼   cup rum
2   teaspoons vanilla

1. In a large heavy saucepan stir together brown sugar and cornstarch. Stir in half-and-half, the water, and corn syrup. Cook and stir over medium heat until thickened and bubbly (mixture may look curdled). Cook and stir for 2 minutes more. Remove from heat. Stir in butter, rum, and vanilla. Let stand at room temperature about 45 minutes or until cooled.
2. Divide sauce among 4 half-pint glass jars. Seal; attach directions for reheating Caramel-Rum Sauce to each jar. Store in the refrigerator up to 1 week.
3. To reheat Caramel-Rum Sauce, empty contents of 1 jar into a small saucepan. Heat over low heat just until warm. Serve warm sauce over ice cream, fruit, pound cake, angel cake, or other desserts. Makes 8 servings.
PER SCANT ½ CUP *378 cal., 10 g total fat (7 g sat. fat,), 30 mg chol., 81 mg sodium, 10 g carbo., 0 g fiber, 1 g pro.*

Hot Fudge Sauce

This classic recipe has two variations—one with kid appeal and a more sophisticated version for grown-ups.

START TO FINISH 15 minutes MAKES 1½ cups

¾   cup semisweet chocolate pieces
¼   cup butter
⅔   cup sugar
1   5-ounce can evaporated milk (⅔ cup)

1. In a small heavy saucepan melt the chocolate and butter over medium heat. Add the sugar; gradually stir in the evaporated milk; stir to dissolve the sugar. Bring to boiling; reduce heat. Boil gently over low heat for 8 minutes, stirring frequently. Remove from heat; cool. Pour sauce into jar. Fasten lid; attach directions for serving sauce.
To Make-Ahead Store in the refrigerator up to 3 days.

To Serve Pour sauce into a small heavy saucepan. Heat over low heat until warm, stirring frequently. Serve warm sauce over ice cream.
PER 2 TABLESPOONS *145 cal., 8 g total fat (5 g sat. fat), 14 mg chol., 41 mg sodium, 19 g carbo., 1 g fiber, 1 g pro.*
Peanut Butter-Fudge Sauce Prepare as directed, except after gently boiling for 8 minutes stir in ¼ cup peanut butter. Makes 1¾ cups.
Hazelnut-Mocha Sauce Prepare as directed, except stir in ¼ cup chocolate-hazelnut spread with the chocolate and butter. After removing sauce from heat, stir in 2 tablespoons coffee-flavor liqueur or strong coffee. Makes 2 cups.

Hot Fudge Sauce

new year's celebration

Ring in the New Year with sophisticated fare that's surprisingly easy to make. Try herb-marinated shrimp, creamy red wine risotto, or goat cheese-stuffed beef tenderloin—to name just a few options. With such a delicious beginning, it's bound to be a very good year.

Roasted Pork Tenderloin with Cranberry-Cherry Chutney, page 139

Holiday Orange-Eggnog Punch

Holiday Orange-Eggnog Punch

This creamy punch tastes a bit like an orange Dreamsicle.

PREP **40 minutes** CHILL **4 hours**
MAKES **22 servings**

6   egg yolks, lightly beaten
2   cups whole milk
½   cup sugar
1   6-ounce can frozen orange juice concentrate,
     thawed
½   of a 6-ounce can frozen lemonade concentrate,
     thawed (⅓ cup)
2   teaspoons vanilla
1   quart French vanilla or vanilla ice cream (4 cups)
1   28-ounce bottle lemon-lime carbonated beverage
     or ginger ale, chilled
     Freshly grated nutmeg (optional)
     Grated white baking chocolate (optional)

1. In a medium-size heavy saucepan stir together egg
yolks, milk, and sugar. Cook and stir over medium heat
just until egg mixture coats a metal spoon; do not boil
(should take about 25 minutes and register 170°F to
175°F on instant-read thermometer). Remove from heat.
2. Place the pan in a sink or bowl of ice water and stir for
2 minutes. Stir in orange juice and lemonade concentrates
and vanilla. Cover and chill for 4 to 24 hours.
3. Just before serving cut ice cream into small chunks
or scoops; put in a punch bowl. Slowly pour lemon-lime
carbonated beverage over ice cream. Stir in chilled egg

mixture. If desired, sprinkle each serving with nutmeg
and/or white chocolate.
PER 4 OUNCES *146 cal., 6 g total fat (4 g sat. fat), 83 mg
chol., 35 mg sodium, 20 g carbo., 0 g fiber, 3 g pro.*

Cranberry-Apple Crush

This warming hot punch is nicely spiced with ginger,
cinnamon, and allspice.

START TO FINISH **15 minutes** MAKES **8 servings**

5   cups apple juice or apple cider
5   cups cranberry juice
1½   cups guava juice or mango nectar
¼   cup lime juice
1   teaspoon ground ginger
½   teaspoon ground cinnamon
½   teaspoon ground allspice
     Honey (optional)
     Lime slices (optional)

1. In a 4-quart Dutch oven combine apple juice, cranberry
juice, guava juice, lime juice, ginger, cinnamon, and
allspice. Bring to boiling; reduce heat. Simmer, uncovered,
for 5 minutes, stirring occasionally. If desired, sweeten to
taste with honey.
2. To serve, pour into mugs. If desired, garnish with
lime slices.
PER 11 OUNCES *182 cal., 0 g total fat, 0 mg chol., 28 mg
sodium, 46 g carbo., 0 g fiber, 0 g pro.*

Prosciutto-Basil Cheese Ball

The classic cheese ball gets a Mediterranean makeover with fontina cheese, fresh basil, prosciutto, and pine nuts.

PREP 35 minutes STAND 45 minutes CHILL 4 hours
MAKES about 2 cups spread

1   8-ounce package cream cheese
1   cup fontina cheese, finely shredded (4 ounces)
¼   cup butter
1   tablespoon milk
½   teaspoon Worcestershire sauce for chicken
2   tablespoons thinly sliced green onion
2   tablespoons snipped fresh basil
2   ounces chopped prosciutto
½   cup coarsely chopped, toasted pine nuts (see note, page 119)
    Apple wedges, assorted crackers, and/or flatbread

1. In a large mixing bowl let cream cheese, shredded cheese, and butter stand at room temperature for 30 minutes. Add milk and Worcestershire sauce. Beat with an electric mixer on medium until light and fluffy. Stir in green onion, basil, and prosciutto. Cover and chill for 4 to 24 hours.
2. Before serving, shape mixture into a ball. Roll ball in nuts and let stand 15 minutes. Serve with apple wedges and/or crackers.
PER 1 TABLESPOON *63 cal., 6 g total fat (3 g sat. fat), 16 mg chol., 62 mg sodium, 1 g carbo., 0 g fiber, 2 g pro.*

Mixed Peppers in Gougère Crust

Traditional Gougère are bite-size French cheese puffs made with choux paste. They are typically served with a glass of wine. Here, that same egg-rich dough is turned into a savory crust for a vegetable tart.

PREP 35 minutes COOK 10 minutes BAKE 50 minutes
OVEN 375°F MAKES 8 servings

3   medium red, yellow, and/or green sweet peppers, sliced
½   a red onion, sliced
1   clove garlic, minced
2   tablespoons olive oil
¼   cup chopped fresh basil
1   tablespoon chopped fresh rosemary
¾   cup milk
5   tablespoons butter, cut up
1   cup all-purpose flour
1   cup blue cheese, crumbled (4 ounces)
4   eggs
¼   cup blue cheese, crumbled (1 ounce)

1. Preheat oven to 375°F. Grease an 11-inch tart pan with a removable bottom; set aside. In a large skillet cook peppers, onion, and garlic in hot oil over medium heat until tender. Stir in basil and rosemary. Season with *salt* and *black pepper;* set aside.
2. In a small saucepan combine milk, butter, ½ teaspoon *salt,* and ½ teaspoon black *pepper.* Bring to boiling. Remove from heat. Using a wooden spoon, vigorously beat in flour. Reduce heat and return saucepan to heat. Stir for 2 minutes. Transfer dough mixture to a large bowl. Add the 1 cup of blue cheese. Using a hand mixer, beat on high for 2 minutes. Add eggs, 1 at a time, beating on medium after each addition until each egg is fully incorporated.
3. Spread dough evenly in the prepared pan. Bake 10 minutes. Spread vegetable mixture on dough. Bake 40 minutes or until puffed and golden brown. Sprinkle remaining blue cheese on tart before serving.
PER SERVING *278 cal., 19 g total fat (9 g sat. fat), 140 mg chol., 345 mg sodium, 17 g carbo., 2 g fiber, 10 g pro.*

Prosciutto-Basil Cheese Ball

Herbed Shrimp and Tomatoes

Also try this dish chilled. Cover and chill the cooked shrimp mixture in the refrigerator up to 4 hours before serving.

PREP 20 minutes MARINATE 10 minutes
COOK 4 minutes MAKES 8 servings

2   pounds fresh or frozen jumbo shrimp (40 to 42 shrimp)
2   tablespoons snipped fresh basil or oregano
1   tablespoon fresh lemon juice
¾   teaspoon salt
¼   teaspoon black pepper
2   tablespoons extra virgin olive oil
2   cups grape tomatoes
     Lemon wedges (optional)
     Snipped fresh basil (optional)
1   recipe Basil Dipping Sauce (optional)

1. Thaw shrimp, if frozen. Peel and devein shrimp, removing tails. Rinse shrimp; pat dry with paper towels. Set aside. In a large bowl combine basil, lemon juice, salt, and pepper. Add shrimp. Toss to coat. Cover and marinate in the refrigerator for 10 to 30 minutes.
2. In a large skillet cook shrimp, half at a time, in hot oil over medium-high heat for 2 to 3 minutes or until shrimp are opaque, stirring often to cook evenly. Transfer shrimp to serving platter.
3. Add tomatoes to shrimp; gently toss to combine. If desired, serve with lemon wedges, snipped basil, and Basil Dipping Sauce. Serve warm.
PER SERVING *162 cal., 5 g total fat (1 g sat. fat), 172 mg chol., 389 mg sodium, 4 g carbo., 1 g fiber, 24 g pro.*
Basil Dipping Sauce In a small bowl combine 1 cup mayonnaise; 1 tablespoon snipped fresh basil; 2 cloves garlic, minced; 1 teaspoon lemon juice; 1 teaspoon Dijon mustard; and ⅛ teaspoon cayenne pepper. Mix thoroughly. Cover and chill up to 3 days before serving.

Prosciutto and Basil Stuffed Turkey Breast

Fresh basil-infused gravy is the final touch on these crisp-skin roasted turkey breasts.

PREP 20 minutes ROAST 1 hour 20 minutes
STAND 10 minutes OVEN 400°F/350°F
MAKES 8 to 12 servings

2   3- to 3½-pound fresh or frozen bone-in turkey breast halves
     Nonstick cooking spray
4   ounces thinly sliced prosciutto
12   small or 6 large fresh basil leaves
½   cup butter, melted
¼   cup finely chopped shallots
2   cloves garlic, minced
½   teaspoon salt
¼   teaspoon freshly ground black pepper
1   14-ounce can chicken broth
¼   cup all-purpose flour
2   tablespoons snipped fresh basil
     Salt
     Freshly ground black pepper

1. Thaw turkey, if frozen. Preheat oven to 400°F. Coat a large shallow roasting pan and rack with cooking spray. Place turkey breast halves, bone sides down, on roasting rack in prepared pan.
2. Starting at breast bone of each breast half, slip your fingers between skin and meat to loosen skin, leaving skin attached at top. Lift skin and arrange prosciutto slices and basil leaves over breast meat. Insert an oven-going meat thermometer into the thickest part of 1 of the turkey breasts, being sure bulb does not touch bone.
3. Roast, uncovered, on lower rack of oven for 20 minutes. Meanwhile, in a small bowl stir together melted butter, shallots, garlic, the ½ teaspoon salt, and the ¼ teaspoon

Prosciutto and Basil Stuffed Turkey Breast

pepper. Reduce oven temperature to 350°F. Roast for 1 to 1½ hours more or until thermometer registers 170°F, juices run clear, and turkey is no longer pink, occasionally spooning butter mixture over turkey breasts. Let stand, covered with foil, for 10 minutes before slicing.

4. Meanwhile, for gravy, pour pan drippings into a 2-cup glass measure, scraping up browned bits. Skim off fat, pouring ¼ cup of the fat into a medium saucepan; discard remaining fat. Add enough broth to the drippings in the measuring cup to equal 2 cups total liquid.

5. Stir flour into fat in saucepan. Stir drippings mixture into flour mixture in saucepan. Stir in snipped basil. Cook and stir over medium heat until thickened and bubbly. Cook and stir for 1 minute more. Season with salt and pepper. Serve gravy with sliced turkey.

PER SERVING *539 cal., 23 g total fat (9 g sat. fat), 240 mg chol., 858 mg sodium, 4 g carbo., 0 g fiber, 76 g pro.*

Rosemary Beef Tenderloin

While still warm, slice this roast (not all the way through) and tuck in a coin of herbed goat cheese between each slice so it gets melty and delicious before serving.

PREP **15 minutes** ROAST **35 minutes**
STAND **15 minutes** OVEN **425°F** MAKES **8 servings**

2   tablespoons Dijon mustard
1   tablespoon extra virgin olive oil
1   tablespoon snipped fresh rosemary
3   cloves garlic, minced
¾   teaspoon salt
¼   teaspoon black pepper
1   2½- to 3-pound center-cut beef tenderloin roast* or boneless pork top loin roast**
1   4- to 6-ounce package garlic and herb goat cheese (chèvre), cut crosswise into 8 slices or ½ of an 8-ounce tub cream cheese spread with chive and onion
    Snipped fresh rosemary

1. Preheat oven to 425°F. In a bowl combine mustard, oil, the 1 tablespoon rosemary, garlic, salt, and pepper. Spread mixture on the beef tenderloin or pork loin. Place roast on a rack in a shallow roasting pan.

2. Place roast in oven. For medium-rare doneness, roast the beef, uncovered, for 35 to 40 minutes or until internal temperature registers 135°F on an instant-read thermometer. Cover with foil; let stand 15 minutes before slicing. Meat temperature will rise about 10°F during standing. (For medium doneness, roast, uncovered, for 45 to 50 minutes or until meat reaches 150°F. Cover and let stand as directed above.)

3. Cut roast into 8 slices, about 1 to 1½ inches apart, cutting to, but not through, base of meat. Tuck a slice of goat cheese or 1 tablespoon cream cheese between each slice. Sprinkle with additional rosemary. To serve, slice through the meat.

Rosemary Beef Tenderloin

*****Note** Order a center-cut tenderloin from the butcher or meat counter ahead of time. The center cut holds its shape best during roasting.

******To Prepare Pork Roast** Preheat oven to 325°F. Spread roast with dijon mixture. Roast for 1¼ to 1¾ hours or until thermometer registers 150°F. Cover with foil; let stand for 15 minutes before slicing. Meat temperature will rise about 10°F during standing. Serve goat cheese with roast.

PER SERVING *275 cal., 14 g total fat (6 g sat. fat), 101 mg chol., 440 mg sodium, 1 g carbo., 0 g fiber, 35 g pro.*

Braised Short Ribs with Orange Gremolata

Braised Short Ribs with Orange Gremolata

Gremolata is a garnish that is usually made from finely shredded lemon peel, fresh parsley, and minced garlic. It is the traditional accompaniment to osso bucco, the classic Italian dish of braised veal shanks. This orange version adds fresh flavor to these braised beef short ribs.

PREP 30 minutes BAKE 2 hours COOK 20 minutes
OVEN 350°F MAKES 6 servings

3   pounds bone-in beef short ribs
¾   teaspoon salt
¼   teaspoon freshly ground black pepper
1   tablespoon olive oil
1½   cups finely chopped carrots (3 medium)
1   tablespoon minced garlic (6 cloves)
1   14.5-ounce can beef broth
½   cup dry red wine or beef broth
1   teaspoon dried thyme, crushed
1   bay leaf
2   cups frozen small whole onions
1   tablespoon Dijon mustard
1   tablespoon prepared horseradish
1   recipe Orange Gremolata
      Soft polenta or mashed potatoes (optional)

1. Preheat oven to 350°F. Trim fat from ribs. Sprinkle ribs with ½ teaspoon of the salt and the pepper. In a 4- to 5-quart oven-going Dutch oven heat olive oil over medium-high heat. Brown ribs on all sides in hot oil. Remove ribs and set aside. Discard all but 1 tablespoon drippings in Dutch oven. Reduce heat to medium-low. Add carrots and garlic to drippings in pan. Cook and stir about 10 minutes or just until carrots are tender.
2. Return ribs to Dutch oven. Add beef broth, wine, thyme, bay leaf, and the remaining ¼ teaspoon salt. Bring to boiling; remove from heat. Cover Dutch oven. Transfer Dutch oven to the oven. Bake ribs for 2 hours or until very tender, adding the frozen onions the last 30 minutes of baking.
3. Transfer ribs to a large, deep serving platter and cover with foil. Skim fat from cooking liquid; discard bay leaf and any bones that have fallen off. If sauce is too thin, bring to boiling and cook, uncovered, about 5 minutes to reduce slightly (you should have about 2½ cups). Whisk in mustard and horseradish. Pour sauce over ribs. Top with Orange Gremolata. If desired, serve with polenta or mashed potatoes.
Orange Gremolata In a small bowl combine 2 tablespoons snipped fresh parsley; 2 cloves garlic, minced; and 2 teaspoons finely shredded orange peel.
PER SERVING *717 cal., 62 g total fat (26 g sat. fat), 126 mg chol., 714 mg sodium, 8 g carbo., 1 g fiber, 25 g pro.*

Roasted Pork Tenderloin with Cranberry Chutney

Few meats offer so succulence as simply as pork tenderloin. Cook the ruby-red chutney while the meat roasts and your entrée is ready in less than one hour.

PREP 45 minutes COOK 30 minutes
ROAST 25 minutes CHILL 4 hours OVEN 425°F
MAKES 12 to 16 servings

3   1- to 1½-pound pork tenderloins
1   tablespoon allspice
2   to 3 teaspoons cracked black pepper
1   teaspoon salt
2   tablespoons cooking oil
1   tablespoon butter
1   large onion, quartered and thinly sliced
1   12-ounce package cranberries (3 cups)
1   10-ounce jar currant jelly (about 1 cup)
1   cup cranberry juice
¼   cup packed brown sugar
3   tablespoons cider vinegar
1   tablespoon grated fresh ginger or ½ teaspoon
      ground ginger
½   teaspoon curry powder
2   bunches watercress

1. Preheat oven to 425°F. In a small bowl combine allspice, pepper, and salt; rub on all sides of tenderloins.
2. In a large skillet brown tenderloins in hot oil over medium heat, turning to brown all sides. Transfer tenderloins to a shallow roasting pan. Roast for 25 minutes or until internal temperature registers 160°F on an instant-read thermometer. Remove from oven and keep warm until ready to serve.
3. Meanwhile, for cranberry chutney, add butter and onion to the same large skillet. Cook about 5 minutes or until almost tender, stirring occasionally. Add cranberries, jelly, cranberry juice, brown sugar, vinegar, ginger, and curry powder to the skillet. Bring to boiling; reduce from heat and simmer 20 to 25 minutes or until thickened to desired consistency and reduced to about 3 cups.
4. To serve, line a serving platter with watercress. Slice pork and arrange on watercress; spoon some of the Cranberry Chutney over pork. Serve remaining chutney on the side.
PER SERVING *227 cal., 7 g total fat (2 g sat. fat), 76 mg chol., 260 mg sodium, 30 g carbo., 2 g fiber, 24 g pro.*

Jeweled Spaghetti Squash

Toothsome strands of nutty-tasting spaghetti squash are coated in an orange glaze and tossed with dried cherries and pan-toasted walnuts.

PREP **20 minutes**   COOK **44 minutes**
STAND **10 minutes**   MAKES **8 servings**

1	3- to 3½-pound spaghetti squash
½	cup water
½	cup orange juice
¾	cup dried tart cherries
¼	cup chopped walnuts
2	tablespoons butter
¼	cup snipped fresh parsley
½	teaspoon salt
⅛	teaspoon black pepper

1. Halve squash lengthwise; discard seeds. Place 1 squash half, cut side down, in a microwave-safe baking dish with ¼ cup of the water. Cover with plastic wrap, turning back a corner of wrap to allow steam to escape. Microwave, covered, on high for 20 to 22 minutes or until tender, turning once. Remove squash and keep warm. Repeat with remaining squash and remaining water. Use a fork to scrape squash pulp from shells into a serving bowl.*

2. In a saucepan bring orange juice to boiling. Remove from heat. Add cherries; let stand for 10 minutes. In a skillet cook nuts in hot butter over medium heat for 2 to 3 minutes or until toasted, stirring occasionally.

3. Add cherries and juice, walnuts, parsley, salt, and pepper to squash. Toss to coat and spoon into a serving dish.

To Make-Ahead Cook spaghetti squash; scrape cooked spaghetti squash into a large bowl. Cover and refrigerate squash for up to 2 hours. To serve, warm squash in microwave, covered and vented, for 3 to 4 minutes, gently stirring twice. Continue as directed in Step 2.

Oven Directions To bake squash in oven, preheat oven to 350°F. Omit water. Place squash halves, cut sides down, in a shallow baking pan. Bake for 75 to 80 minutes or until tender. Continue as directed in Step 2.

***Note** Cool cooked squash first or protect your hands with oven mitts.

PER SERVING *135 cal., 6 g total fat (2 g sat. fat), 8 mg chol., 190 mg sodium, 20 g carbo., 1 g fiber, 2 g pro.*

Orange, Red Grape, and Watercress Salad

Blood oranges, also called Moro oranges, are so named because their juicy, sweet flesh has a deep ruby-red hue.

PREP **20 minutes**   CHILL **1 hour**   MAKES **8 servings**

3	tablespoons olive oil
1	tablespoon Spanish sherry vinegar or red wine vinegar
¼	teaspoon sea salt
⅛	teaspoon paprika
3	blood oranges, peeled and sliced
1	cup seedless red grapes, halved
4	cups watercress, arugula, or fresh spinach
¼	cup fresh mint leaves
	Paprika
	Cracked black pepper

1. For dressing, in a medium bowl whisk together the oil, vinegar, salt, and paprika. Carefully stir in oranges and grapes; cover and chill at least 1 hour.

2. Trim stems from watercress, arugula, or spinach and place in a salad bowl. Tear large mint leaves into smaller pieces; leave small mint leaves whole and add to salad bowl.

3. To serve, drain dressing from fruit mixture; pour dressing over watercress and mint. Toss lightly to coat. Divide greens among 8 salad plates; arrange fruit on greens. Sprinkle with paprika and pepper.

PER SERVING *72 cal., 5 g total fat (1 g sat. fat), 0 mg chol., 58 mg sodium, 6 g carbo., 1 g fiber, 1 g pro.*

Jeweled Spaghetti Squash

Tuscan Cheese Potato Bake

A cross between mashed potatoes and gratin, this creamy potato dish consists of coarsely mashed red potatoes flavored with garlic, herbs, buttermilk, and three cheeses, then baked under a crust of seasoned bread crumbs until golden and bubbly.

PREP **30 minutes** BAKE **20 minutes** OVEN **400°F**
MAKES **8 to 10 servings**

2   pounds red potatoes
3   or 4 cloves garlic, minced
1½   teaspoons snipped fresh thyme or ½ teaspoon
      dried thyme, crushed
¼   cup butter
1   cup buttermilk
1   cup fontina cheese, shredded (4 ounces)
1   cup Parmesan cheese, finely shredded (4 ounces)
⅓   cup crumbled blue cheese
½   cup panko (Japanese-style bread crumbs)
¼   teaspoon dried Italian seasoning, crushed
1   tablespoon olive oil
      Snipped fresh parsley (optional)

1. Preheat oven to 400°F. Lightly grease a 2-quart square baking dish; set aside. Scrub potatoes; cut into 1-inch pieces. In large saucepan cook potatoes in lightly salted boiling water 12 to 15 minutes or until tender; drain.
2. In a large skillet cook and stir garlic and thyme in butter over medium heat for 1 minute; add potatoes. Coarsely mash potatoes. Stir in buttermilk, ½ teaspoon *salt,* and ¼ teaspoon *black pepper.* Fold in fontina cheese, half the Parmesan cheese, and the blue cheese. Evenly spread in baking dish.
3. In a small bowl combine remaining Parmesan, panko, Italian seasoning, and oil; toss with a fork to combine. Evenly sprinkle over potato mixture in dish. Bake for 20 minutes or until bubbly and top is golden. If desired, sprinkle with snipped fresh parsley.
PER SERVING *304 cal., 18 g total fat (10 g sat. fat), 47 mg chol., 653 mg sodium, 23 g carbo., 2 g fiber, 14 g pro.*

Risotto with Lentils and Pancetta

French green lentils, also called Du Puy lentils, are smaller and more delicate than the more common brown lentils and hold their shape better when cooked. If your supermarket doesn't have them, look at a specialty or natural foods store.

START TO FINISH **55 minutes**
MAKES **8 to 10 servings**

2   tablespoons butter
1   tablespoon olive oil
8   ounces pancetta, chopped
½   cup finely chopped onion
2   cloves garlic, crushed
2½   cups uncooked Arborio rice

Tuscan Cheese Potato Bake

½   cup dry red wine
3   14.5-ounce cans reduced-sodium chicken broth
1½   cups water
1½   cups cooked lentils*
1   cup grated Parmigiano-Reggiano cheese
2   tablespoons butter
      Finely shredded Parmigiano-Reggiano cheese
      (optional)

1. In a 4-quart Dutch oven heat 2 tablespoons butter and the oil over medium heat. Add pancetta; cook and stir until nicely browned. Using a slotted spoon, remove pancetta and drain on paper towels, reserving drippings in Dutch oven. Add onion and garlic to reserved drippings; cook until onion is tender. Using the slotted spoon, remove and discard garlic.
2. Add rice to Dutch oven; cook and stir for 3 to 4 minutes or until rice is lightly browned. Stir in half of the cooked pancetta. Carefully add wine.
3. Meanwhile, in a large saucepan combine broth and the water. Bring to boiling; reduce heat and simmer. Slowly add 1 cup of the broth mixture to rice mixture, stirring constantly. Continue to cook and stir over medium heat until liquid is absorbed. Add the remaining broth mixture, ½ cup at a time, cooking and stirring just until rice is tender (should take about 30 minutes total). Stir in lentils, the 1 cup cheese, and 2 tablespoons butter.
4. Divide risotto among 8 to 10 dinner plates. Sprinkle with the remaining cooked pancetta and, if desired, additional cheese.
*Note To cook lentils, rinse and drain ½ cup brown, yellow, and/or French (green) lentils. In a small saucepan combine lentils and 1½ cups water. Bring to boiling; reduce heat. Cover and simmer about 15 to 20 minutes or until lentils are tender and most of the liquid is absorbed. Drain.
PER SERVING *504 cal., 20 g total fat (9 g sat. fat), 44 mg chol., 1,073 mg sodium, 57 g carbo., 11 g fiber, 22 g pro.*

Easy Sage Potato Rolls

2. After dough has rested, divide into 20 pieces. Shape pieces into balls. Place rolls on prepared baking sheets about 2 inches apart. If desired, brush tops of rolls lightly with egg white and top each roll with a small sage leaf; brush leaves lightly with egg white. Cover and let rise 30 minutes or until double in size.

3. Preheat oven to 350°F. Bake rolls 15 to 18 minutes or until golden, rearranging baking sheets halfway through baking time. Remove rolls from baking sheets; cool slightly on wire rack. Serve warm.

PER ROLL *101 cal., 2 g total fat (0 g sat. fat), 10 mg chol., 150 mg sodium, 18 g carbo., 0 g fiber, 3 g pro.*

Honeycrisp Apple and Browned Butter Tart

Honeycrisp apples are a fairly new variety. Their ambrosially sweet flavor and crisp texture have made them wildly popular. Here they star in a tart with a browned butter custard.

PREP **45 minutes** BAKE **48 minutes**
COOK **10 minutes** OVEN **450°F/350°F**
MAKES **12 to 16 servings**

1   recipe Pate Sucré (sweet pastry)
2   tablespoons butter
½   cup sugar
5   large Honeycrisp apples, cored and cut into
       8 wedges each (3½ pounds)
½   cup butter
3   egg yolks
⅓   cup sugar
¼   teaspoon salt
¼   teaspoon almond extract
⅓   cup all-purpose flour

1. Preheat oven to 450°F. Prepare Pate Sucré. On a lightly floured surface use your hands to slightly flatten the pastry dough. Roll from center to edges into a circle 12 inches in diameter. To transfer pastry, wrap it around the rolling pin. Unroll pastry into a 10-inch tart pan with removable bottom. Ease pastry into pan without stretching it. Press pastry into fluted sides of tart pan and trim edges. Line pastry with a double thickness of foil. Bake for 8 minutes. Remove foil. Bake for 5 minutes more or until crust is golden. Cool on a wire rack. Reduce oven temperature to 350°F.

2. In a large skillet melt 2 tablespoons butter over medium heat. Stir in ½ cup sugar. Cook and stir constantly until sugar begins to brown. Add apple wedges. Cook and stir for 10 to 12 minutes or until apples are lightly caramelized. Remove skillet from heat.

3. In a small saucepan melt ½ cup butter over medium heat. Reduce heat to medium-low. Continue to cook, without stirring, for 5 to 6 minutes more or until butter becomes brown and fragrant. Remove from heat; cool slightly.

Easy Sage Potato Rolls

These herbed rolls start with a hot roll mix. Instant mashed potatoes give them fluffy, tender texture.

PREP **35 minutes** RISE **30 minutes**
BAKE **15 minutes** OVEN **350°F** MAKES **20 rolls**

1   16-ounce package hot roll mix
⅔   cup instant mashed potatoes
2   tablespoons snipped fresh sage
1   egg white, lightly beaten (optional)
       Small sage leaves (optional)

1. Prepare hot roll mix according to package directions, except increase hot water to 1½ cups and add instant potatoes and snipped fresh sage to the hot water. Line 2 large baking sheets with parchment paper; set aside.

4. In a medium mixing bowl beat egg yolks, ⅓ cup sugar, salt, and almond extract with an electric mixer on medium until mixture is thickened. Beat in ⅓ cup flour on low. Add browned butter and beat on low just until combined.

5. Spread custard mixture into prebaked crust. Remove apple wedges from skillet with a slotted spoon; arrange attractively on custard. Drizzle cooking liquid in the skillet over apples. Cover edges of pastry with foil. Bake for 35 to 45 minutes or until custard is puffed and set in the center.

Pâte Sucré Place a steel blade in a food processor. Add 1¼ cups all-purpose flour and 2 tablespoons sugar. Cover and process just until combined. Add ½ cup cut-up butter. Cover and process with on/off turns until pieces are pea size. In a small bowl combine 2 tablespoons whipping cream and 1 lightly beaten egg yolk. With the food processor running, quickly add the whipping cream mixture through the feed tube. Stop food processor as soon as the mixture is added; scrape down sides. Process with 2 on/off turns (mixture may not be all moistened). Remove dough from the bowl; shape into a disk. If necessary, cover and chill for 1 hour or until dough is easy to handle.

PER SERVING 364 cal., 20 g total fat (12 g sat. fat), 119 mg chol., 176 mg sodium, 45 g carbo., 3 g fiber, 3 g pro.

Bourbon-Brownie Petits Fours

These spirited brownies are a step up from the average. Coated in chocolate glaze and topped with frosting rosettes, they merit formal occasions.

PREP **35 minutes** BAKE **30 minutes**
OVEN **350°F** MAKES **about 64 petits fours**

½ cup butter
3 ounces unsweetened chocolate, coarsely chopped
¼ cup bourbon or milk
3 tablespoons instant coffee granules
1 cup sugar
2 eggs
1 teaspoon vanilla
¾ cup all-purpose flour
¼ teaspoon baking soda
1 recipe Milk Chocolate Glaze and Frosting

1. In a medium saucepan stir butter and unsweetened chocolate over low heat until melted and smooth. Remove from heat; cool.

2. Preheat oven to 350°F. Line an 8×8×2-inch baking pan with foil, extending foil over the edges of pan. Grease foil; set pan aside. In a small bowl stir together bourbon and coffee granules; set aside.

3. Stir the sugar into the cooled chocolate mixture in saucepan. Add the eggs, 1 at a time, beating with a wooden spoon just until combined. Stir in vanilla and bourbon mixture.

4. In a bowl stir together the flour and baking soda. Add flour mixture to chocolate mixture, stirring just until combined. Spread batter in the prepared baking pan.

5. Bake for 30 minutes. Cool in pan on a wire rack. Using the edges of the foil, lift the uncut brownie out of the pan. Cut off the edges of brownie; save for another use. Cut brownies into 1- to 1½-inch squares. Coat petits fours with Milk Chocolate Glaze. For Milk Chocolate Frosting, beat the reserved cooled Milk Chocolate Glaze with an electric mixer for 30 seconds or until fluffy. Spoon frosting into a decorating bag fitted with a large star tip. Pipe a large rosette in the center of each petit four.

Milk Chocolate Glaze and Frosting In a medium saucepan bring 1 cup whipping cream just to boiling over medium-high heat. Remove from heat; add milk chocolate pieces from one 12-ounce package (do not stir). Let stand for 5 minutes. Stir until smooth. Pour half of chocolate mixture into a large bowl; cover loosely and chill for 1 to 2 hours to reserve for Milk Chocolate Frosting. When ready to glaze petits fours, reheat and stir remaining Milk Chocolate Glaze in pan over medium-low heat until it is drizzling consistency.

PER PETIT FOUR 157 cal., 10 g total fat (6 g sat. fat), 43 mg chol., 90 mg sodium, 18 g carbo., 1 g fiber, 2 g pro.

Bourbon-Brownie Petits Fours

weekend guests

The holidays are all about hosting and being hosted for good food and good times. When company is coming to your house, be prepared with these easy recipes for soups, casseroles, sandwiches, snacks, and simple desserts. They deliciously satisfy hunger pangs when you serve casual meals.

Turkey Panini with Basil Aïoli, page 147

Cheesy Shell-Stuffed Shells

Cheesy Shell-Stuffed Shells

Double the shells, double the yum. These tomato-sauced jumbo shells are stuffed with a creamy mac 'n' cheese filling made with tiny shell macaroni and two cheeses.

PREP 40 minutes BAKE 45 minutes STAND 10 minutes OVEN 350°F MAKES 6 servings

24 dried jumbo shell macaroni
8   ounces dried tiny shell macaroni (2 cups)
2   cups Gruyère cheese, shredded (8 ounces)
2   cups shredded sharp cheddar cheese (8 ounces)
¾   cup half-and-half or light cream
⅛   teaspoon white pepper or black pepper
1   24-ounce jar vodka sauce or tomato pasta sauce
4   ounce brick cheese or mozzarella cheese, shredded (1 cup)
    Fresh basil leaves (optional)

1. Preheat oven to 350°F. Cook jumbo shells according to package directions. Using a large slotted spoon, transfer shells to a colander. Rinse with cold water; drain well and set aside. In the same pan cook tiny shells according to package directions. Drain; set aside.
2. Meanwhile, in a large saucepan combine Gruyère cheese, cheddar cheese, half-and-half, and pepper. Heat over medium-low heat until cheese is melted and smooth, stirring frequently. Stir in tiny shells.
3. Spread about ½ cup of the vodka or pasta sauce in a 3-quart rectangular baking dish. Spoon cheese-shell mixture into drained jumbo shells; place stuffed shells in prepared baking dish. Top with remaining sauce.
4. Bake, covered, for 30 minutes. Uncover and sprinkle with brick cheese. Bake, uncovered, about 15 minutes more or until heated through. Let stand 10 minutes before serving. If desired, top with fresh basil.
PER SERVING 858 cal., 42 g total fat (25 g sat. fat), 128 mg chol., 1,035 mg sodium, 79 g carbo., 3 g fiber, 40 g pro.

Turkey Panini with Basil Aïoli

Make these toasty, cheesy sandwiches as a fancy and fun lunch for holiday company.

START TO FINISH 30 minutes MAKES 4 sandwiches

2   tablespoons mayonnaise or salad dressing
1   tablespoon purchased basil pesto
4   ciabatta rolls, split, or 8 slices sourdough bread
8   ounces thinly sliced cooked turkey breast
1   3.5-ounce package thinly sliced pepperoni
½   cup bottled roasted red sweet peppers, sliced
4   slices provolone cheese (about 4 ounces)
1   to 2 tablespoons olive oil

1. Preheat an electric sandwich press, covered indoor grill, grill pan, or skillet. In a small bowl combine mayonnaise and pesto. Spread pesto mixture on the cut sides of the rolls. Divide turkey, pepperoni, peppers, and cheese among roll bottoms. Add roll tops. Lightly brush tops and bottoms of sandwiches with olive oil.
2. Place sandwiches (half at a time if necessary) in the sandwich press or indoor grill; cook, covered, for 7 to 9 minutes or until bread is toasted and cheese melts. (If using a grill pan or skillet, place sandwiches on grill pan. Weight sandwiches with a heavy skillet and grill about 2 minutes or until bread is lightly toasted. Turn sandwiches over, weight, and grill about 2 minutes or until second side is lightly toasted.)

PER SANDWICH *506 cal., 30 g total fat (11 g sat. fat), 80 mg chol., 1,534 mg sodium, 30 g carbo., 2 g fiber, 29 g pro.*

Baked Risotto with Sausage and Artichokes

This baked risotto doesn't have the creamy texture of traditional stovetop stirred risotto, but it is hearty, savory, delicious, and doesn't require the cook's constant attention!

PREP 30 minutes BAKE 1 hour 10 minutes
STAND 5 minutes OVEN 350°F MAKES 6 to 8 servings

1   pound bulk Italian sausage
1   cup fennel bulb, cored and chopped (1 medium)
½   cup onion, chopped (1 medium)
2   cloves garlic, minced
¾   cup uncooked Arborio or long grain white rice
2   14-ounce cans quartered artichoke hearts, drained
1   cup carrots, shredded (2 medium)
2   teaspoons snipped fresh thyme
½   teaspoon black pepper
2   cups chicken broth
⅓   cup dry white wine or chicken broth
½   cup panko (Japanese-style bread crumbs)

¼   cup finely shredded Asiago cheese or Parmesan cheese (1 ounce)
½   teaspoon finely shredded lemon peel
1   tablespoon butter, melted

1. Preheat oven to 350°F. In an extra-large skillet cook sausage, fennel, onion, and garlic over medium-high heat until sausage is browned and vegetables are tender. Drain off fat. Add rice; cook and stir for 1 minute.
2. Add artichoke hearts, carrots, thyme, and pepper. Stir in broth and wine. Bring just to boiling. Transfer mixture to an ungreased 2½-quart casserole. Bake, covered, about 1 hour or until rice is tender, stirring once halfway through baking.
3. Meanwhile, in a small bowl combine panko, cheese, and lemon peel; stir in melted butter. Sprinkle over sausage mixture. Bake, uncovered, about 10 minutes more or until mixture is heated through and crumbs are lightly browned. Let stand for 5 minutes before serving.

PER SERVING *473 cal., 28 g total fat (11 g sat. fat), 68 mg chol., 1,429 mg sodium, 36 g carbo., 7 g fiber, 18 g pro.*

Baked Risotto with Sausage and Artichokes

Ham and Pea Soup

Ham and Pea Soup

Substitute fresh basil for the fresh tarragon in this soup if you like.

PREP **20 minutes** COOK **15 minutes** MAKES **8 servings**

12 ounces lower-sodium ham (2 cups), cut into bite-size pieces
4 teaspoons canola oil
24 ounces fresh peas or two 10-ounce packages frozen baby peas
4 cups water
2 14.5-ounce cans reduced-sodium chicken broth
4 medium carrots, sliced ¼ inch thick
4 stalks celery, sliced ½ inch thick
2 bunches green onions, bias-sliced
2 tablespoons snipped fresh tarragon or 1 teaspoon dried tarragon
1 8-ounce carton plain yogurt
    Lemon wedges
    Freshly cracked black pepper (optional)

1. In a Dutch oven brown ham in hot oil over medium heat without stirring for 3 minutes. Stir and brown the other side for 2 to 3 minutes.
2. Add peas, water, broth, carrots, celery, green onions, and tarragon. Bring to boiling. Reduce heat; simmer, covered, for 5 to 10 minutes or until peas and carrots are tender.
3. To serve, divide soup among 4 soup bowls. Pass yogurt, wedges, and if desired, black pepper, .
PER SERVING *176 cal., 4 g total fat (1 g sat. fat), 19 mg chol., 586 mg sodium, 21 g carbo., 6 g fiber, 14 g pro.*

Romaine with Creamy Garlic Dressing

The creaminess in this dressing comes from yogurt, which keeps it light. Yogurt adds a nice tangy flavor too.

START TO FINISH **5 minutes** MAKES **6 servings**

½ cup plain yogurt
⅓ cup bottled Italian salad dressing
1 clove garlic, minced
1½ heads romaine lettuce, quartered lengthwise
2 to 3 ounces Parmesan cheese, shaved*
    Freshly ground black pepper (optional)

1. For dressing, in a small bowl stir together yogurt, salad dressing, and garlic.
2. Arrange romaine on 6 salad plates. Drizzle each salad with 1 tablespoon of the dressing. Sprinkle salads with Parmesan cheese. If desired, sprinkle with freshly ground pepper.
*Note Use a vegetable peeler to shave Parmesan cheese into thin strips.
PER SERVING *257 cal., 19 g total fat (7 g sat. fat), 26 mg chol., 744 mg sodium, 7 g carbo., 1 g fiber, 15 g pro.*

Seeded Breadsticks

Nuts and seeds add crunch and flavor to these quick to fix breadsticks. They make a nice accompaniment to soups and salads.

PREP 25 minutes   BAKE 8 minutes per batch
OVEN 425°F   MAKES about 24 breadsticks

1   pound loaf frozen wheat bread dough
1   egg, lightly beaten
1   to 3 tablespoons pumpkin seeds, sesame seeds, and/or poppy seeds
    Coarse salt or salt

1. Thaw dough according to package directions. Preheat oven to 425°F. Lightly grease 2 large baking sheets; set aside. Roll dough into a 12×9-inch rectangle.
2. Brush dough with some of the egg. Sprinkle with seeds and lightly sprinkle with salt. Flour a long knife or pizza cutter to cut dough crosswise into ½-inch-wide strips.
3. Place strips on the prepared baking sheets. Bake, one sheet at a time, for 8 to 10 minutes or until golden. Transfer to wire racks; cool.
To Store Place breadsticks in an airtight container; cover. Store at room temperature up to 2 days or freeze up to 1 month.
To Reheat Place breadsticks on a baking sheet and heat in a 350°F oven for 5 to 8 minutes or until heated through.
PER BREADSTICK *52 cal., 1 g total fat (0 g sat. fat), 9 mg chol., 148 mg sodium, 9 g carbo., 1 g fiber, 3 g pro.*

Oven-Fried Veggies

Panko bread crumbs, cheese, and seasonings create a crisp coating on your choice of vegetables. Kids gobble them up!

PREP 25 minutes   BAKE 20 minutes   OVEN 400°F
MAKES 6 servings

1   cup panko (Japanese-style bread crumbs)
½   cup grated Parmesan cheese
1   teaspoon dried oregano, basil, or thyme, crushed
½   teaspoon garlic powder
½   teaspoon black pepper
1   egg, lightly beaten
1   tablespoon milk
4   cups cauliflower florets, broccoli florets, whole fresh button mushrooms, and/or packaged peeled baby carrots
¼   cup butter or margarine, melted

1. Preheat oven to 400°F. Lightly grease a 15×10×1-inch baking pan; set aside. In a resealable plastic bag combine panko, Parmesan cheese, oregano, garlic powder, and pepper. In a small bowl combine egg and milk.
2. Toss 1 cup of the vegetables in the egg mixture. Using a slotted spoon, transfer vegetables to the plastic bag. Close bag and shake to coat well. Place coated vegetables on the prepared baking pan. Repeat with remaining vegetables. Drizzle melted butter over vegetables.
3. Bake for 20 to 25 minutes or until golden brown, stirring twice.
PER ⅔ CUP *169 cal., 11 g total fat (6 g sat. fat), 62 mg chol., 222 mg sodium, 12 g carbo., 2 g fiber, 7 g pro.*

Oven-Fried Veggies

Roasted Pepper Muffins

Make a batch of these muffins up to 3 days before serving. Cool completely, then place in a single layer in a covered container and refrigerate. To serve, wrap in foil; heat in a 350°F oven for 15 minutes or until warmed through.

PREP 20 minutes BAKE 18 minutes COOL 5 minutes
OVEN 375°F MAKES 12 muffins

2   cups all-purpose flour
2   teaspoons baking powder
½   teaspoon salt
½   teaspoon baking soda
1   cup buttermilk
1   egg, slightly beaten
¼   cup olive oil
¾   cup crumbled feta cheese
½   cup chopped roasted red sweet pepper, drained
3   tablespoons snipped fresh basil

1. Preheat oven to 375°F. Grease twelve 2½-inch muffin cups; set aside. In a medium bowl combine flour, baking powder, salt, and baking soda. Make a well in the center of flour mixture; set aside.
2. In another bowl combine buttermilk, egg, and olive oil. Add egg mixture all at once to the flour mixture. Stir just until moistened (batter should be lumpy). Gently fold in cheese, roasted red pepper, and basil.

3. Spoon batter into prepared muffin cups, filling each two-thirds full. Bake for 18 to 20 minutes or until golden and a wooden toothpick inserted near the centers comes out clean. Cool in muffin cups on a wire rack for 5 minutes. Remove from muffin cups; serve warm.
PER MUFFIN *157 cal., 7 g total fat (2 g sat. fat), 27 mg chol., 342 mg sodium, 18 g carbo., 1 g fiber, 5 g pro.*

Bit O' Everything Bars

Craving something sweet but can't decide just what? These pretzel-crusted, sweet-salty bars layered with caramel, chocolate, peanuts, and toffee have something for everyone.

PREP 30 minutes BAKE 25 minutes OVEN 325°F
MAKES 36 bars

3   cups crushed pretzels (about 8 ounces)
1   cup butter, melted
⅓   cup granulated sugar
½   cup butter
½   cup whipping cream
¼   cup packed brown sugar
1   11-ounce package miniature round caramel bits or one 14-ounce package vanilla caramels, unwrapped
2   cups cocktail peanuts
1   cup dark chocolate or semisweet chocolate pieces
1   cup milk chocolate pieces with peanut butter swirls
1   cup toffee pieces

1. Preheat oven to 325°F. Line a 13×9×2-inch baking pan with foil, extending the foil over edges of pan. Grease foil; set pan aside. In a medium bowl combine pretzels, melted butter, and granulated sugar. Press mixture firmly and evenly onto the bottom of the prepared baking pan.
2. In a medium saucepan combine ½ cup butter, cream, and brown sugar. Cook and stir over medium-low heat until butter is melted and brown sugar is dissolved. Stir in caramel bits. Cook and stir until caramels are melted and mixture is smooth. Stir in peanuts.
3. Quickly pour caramel mixture over crust, spreading evenly. Sprinkle with dark chocolate pieces, milk chocolate pieces with peanut butter swirls, and toffee pieces.
4. Bake for 25 minutes or until edges are bubbly and lightly browned. Cool in pan on a wire rack. Using the edges of the foil, lift out of pan. Cut into bars.
To Store Layer bars between sheets of waxed paper in an airtight container; cover. Store at room temperature for up to 3 days or freeze for up to 3 months.
PER BAR *291 cal., 20 g total fat (10 g sat. fat), 30 mg chol., 232 mg sodium, 26 g carbo., 1 g fiber, 3 g pro.*

Roasted Pepper Muffins

Best-Ever Carrot Cake

This classic carrot cake takes on a nontraditional shape—it's baked in loaf pans instead of round cake pans.

PREP 50 minutes STAND 30 minutes
BAKE 50 minutes COOL 2 hours OVEN 350°F
MAKES 2 loaves (16 servings)

¾   cup butter
½   an 8-ounce package cream cheese
4   eggs
2½ cups all-purpose flour
1   tablespoon baking powder
1   tablespoon finely shredded lemon peel
½   teaspoon salt
1   pound carrots, cut up
1   cup pecans, toasted (see note, page 119)
1½ cups sugar
1   8-ounce can crushed pineapple (juice pack), drained
½   recipe Cream Cheese Frosting
    Fresh or canned pineapple slices, drained and
    halved (optional)

1. Let butter, cream cheese, and eggs stand at room temperature for 30 minutes. Grease the bottoms and 1 inch up the sides of two 8×4×2-inch loaf pans. Set pans aside. In a large bowl stir together flour, baking powder, lemon peel, and salt; set aside.
2. Preheat oven to 350°F. In a food processor process carrots with on/off turns until finely chopped. Add pecans and ½ cup of the sugar; process until pecans are finely chopped.
3. In an extra-large mixing bowl beat butter and cream cheese with an electric mixer on medium to high for 30 seconds. Gradually beat in the remaining 1 cup sugar until well combined, scraping sides of bowl. Add eggs, 1 at a time, beating until combined after each addition. Stir in carrot mixture and drained pineapple until combined. Stir in the flour mixture.
4. Divide batter evenly between the prepared pans. Bake for 50 to 55 minutes or until a wooden toothpick inserted near centers of cakes comes out clean. Cool cakes in pans on a wire rack for 10 minutes. Remove from pans; cool completely.
5. Frost with Cream Cheese Frosting. Serve immediately or cover and store in the refrigerator for up to 3 days. If desired, just before serving top with pineapple slices.
Cream Cheese Frosting In a large mixing bowl combine 4 ounces softened cream cheese, ¼ cup softened butter, and 1 teaspoon vanilla; beat with an electric mixer on medium until light and fluffy. Gradually beat in 2¾ to 3 cups powdered sugar to reach spreading consistency.
PER SERVING *470 cal., 23 g total fat (11 g sat. fat), 99 mg chol., 340 mg sodium, 63 g carbo., 2 g fiber, 6 g pro.*

Best-Ever Carrot Cake

holiday menus

A thoughtfully created menu makes the sum of any meal even greater than its parts (although the parts are all pretty great)! Think of these menus as your go-to guides for holiday party planning—whether you host a small gathering or a hungry crowd.

menu 1

Soup Supper

On a cold winter day nothing warms like a bowl of homemade soup and all the trimmings.

Ham and Pea Soup, page 148

Christmas Potato Soup, page 29

Waldorf Wilted Salad, page 31

Roasted Pepper Muffins, page 150

Cheddar Cornmeal Sticks, page 127

Linzer Pinwheels, page 107

menu 2

Small Plates Celebration

These dishes are packed with big flavors and provide a variety of tastes, textures, and seasonings.

Goat Cheese-Olive Tart, page 41

Herbed Shrimp and Tomatoes, page 136

Mixed Peppers in Gougère Crust, page 135

Bacon-Filled Medjool Dates, page 41

Teriyaki Chicken Rumaki, page 38

Italian Mini Meatballs, page 36

menu 3

Holiday Open House

The holidays are a wonderful time to host a casual Sunday afternoon gathering.

menu 4

Sports Day Buffet

Relax with family and friends while enjoying savory and sweet bites—perfect to nosh on while cheering for your favorite team.

menu 5

Holiday 101

When preparing a festive spread for the first time, keep it simple and let this menu be your guide.

Herb-Crusted Pork Tenderloin with Red Currant Sauce, page 10

Walnut-Lemon Rice Pilaf, page 17

Green Beans with Sage and Shiitake Mushrooms, page 27

Creamed Corn Casserole, page 20

Cheesy Garlic Rolls, page 76

Apple Tart with Cheddar Cheese Crust, page 91

menu 6

New Year's Brunch

Kick off the New Year with this easy to compose brunch menu.

Tomato, Spinach, and Feta Strata, page 51

Smoked Salmon Platter with Dilled Crème Fraîche, page 53

Lemony Scones with Dried Fruit, page 73

Fruit and Yogurt Parfaits, page 60

Gooey Ginger Coffee Rolls, page 74

Pineapple Mimosas, page 60